GW00503630

PAT NEVIN

football
and how to survive it

monoray

First published in Great Britain in 2023 by Monoray,
an imprint of Octopus Publishing Group Ltd
Carmelite House
50 Victoria Embankment
London EC4Y 0DZ
www.octopusbooks.co.uk

An Hachette UK Company
www.hachette.co.uk

Text copyright © Pat Nevin 2023
Design and layout copyright © Octopus Publishing Group Ltd 2023

All rights reserved. No part of this work may be reproduced or utilized in any form or by any means, electronic or mechanical, including photocopying, recording or by any information storage and retrieval system, without the prior written permission of the publisher.

Pat Nevin asserts the moral right to be identified as the author of this work.

Photographic credits: 1, 2a & b Lloyd Wright/Liverpool Echo/Mirrorpix; 3 Bob Thomas/Popperfoto/Getty Images; 5a Bob Thomas/Getty Images; 6a Colin Lane/Liverpool Echo/Mirrorpix; 6b courtesy PFA; 7, 9, 11b Craig Halkett/Daily Record/Mirrorpix; 8 SNS Group via Getty Images; 11a Mark Runnacles/Daily Record/Mirrorpix; 12a Stuart Farmer/Daily Record/Mirrorpix; 12b, 13 Jim Galloway/Herald and Times Group; 14a, 15a SNS Group; 14b Ben Curtis/PA Images/Alamy Stock Photo; 15b Henry McInnes/Sunday Mail/Mirrorpix; 16a SNS Group; 16b David Davies/PA Images/Alamy Stock Photo. All other images are courtesy of the author.

Every effort has been made to establish copyright ownership of the photographic material included in this publication. Please contact the publishers if any errors or omissions have been made in order that any future editions can be corrected.

ISBN 978-1-80096-113-5 (Hardback)
ISBN 978-1-80096-116-6 (Trade Paperback)

A CIP catalogue record for this book is available from the British Library.

Printed and bound in the UK.

1 3 5 7 9 10 8 6 4 2

Typeset in 12/16pt Adobe Garamond Pro by Jouve (UK), Milton Keynes

This FSC® label means that materials used
for the product have been responsibly sourced.

To Bella, Simon and the Cat. Every day is worth living because you are around.

Contents

Introduction

Maybe I always had unconventional attitudes and these in turn led me to being a natural outsider. In my late teens, back in the early 1980s, I tried hard not to become a full-time professional footballer, then totally failed by subsequently having a 19-year playing career. After being persuaded to join Clyde part-time for a couple of years in Scotland's lower leagues, while studying for a degree, I was subsequently lured south for a further nine seasons at the top level in the English professional game. Initially I reluctantly signed for Chelsea before moving on to Everton after five years while also representing Scotland, in what to my amazement became a very successful occupation.

I always loved playing football, including the hard physical training. I also curiously enjoyed the pressure from the high expectations at the top level. So why the initial reticence to become a pro? It was because just about everything else surrounding the sport, other than the actual playing, didn't appeal to the earnest young man I was back then.

I didn't like the idea of the fame and the notoriety, the weird bubble surrounding the players in the game, the strange way people treated you: with either too much respect or downright disdain or even sometimes open hatred. I also loathed the intrusions of the untrustworthy hangers-on who seemed to survive like leeches on the periphery of the sport's bloated body, and I railed against the laddish gang-culture attitudes, be they in the dressing rooms or on the terraces.

OK, so it wasn't that bad most of the time, once I eventually settled into the sport; in fact, it was generally great fun after I'd figured out a few survival strategies. During those years there were many glorious days and fabulous successes at Stamford Bridge and Goodison Park, as well as the inevitable disappointments. I managed to deal with them all, usually with some equanimity, probably due to the loving and happy home and school life I had enjoyed growing up.

My method of surviving during the first part of my career was to keep the 'football life' at arm's length from my real life. I would do the job to the best of my ability and enjoy it, but when I left training or a game, I would sink back into my own little life, rarely considering football until the next training session.

Sometimes the two worlds would collide, which initially led to confusion and misunderstandings, but I quickly decided to take as much joy as I could from the madness of an industry that so intrigues large parts of the planet's population. Being an outsider looking in provided the perfect vantage point to see its virtuous and glorious sides as well as the grotesque and unscrupulous underbelly.

I was initially bewildered by outlooks that were so different from my own. In what sensible walk of life would you get fined for being sober, especially when your fitness was vital to the success of the job? At Everton Howard Kendall had tried just that, even if I did refuse to pay up in the end.

As a student in Glasgow me and my friends made a silly fun-loving group, but the idea of us regularly fighting with each other, trading blows, sometimes while stark naked in a bath, was unthinkable. Pro football life, on the other hand, delivered that sort of bedlam regularly.

My interests in the arts and music were considered suspect by many, but I refused to be anything other than myself which, fortunately and maybe surprisingly, didn't lead to me being ostracised. I wasn't picked on by players for my 'otherness', though I admit I was luckier than some who weren't internally wired to cope quite as well with being an outsider in that enclosed world.

Back then in the 1980s I was a staunch anti-racist activist, but around the game there were many racists on the terracing and even some on the field. To my amazement few others seemed to think that that behaviour was offensive enough for them to speak out against it. My earnest attitudes were seen as unusual, but I came to accept that it was education that was needed, not anger from me towards my colleagues. As the years progressed, the game and indeed our society moved on at least a little way down the road. After a while I came to better understand, like, and even respect footballers and their foibles as I spent more time working and travelling with them.

I couldn't change every player's attitudes, though. Trips to learn more about the cultures of the countries we visited while playing were beyond my limited powers of persuasion. 'If you've seen one wall, you've seen them all,' was the reply when I suggested going to see the Great Wall of China while in Beijing!

Back on the pitch I couldn't get my head around the desire to play long-ball simplistic football when it was supposed to be an entertainment. Surely focusing a bit more on the skilful side of the sport might have been more rewarding. I will admit that, selfishly, it would have been more rewarding first and foremost for me, but I suspected it would be a lot more enjoyable for many of the fans too. That purist attitude had ultimately finished my career at Chelsea, and just being an outsider who was keen on fitness was eventually part of the reason why I was later jettisoned from Everton. I still thought I was in the right, even as I eventually trudged out of those clubs!

The truth was that for all the distance I kept from my fellow players, it didn't mean I disliked them – quite a few became lifelong friends. But I admit that there was an attitude from one or two who saw my non-conforming 'otherness' as me thinking I was 'better' than them. This never came from me, but I did understand that being different from the group could breed fear or distrust. I knew it was something I would have to work on as I got older, but my instinctive path was always to stick to my guns. By the time I finished at Everton and signed for Tranmere Rovers I was finally ready to at last grudgingly accept that football was my career, for a little while longer anyway. By then I had started to seek out and enjoy watching, if not always embracing, some of the peculiarities of the sport's attitudes, players, and coaches.

From a distance, with a slightly skewed perception, the first half of my career had been exciting but also fairly standard in at least one way. I'd started with a small Scottish club after being spotted at youth level, then had forged that initially accidental football career all the way to the top of the game for the best part of the next decade. Now, however, in the early 1990s, I was at Tranmere Rovers, living in provincial Chester far from the swinging rock 'n' roll, gig-going life in Chelsea just five years earlier. The whistle was about to blow for the second half of my career, and different considerations had to be faced. I was less focused on hanging out with John Peel and going to see lots of bands and more dedicated to my new family and fatherhood; they were the most important things in my life now, way above the music or, indeed, playing football. Annabel and I had now been married for three years and our son Simon had recently turned one, so me toddling off regularly to gigs would have to wait until he stopped being a toddler.

If this sounds to you like it might not make for a very interesting read, don't worry, because it was from this rather safe existence that my life and career took several unpredictable and wild turns.

Football and How to Survive It is about what happened next, when I played for my slightly less glamorous clubs – Tranmere, Kilmarnock and Motherwell. Some people thought that my real football career finished on the eve of my 29th birthday when I left Everton and indeed the top level in England in 1992. As it turned out, there was more extreme madness, higher levels of fun and deeper levels of pain to come.

The initial challenge facing the young me at the start of this book is that I was working in an industry where your 30th birthday is considered a day of mourning, and I was closing in on 29 at an alarming rate. The nagging was certainly already there in the back of my mind. I would eventually have to consider what would follow the inevitable retirement a few short years later, and start wondering if it was finally worth having a vague plan for the next stage of my life.

Fortunately, I didn't put a strict plan in place as it would have been pointless considering some of the insane curve balls that would fly towards me over the coming decade.

The conclusion I had reached was that I absolutely loved playing football, even if I had no great desire to spend a lifetime within the business. So, as long as I was playing every week, I'd be happy. But the reality is that the older you get the harder it is to stay in the first eleven, especially at the higher levels.

What was important to me was that I wanted to leave the industry at the end of the career with my love, passion and enthusiasm for it still intact. This had been ingrained in me by my dad, who coached, helped and watched me through my entire career. With any luck surviving would be easy enough, but I knew that surviving without resentment or regret might be trickier. I had watched too many other players come out of the game scarcely able to hide a bitterness that seemed to gnaw at their souls, often for years, sometimes for the rest of their lives.

That is what I meant when I told myself I wanted to 'survive' football. I didn't want to be defined by the job, I just wanted to enjoy it, be as successful as possible and then move on. I had always been fiercely determined that the sport wouldn't take over my entire life; if I could continue to grasp the joy, the glory and the opportunities to be creative then, I reasoned, I would be fine.

But, as it turned out, that would be a much tougher test than I – or anyone else – would have expected.

PART ONE
PRENTON PARK

1/
UPSIDE DOWN

I am not the first ex-professional footballer to openly admit that I had an alcohol problem during my career. Some people in the game thought that I didn't drink enough, and that was a problem. The drinking culture was one of the things that infuriated me during my time at Everton but now that I had left to join Tranmere Rovers I was looking forward to a bright new dawn at their delightful, homely little stadium, Prenton Park.

I might have been dropping down a division after spending nine years at the top level of English football – there would be no more Shed End at Chelsea to impress, just the Cowsheds at Tranmere – but I was happy and excited by the new challenge and by the surprisingly high quality of my new teammates. The manager Johnny King was on my side because he loved attacking instinctive skilful players, even if his team talks and attitudes were unconventional, sometimes even baffling but always colourful. While trying to talk me into signing from Everton, he had prepared one of his classic idiosyncratic lines that no other boss would have considered. 'Tranmere Rovers may never be able to compete with Liverpool or Everton, Pat – they are big liners, like the *Queen Mary*. However, I see Tranmere as a deadly submarine, attacking them silently from beneath with a torpedo.'

My first league game under Kingy for the Rovers was away at Roker Park, the home of Sunderland. We stayed overnight in a local hotel, which was the professional thing to do, and after dinner there was a short team meeting and a pep talk by the coaching staff. Tactics talks weren't high on the agenda with Kingy – his attitude was straightforward and deliciously refreshing when asked about it: 'Some managers spend weeks on complicated tactical plans and formations. We just sign good players and let them play.' Some of those off-the-cuff remarks probably took him weeks to invent!

As the team walked out of the meeting together I made to turn left and upstairs to the bedrooms, but everyone else languidly swerved right towards the hotel exit. 'Oh, of course,' I thought. 'An evening stroll after dinner to loosen the legs. Very sensible.' I joined the rest of the team and casually asked one of the players, 'Where are we walking to?'

'To the pub, obviously.'

I couldn't believe it. 'What?! You mean the night before an away match, everyone goes down the pub? That's mental, even Everton didn't do that!' My heart was sinking fast. Had I jumped out of a gentlemen's drinking club and landed up in Club 18–30? Two hundred yards later we reached the pub with pints immediately being ordered all round. I turned to John Aldridge, the former Liverpool and Irish international striker, for an explanation: 'Is this really happening? Is this a regular thing with this lot?'

He shrugged and explained that, 'It's pretty normal for them. But, to be fair, most of the lads don't overdo it.'

'Well, that's a relief. What about the manager, what if he finds out?' Aldo nodded towards the bar, where the boss was casually getting the first round in!

In truth, the lads generally only had a couple at most. Hypocritically, St Patrick here wouldn't be against having a glass of wine with a meal the night before a game, so perhaps, I said to myself, I just had to start easing up a bit on the moral judgements. There were others on the team who didn't drink much, or at all, and they seemed to have a laidback attitude about the pub visit. Maybe it was time for me to relax a little and just enjoy the ride without worrying too much about the curious culture at my new club this time.*

The year is 1992 and lots of things have led to me choosing Tranmere Rovers. There was a good group of young players there and the more senior ones were impressive too, notably striker John Aldridge. I had played against Aldo many times before, memorably when he scored against us while I was playing for Everton in the FA Cup final of 1989. Before I came to Tranmere I thought he was a very good goalscorer; after playing alongside him for a few weeks I realised I was very wrong: he was a world-class finisher.

I was convinced I was now playing at a level below my capabilities – to my mind circumstances had conspired against me – but what on earth was a talent like his doing outside the Premier League? He might have been 33 years old, but he was still lightning-quick and as natural a goalscorer as I had ever worked with. If I put the ball in his area in the box and he got on the end of it, then it invariably landed in the back of the net. He could score every type of goal, and his numbers were off the scale year in, year out. Often compared to Liverpool legend Ian Rush, his scoring averages throughout his career were even better than the iconic Welshman's. Scoring goals in training seemed just as important to him. He would be furious if his team didn't win in the small-sided games, and it was even worse if he hadn't scored the most goals. That, however, was a rarity.

There was a lot of fun to be had at the club with a variety of unusual characters in the team, so wind-ups were part of their daily routine. When choosing the teams for those small-sided games, particularly at the end of the week, just like back in the school days, nobody wanted to be last pick. It is embarrassing enough at school, but this is your job, and the implication

---

* We lost 1–0 the next day and, although it wasn't a bad performance, I couldn't help thinking that those one, two or even three drinks for some of the lads might have made all the difference to the tight scoreline.

is that all the others rate you as the worst player in the team if you are chosen last. For a time at the club, it was the accepted practice that the rest of us would select Aldo last, just to annoy him – and it did, particularly when kids, injured players or an extra goalie would sometimes be picked before him.

The idea we peddled was that Aldo, like many centre-forwards, should be treated with utter disdain by the rest of us 'real' footballers who could actually play a bit. After all, the only thing the strikers can do is put the ball in the net after all our combined hard work and creativity. Technical stuff, skills and tactical acumen are clearly beyond their ability, knowledge or even interest. So why would we pick these crap footballers in our seven-a-side team when technical ability was needed? Strikers do not have the spatial awareness to be midfielders, or the game awareness to be defenders; complex team tactics fly over their heads, they are selfish beings – and, as such, creation is something that is provided for them not by them.

As soon as the training game started, Aldo would vent his anger by haring around diving into tackles and risking injury, which just made it all the more likely we would do exactly the same thing the next week.

There were intriguing, funny characters everywhere I looked at Tranmere Rovers. Our two centre-halves at the time were Dave Higgins and Steve Vickers, an impressive double act on and off the field. This left little or no room in the team for the talented and classy sweeper Mark Hughes. He was unlucky not to be getting a game and wanted to move to another club so he could play every week. But the manager needed him in case his first choices were injured, so there he languished, on the bench or in the reserves.

'Yosser' reacted to the disappointment in a singular way. Every day, as he entered the dressing room at the training ground, he would sing loudly and very passionately to everyone at the club, in his pleasantly rich Welsh baritone, *'Please release me, let me go/For I don't love you, any more . . .'* I think he was channelling Tom Jones more than Engelbert Humperdinck, though it was a close call. Unsurprisingly, some of the youngsters didn't get the reference.

The two players in his way, Higgins and Vickers, were the club surrealists and spent most of their time together thinking up ways to take the rise out of anyone and everyone. As a new player, but one who was an established international, obviously I would be given some respect. Yeah, right! They were straight on the wind-ups, and Higgy eventually christened me 'Buffy the Vampire Slayer'. If you don't know who 'she' is, then Google the name. I reckon I wasn't getting the respect that most in my position would have expected, and luckily I loved it.

During one evening game early on in the season, our resident Dadaist defender Higgy went down screaming in our own half after what appeared to be a fairly robust challenge on him. The play thundered on up field, but he sounded so badly hurt that I ignored our attack and raced over to him as fast as I could to make sure he was OK. As I got there, I could hear his scream as he pointed towards something in the middle distance, '*Aaaah! Aaaah, Aaaah . . .! Ah* can see my house from here.' The rest of the team knew there was nothing wrong with him, physically anyway, but I fell for it hook, line and sinker. But who goes for laughs during a tight league game, while play is still raging on?

After a sluggish start to the season, we quickly began to improve. Making chances for John Aldridge wasn't difficult: he was always hungry to score, in fact he was insatiable. This wasn't a bad thing, but he was always frustrated if he didn't get precisely the pass he expected, which is the classic attitude of most strikers. Even so, soon it was so much fun that, like a young kid, I couldn't wait to get to the matches to play.

One noticeable difference surfaced for me on the pitch because Tranmere already had a talented and extremely popular right-winger in Johnny Morrissey, which created a problem. Me coming in to take his place looked like it could annoy some of the fans but, even more likely, antagonise quite a few within the team group.

Manager John King figured it out after a few weeks. He called me in to the office: 'Pat, do you think you might be able to do a job for us on the left wing? I know it is not your usual position, but it would help balance the team with Moggsy on the other side. It could be bloody exciting with both of you providing ammunition for my gunslinger.' That was his pet name for Aldo. Kingy loved to serve up a metaphor, usually badly mixed.

'Of course, I can do that. I couldn't care less if I am right, left or central. As long as I get enough of the ball in the final third it doesn't really matter to me where I am on the pitch.'

If anything, playing on the left suited me and my style slightly more than playing on the right-hand side. It also led to me developing a fantastic understanding with a line of left full-backs over the coming seasons. Fellow Scot Stevie Mungall played there for a while and was one of the footballers I most enjoyed playing with throughout my career. Throughout his over 650 appearances for Tranmere over the years Mungy slotted in efficiently just about everywhere on the field – think of James Milner of Liverpool and England and you will not be far off a decent image of the versatility and the perfect professionalism of this rugged but friendly Scotsman.

I had played against him for Everton in pre-season games and well-remember those first welcoming words he said to me: 'Dae that again, ya wee bastert and I'll hoff ye in two.' How pleasant to hear a fellow, friendly west-of-Scotland accent warning me of the dangers the future may pose. In fact, it was said with a smile and although most wouldn't have noticed the kindly lilt behind the gruff Bellshill (home of Teenage Fanclub) brogue, I smiled and laughed back. We were kindred spirits clearly, even if, yes, us Scots do have an odd way of showing it.

Following on from him at left-back was a youngster signed from local part-timers Marine, Ian Nolan. I explained to the eager colt, 'You just overlap using that searing pace and don't worry about defensive positioning while I'm on the ball. I'll deliver it at the right moment near the byline. If I lose it, that's my problem.' He followed the instructions unquestioningly to the letter and between us we created a whole load of goals with that one move. He was eventually sold on for £1.7 million to Sheffield Wednesday. His replacement in time was Alan Rogers. I explained the same concept to him and off he sped merrily to the byline at every opportunity. I would beat a player or two, draw a couple of others before slipping it into his path in the space I had developed near the byline. All this was very impressive as his more natural left foot created as many goals as his predecessor's, so in time he was also sold on, this time to Nottingham Forest for around £3 million.

Did anybody actually notice who was the brains behind this particular operation?!

Ged Brannan filled in behind me at left-back quite a few times, and although a much more complete player than the two specialist full-backs mentioned above, being a real class act in midfield, he was also later sold on for £800,000, this time to Manchester City. I tried not to take being overlooked by the Premier League teams too personally! I did, however, feel I was helping make the club some very good money by training these lads up, which I was delighted to do.

It all slotted into place in that first season and soon enough we became a hugely attractive team to watch. We were scoring plenty of goals while delighting our fans and the local media with our devil-may-care approach and non-stop attacking style.

It was nothing less than glorious for me, something I desperately wanted. After a less than joyous last year and a half at Everton, I had rediscovered my boyish love of playing. I liked everything about this club, particularly its curious, homely, mad-cap personality. The ground itself was tight: a real old-school stadium that needed less than 10,000 fans inside to have it rocking, but when it was busier than that the noise could be earsplitting. The club had been in the fourth tier as recently as six seasons earlier, only missing relegation to the Conference by two points, but John King had already built a side that could make a decent challenge of getting into the Premier League itself, generally accepted as the Holy Grail not only at Tranmere but for every club outside the top division. With the money on offer in the Premier League, it felt more financially valuable than finding the original chalice from the Last Supper, though the lads would probably have filled that with lager given the chance. This was an unthinkable rise in such a short time, for a small club with limited financial resources and no history whatsoever in the top flight.

We also had another unique advantage: we often played our home games on Friday nights. This was originally a ploy to attract some fans who would otherwise go to Liverpool or Everton on a Saturday afternoon, those giants being only six miles away across the Mersey, after all. The upshot was that our games under floodlights had a special quality: the atmosphere could feel twice as good as a daytime fixture with the same attendance. This after-dark ambience is not uncommon in football, and there was also the fact that the darkness hid some of the few empty spaces in the stands and the enclosures. We had plenty of those floodlit home games, far more than all our competitors, and we made good use of the advantages; of how it lifted us and added to the oppression of our opponents. Some Everton and Liverpool fans would come to Prenton Park to start their weekends on a Friday night, and plenty told me they became regulars after enjoying our style.*

A classic example of our cavalier style came against Brentford on a mid-November evening. Two-nil down and struggling, the fans got behind us and we roared back to an impressive 3–2 victory. I managed to score a couple, for once beating Aldo's tally on the night, but the feeling in the ground was electric and ecstatic. I think some of us, fans and players alike, began to think then, less than halfway through the season, that maybe, just maybe, we could make this miracle happen. It moved us up to third place in the league, a third place that was thrilling to watch.

Picking up my Man of the Match award after the game, however, I already felt ill, just as I had recently in a few other games, but thought

---

* Premier League football wasn't to everyone's taste at the time, including mine. The over-simplistic, insular and dated coaching methods inspired by Charles Hughes still held sway with too many. I interviewed Everton manager Joe Royle for *GOAL* magazine in the mid-1990s, and he was disarmingly direct: 'The way it has gone with pace and power, there are fewer players coming through like yourself and Peter Beardsley. That's why we are now importing those creative players; we aren't developing them here. With the exception of Manchester United, who have the perfect balance of pace, power and skill, many of these players are like professional athletes first and foremost.'

nothing of it, just putting it down to 90 minutes of over-exertion. A medic checked me out and said, 'It could be a number of things, but it definitely isn't appendicitis.' Against Swindon a few weeks later, the excruciating stomach pains were back after the game. Again, I was assured I was going to be OK, and, 'The one thing that is certain is that it is not appendicitis.'

Of course, I was rushed to hospital the next day to have my appendix removed in an emergency operation.

After an appendix removal you would expect a slow and drawn out recovery, but I had two things in my favour. First, I was a weirdly quick healer and, secondly, I had the offending body part removed by what was, for the time, pioneering keyhole surgery. I was back in training by the end of the week and fit to play seven days later. I clearly didn't want to miss a moment of the pleasure at Prenton Park.

As the season took off, I continued to enjoy the incredibly excited air in the Tranmere dressing room and on the training ground. Although, having said that, the high spirits often seemed to be fuelled at least as much by the upcoming Christmas party as the prospect of promotion to the Premier League. The preparation for the party, organised solely by the players not the club, was discussed more than any other topic, including winning football games.

When I signed for the Rovers, Johnny Morrissey's first words were, 'How do you want to pay your costs for the Christmas party? All up front? Or monthly?' A simple 'nice to have you here, Pat' might have been the more customary greeting to a newly signed player, so I knew right away they took their 'Chrimbo party' seriously. The Everton bash could be wild, but even before I got to the Tranmere event I knew it would make the Toffees night feel like a dull suburban dinner party in comparison.

One of the odd things about these nights, which was the same for the Liverpool FC party too, was that all the local sports journos were invited along to join in the fun. As such, any misbehaviour was never reported, those nights were sacrosanct. I thought the mafia had it sewn up with their omerta code, but this was a different league. Now, I was far from the biggest partygoer in the football world, but after underestimating it at Everton, a little older and wiser, I now understood the importance of this blow-out for the players. This was their ultimate bonding night; I wouldn't be able to duck this one with some feeble excuse.

As with the Everton party, it was held at the Continental ('Conty') nightclub, the entry tickets were extortionately priced for guys but completely free for the local Liverpool and Wirral girls. I say it was held at the nightclub, but that was only where the team eventually landed at 9pm, having been drinking and partying from roughly 2pm, right after training.

Just as with the other parties for the Merseyside clubs, it was strictly fancy dress. You could tell immediately who was really 'on the pull' by what they wore. Those turning up in Navy whites, cowboy outfits and superhero costumes wanted to turn the girls' heads. Those of us turning up as, say, a particularly impressive version of Michelle Pfeiffer's Cat Woman character (even if she was also a superhero), were less likely to be on the prowl.

Back in those days it was considered not at all unusual to have strippers as part of the entertainment. Even back then it was something I felt very uneasy with. I couldn't help but think how demeaning it was to the women and how obviously faked it was as well. I would, and not just because I am writing in a book, quietly absent myself from the proceedings at this point. Maybe in hindsight I should have done more to discourage the behaviour, but this was the players' affair, and I would have been given short shrift for spoiling the 'fun' for my new teammates. I always brought my brother-in-law Liam along for the night and both of us would sit at the bar with our other great friend Danny Lloyd while that part of the 'entertainment' was going on.

At one Christmas party I was (shock, horror!) drawn into the room where the girls were stripping, just briefly, simply because I could not believe what I was hearing. Astonishingly, emanating from there, was the sound of 'Sugar Hiccup' by the Cocteau Twins, my favourite band, who made the most heartachingly beautiful, sensitive and ethereal music. One of the girls was 'dancing' to the track. I couldn't imagine anything more incongruous. While I applauded her taste in music, I couldn't at that moment imagine how anyone could love that sound and actually enjoy doing that job. I suspected it was a mournful cry of, 'If there is anybody with a soul in here, I have one too, just in case you were wondering.'

There was also one very strange occurrence at one of the Christmas parties. A girl turned up and sidled over to me, wearing very little indeed. It was impossible not to notice that she was also rather beautiful, but her opening line was maybe a bit more forward than I was used to. 'I have come all the way up from Essex for this party, just to meet you. I have booked a hotel room, shall we go?' I had been drinking wine, quite a bit in fact, but was aware of myself enough to say politely, 'It is a lovely offer and you look lovely as well, but I am actually married and very happily too.' She made a halfhearted effort to carry on but seemed oddly relieved when she walked away. Some months later another footballer was outed in the tabloids for having a brief liaison with a girl, and in the photos she looked awfully like the same girl to me.

Honey traps were considered fair game by the red tops back then, but I was amazed that anyone would have targeted me. I mean, I was not then and never have been that kind of big star player. But thinking about it later, I suspect it was nothing to do with my playing fame but more likely to have been about my involvement with the PFA and the fact that sections of the press were out to get Gordon Taylor or, indeed, anyone close to him. Does this sound a bit far-fetched? Maybe so, but years later when the *News of the World* phone-hacking investigation was going on, I got a call from the police to ask if there was any reason why Glenn Mulcaire should have my details in his notebooks. There was no reason why the man at the epicentre of the phone-hacking scandal should have my number, other than the blindingly obvious one that he was trying to get inside information on me and possibly Gordon Taylor, our chief executive. Everyone was fair game for the tabloids using any unfair, underhand or even illegal methods.

I survived the Christmas party that first season and felt better than I had done at any point in my entire career. The appendix had obviously been dragging me down for a while, maybe even years, but at Prenton

Park I now suddenly felt as if I was 21 again. I was back in the Scotland international squad, I had the benefit of ten years' experience in the professional game and, all around me, I could see players playing well and growing in belief.

While our gunslinger was hitting the target every week, the rest of the players were just as impressive in their own ways. Two I particularly liked were the experienced midfielders Neil McNab and Mark Proctor. Both were true gentlemen and superb pros as well as very good footballers who had played at the top level. They were slightly older than me, but suddenly I realised that these were the people I could relate to on a personal level, more so than the excitable youngsters. Maybe it was getting close to the time for my 'maverick young outsider' status to be replaced by that of the 'seasoned sensible old pro'.

I thought I had always been quite level-headed, but there was no getting away from it, having just turned 29, suddenly I was considered more than just a sensible chap: I was now the venerable, sagacious old man to some of these younger players. In that I was also the responsible PFA union man by this point, the 20-year-olds were sometimes uncomfortably respectful towards me, even a little deferential at times, and I disliked that attitude intensely. A frankly disturbing moment came when another young player was drafted into the first team for his debut. He sidled over to me nervously in the dressing room pre-match and, trying not to be heard by the others, plucked up some courage and eventually said, 'Can I ask for some advice, Mr Nevin?'

I kept calm but internally I screamed, '"Mister! Nevin?" Am I that ancient?'

My point of view was that we should all treat each other as equals in a football team. I couldn't be doing with hierarchies due to age, fame, status, ability or anything else. My legs might have felt just a little heavier as I walked onto the pitch that day. Happily, the football was such a joy that it made up for those moments when I was treated like a distinguished grey-haired old man instead of a scruff whose thatch was just thinning a little on top.

2/
CLOUDS

I was so happy playing football again. Some of my attitudes had begun to change from my unplanned, accidental early days in the sport. Specifically, I seemed to be laughing and smiling a lot more at work. I wasn't always rushing away from the lads' company in an unseemly way to get home, go to a gig, catch an art show or get back out to do some extra training on my own. I lingered just a bit longer now, because I enjoyed the companionship of some, if not most, of these guys. It was difficult to know if it was this group that was different or if it was me who had changed, at least a little. This enjoyable life is probably exactly the way the sport looks from the outside, and it was also the way I always wanted it to be.

Life at home was blissful too, with Annabel, Simon and me enjoying as many of those long warm afternoons and evenings together as possible at our cosy little home in Chester. The only blot on the landscape was that my angelic mum had been diagnosed with cancer, but the treatment had started, and we all hoped for and expected a good outcome. Life is never totally perfect, and this was just about the only negative thing that was affecting our world. I wanted to keep this part of our lives happy, carefree and apart. Lying in bed listening to the gorgeous, romantic Go-Betweens album *16 Lovers Lane* summed up what our life was about at this time:

beauty, love and happiness. Somewhere in the background however, mum's illness was a worry, but one that hopefully wouldn't become a critical concern for many years to come.

As the season developed towards Christmas 1992 things were improving in the league and we generally hovered around second or third place. There was even finally a chance to play in a European club football tournament. For almost my entire career up until then, English football had been rightly banned from European competition following the Heysel Stadium disaster at the European Cup final between Liverpool and Juventus. Now we were at last allowed to compete again, so my first ever European club games were not in the Champions League, but in the Anglo-Italian Cup with Tranmere. It was not against the mighty Juventus or AC Milan, but it was still a good experience.*

We had a decent run and were far from outclassed in any of the games against our Italian opponents. After playing Cremonese at home, the Italian club asked John King if he would be willing to sell me to them. I thought it would have been a bit harsh on the gaffer had I accepted the offer only three months into my Tranmere contract. Kingy was always good enough to tell me up front, as he promised he would, when a team wanted to buy me, but in this case I didn't even consider it. The odd thing was that I hadn't even got dressed after my post-match shower before he sidled over to inform me of the Italian interest. He seemed to be enjoying the international intrigue while I awkwardly tried to dry myself.

The most memorable trip was to Reggiana. The 0–0 draw could be described as a classic, but only in terms of it being a classic example of Italian football's dull, defensive dourness. However, the build-up the day before was impossible to forget.

As ever with my travels abroad, I wanted to get out and explore the local culture and the architecture of the area. Reggio Emilia itself is a

---

* We beat Pisa 1–0 in Tuscany, and in their team was a young Christian Vieri, soon to be the most expensive player in the world, so there was a little stardust.

historical and beautiful little town not far from Parma. So, while the rest
of the team headed off to bed for an afternoon's rest the day before the
game, I popped out for a walk into the town to enjoy a coffee in the pretty
piazza. I immediately bumped into a few Tranmere fans who were taking
advantage of the club's first ever foray into Europe. There was a lazy, calm
and restful atmosphere as we enjoyed a nice relaxed chat standing in the
late-afternoon autumn sunshine. There might even have been the muffled
sound of an old donkey's hooves moving slowly over the flagstones in the
background, just to add to the general languid air.

Suddenly a man came sprinting out from nowhere and ripped the
expensive camera from the shoulder of one of the fans I was talking
to. As they stood motionless, shocked and confused by what had just
happened, I was already haring off after the thief. My east end of Glasgow
background kicked in and within 50 yards I knew I was going to catch
the sprinting Italian mugger. Now, as a footballer, yes even a cultured
creative type, if I am running behind anyone, I know exactly how to
bring him down with a judicious trip. I tapped his trailing leg onto his
other with my right foot and sent him flying into a parked car on the
narrow one-way street. When he stopped rolling, while clearly still in
some pain from the fall, I leaned down to wrench the camera from his
hand. As I bent over, he reached for his inside jacket pocket and, in what
felt like slow motion, pulled out something long, metallic and shiny that
glinted in the fading sunlight.

At that moment I decided it wasn't worth facing a large knife for a
camera, however expensive it was. I was just about to resign from my new
'have-a-go hero' role with immediate effect when, fortunately, the 'knife'
turned out to be the handle of an umbrella. What did he think he was going
to do, open me to death? I will admit to a swift kick that was probably a
straight red, even back then, to keep him down, before making my way
back to the fans, camera in hand. They were still standing gaping, rooted to
the spot in the piazza. Clearly they were from a nice leafy part of the Wirral
and not Toxteth, just over the Mersey. They were very thankful, but I had
to explain one very important thing to them and a handful of other Rovers

followers who had by now joined them: 'You know, I'm not supposed to be out of the hotel just now, so if you could keep this to yourselves, I would be very grateful.' They gave me their word they would.

Two days later the story appeared in the *Sun* newspaper.

A few weeks later back on Merseyside there was a midweek League Cup match between Everton and Chelsea at Goodison Park. I fancied going along to watch my old teammates from both sides, but there was a problem: where would I watch the game from? In those days you could just turn up and pay in. Walking towards the ground after parking up, I had to decide which end I would go into. I liked both clubs, but instead of it being a major moral dilemma it just felt natural to pay into the Park End stand where the Chelsea fans were gathered. I got the coat collar up and sat there behind the goal as the game started, hoping not to be noticed. The Everton fans would be none the wiser as long as I kept a low profile.

Five minutes into the game I was recognised by a few of the thousands of Chelsea fans around me. Within moments they were all standing up, turning towards me and singing my name. Kind though it was, I could have done without it. I had just left the Toffees a few months before yet here I was in the away end supporting the opposition; it wasn't a good look. Have you ever been to an event or party you said you weren't going to, or weren't supposed to be at, and then you were spotted, rumbled by someone who is going to shop you? Well, multiply that discomfort by about 10,000!

The Everton fans had every right to think, 'What an ungrateful little creep. After how kind we had been to him in his time here.' I suppose it was the moment that I knew for certain that when my career was over, my English team would always be Chelsea, and that is still the case to this day. Sometimes your heart makes the decision for you, and you have no choice. Having said that, Everton v Chelsea is still my least favourite game every season – I hate seeing either team lose.

It was an exciting time internationally as well, as I was back in the Scotland squad and among the trips abroad there was one to Switzerland for a

World Cup qualifier. We lost 3–1 over there and, to add to my personal disappointment, I didn't even make the bench.*

The day before the game Andy Roxburgh had given a team talk at the hotel and at the end, being a teacher at heart, he had a few extra wholesome educational words for the lads: 'Right, boys, this hotel is one of the oldest in the country and it's of great historical importance. Have a look at the furniture around you and the carvings, they are all original and they were all made by real craftsmen. The management have told me to remind everyone that this place is made entirely of wood and its tinder dry. So don't take any chances, I don't want anyone having a sneaky cigarette in their room as the slightest mistake could lead to a disaster.'

When the game had finished we went back to the hotel and had a couple of drinks in the rooms. I was sitting chatting with the 'nice' boys – Celtic's Tom Boyd and Paul McStay, along with Brian McClair and Kevin Gallagher. As I walked out of their room, I bumped into my old Everton teammate Stuart McCall, now at Rangers, and we walked upstairs together to go to our rooms.

Outside one room big Duncan Ferguson, another sub who hadn't got on, was pushing a gigantic heavy wardrobe that only he could have moved, in front of the door. Inside that room were Ally McCoist, Ian Durrant, Gordon Durie and maybe a few others. 'What are you doing, Duncan?' 'Those bastards were takin' the piss oot o me, so am gettin' them back.'

This sort of hi-jinks is par for the course, and funny up to a point. I smiled, walked past and went on my way towards my own room. Realising I had forgotten something down in the 'Celtic' room I doubled back a few moments later to see the big man lighting a match beside the tinder dry furniture. '*What are you doing?!*' I shouted.

---

* This was a regular occurrence. I more often travelled and was left out than got on the field with Scotland, but I always felt I should be there anyway, in case my country needed me. The idea of it being beneath me not being in the starting line-up or even making one of three spots on the subs' bench never occurred to me. It was an honour to be there, period.

He grinned as he explained, 'I told you, they were taken the piss. I'm gonnae gie them a fright by smokin' them oot, but they cannae git oot.'

I am sure he didn't plan on frying them and the rest of us in this ancient wooden hotel, but I quickly got the matches from him and suggested he just went to bed. The wardrobe-in-front-of-the-door trick would be quite enough on its own. Duncan never meant any harm, he just thought of things very differently from the rest of us. He, of course, changed in time to become a hugely respected coach and a very sensible chap. Every time I was in his company, however, I was rarely ever less than totally entertained by his antics, which are still legendary on Merseyside, in particular. This time, though, he might have gone a bit too far.

Back in normality, or something approaching it anyway, the season was still going along splendidly for Tranmere. By January we were solidly in second place, a position that would give us automatic promotion to the Premier League if we stayed there. We then beat Oldham in the FA Cup after a replay, where I managed to score an impressive diving header from a Johnny Morrissey cross.

It all felt close to perfection, helped by the fact that there was minimal pressure in comparison to England's top league. There were also limited expectations at Tranmere compared to my previous clubs, but, even so, we were outperforming any there might have been by some distance. The games were exciting and open, while every training session had its fair share of fun. I walked out onto the training ground one freezing cold day that winter. The area was wide open, and the sleet was battering in vertically on a howling gale from the nearby Irish Sea. As I looked around, the players were all huddled in a group in exactly the same formation as you would see emperor penguins huddled together against an Antarctic storm on a David Attenborough documentary. The manager walked out and could not stop laughing at them shuffling round replacing the outer 'human penguins' from the elements.

I enjoyed the company of this group of players as much as any I had spent time with before. If, however, I thought I was beginning to actually fit in just a little at some points, it usually didn't last long. In a tense cup game at Prenton Park we had a free-kick against us 25 yards out. With ten minutes to go and us defending a fragile single-goal lead, the wall was lined up. I was the designated player to charge the ball down from the side of the wall. I was out to the side just a little, but still on an arc, ten yards from the ball, getting ready to charge.

The referee shouted at me, 'Get back the whole ten yards.'

'I am back the whole ten yards,' I screeched, prepped and strained to sprint at his whistle.

Tension building, fans screaming, nerves fraying, he called out to me again: 'Get back the full ten yards or I'll book you.'

'But, ref, it's an arc of ten yards – we are all equidistant.'

At that point my teammates stopped and turned round to me: '*Equidistant!!!???*'

Even the opposition players turned on me: 'Ooh, so it's "equidistant", is it?'

Next the referee looked over and shook his head as if to say, 'We don't use that kind of language here, sonny.'

So much for the tension of the moment. When one of our lads shouted at the referee with a minute to go, 'Ref, he nearly decapitated me at the knee,' I let it slide.

For the next round of the FA Cup, the squad was beginning to look thin because of a few injuries. Aldridge was out and I agreed to have an injection in my ankle to allow me to play. After years of tackles and injuries on many parts of my body, I was beginning to creak just a little at the edges. The ankles in particular had to be strapped up most weeks and, on this occasion, I had been crocked in the game the week before by a scything agricultural tackle that had damaged the ligaments yet again. We all knew we would pay for these injections later, but most players accepted the risks and the pain to come afterwards. The suffering would kick in right after the game when the painkillers wore off, as well as at the end of our careers with the early onset of arthritis.

On the Friday I was miles away from being fit to play because of the ankle injury. On Saturday morning I was not much further on in the recovery – but by the time I got to the ground the drugs were kicking in and I had my ankle strapped up so tight that I couldn't even feel my left foot. It didn't matter – I was able to start against Premier League Ipswich Town at Prenton Park, which was all the club and, crucially, I cared about. I scored the opener and felt confident; had we had our star striker on the field, we would have won the game. We didn't and were unlucky to lose 2–1.* It did however show that we were as good as some Premier League teams – we just needed more strength in depth. This was only January and the run-in would be difficult, particularly as the bigger clubs' resources, even in this division, were miles beyond ours.

We hung on in there but by March the manager called me into his room and asked, 'Do you reckon you could do a job for us up front against Bristol City while Aldo is injured again?' It was music to my ears, of course. At heart I still, 12 years into my career, thought of myself more as a centre-forward or a second striker (that is, a number 10) than the restrictive old-school winger that had been foisted on me over the years. That had been my position until I turned professional, and I still felt much more comfortable there.

I scored one and made another for my playing partner Chris Malkin. I loved playing with him whether I was up front or out wide. He was lightning quick, brave and utterly selfless, a fairly unusual trait for a striker. He always ran beyond the defence, which made them drop back, developing space for me to create in the pockets he left.

The next game was a midweek away match at Brentford where Chrissy and I linked up again for me to score the only goal. The real satisfaction that night was that Everton were playing in London the next day against Chelsea and their entire team came along to watch us. Apparently, Howard Kendall, the manager who had got rid of me from Everton just months

---

* At this point in the FA Cup struggling Everton got a home crowd of only 4,000 more than Tranmere Rovers, an incredible relative change in fortunes.

before, had organised a sweepstake on the first goalscorer and had laughed at the player who had drawn me – he couldn't imagine me as a striker. To be fair, he clearly couldn't imagine me anywhere in his team. Apparently, he was very disgruntled when I scored, and my old teammates were made to leave immediately after that goal. A small (-minded) victory for me inside the bigger victory for the team.

Ultimately, our own manager felt that the balance of the team wasn't right, and even though I was a capable makeshift striker, I was no Aldo and he wanted me back out wide providing as well as scoring goals from there.*

Unsurprisingly, without our world-class scorer we were slipping down the table a bit. In March the decision was made to buy Tommy Coyne from Celtic for £400,000. This was a huge investment for Tranmere, but it seemed worth it. TC was a very reliable scorer; an incredibly intelligent player and also an Irish international who played alongside Aldo for Jack Charlton's side. It seemed an inspired move and, when he arrived in the dressing room, I liked him immediately. A fellow Glaswegian, he had that ultra-dour Scottish humour that I always warm to. Even though we had fallen to sixth over the past couple of months, I felt we had a good chance of promotion even if it was through the play-offs. First though, I had to give 'TC' the obligatory warnings about the manager John King and his idiosyncrasies: 'Tommy, just to let you know, the manager's team talks can sometimes be a bit . . . out there. He does like to add a little or indeed a lot of colour when he is in a particular mood. With you being a new player, he is sure to go for it before your first game, just don't worry about it too much, let it wash over you. OK?'

Tommy looked confused. 'How weird can it be? I've talked to him a few times already and he doesn't seem that far from normal . . . for a manager.'

An hour before Tommy's debut, the dressing-room door opens and Johnny King ambles in.

---

* The manager was still entertaining everyone with his thoughts on Aldo: 'He might be injured but Aldridge is like El Cid. Even when he's dead, you could strap him to a trolley, wheel him to the back post, and he'd still knock one in for you.'

The team is read out in a perfunctory way and then he goes into one: 'Right, lads, I want to imagine you are in the Wild West. Just like the old movies, you are in a saloon bar and there is danger all around, especially from that guy in the corner all in black. The piano player stops, and you know you have to get out of there fast. But you don't panic, no. The first thing you have to do is get your two Smith & Wesson pistols out and have them cocked ready to fire. You face everyone in the bar, and then you walk slowly backwards keeping an eye on everyone and keeping those guns pointed at all the other cowboys.'

At this point Tommy Coyne stole a glance over at me, his questioning eyes filled with confusion. The question seems to be, 'Is he all right?' We look at the rest of the team. They have seen it all before, there are a few suppressing giggles, though others are just shaking their heads.

By now, Kingy, our 'respectable' manager, is down on his hunkers in the middle of the dressing room going backwards, getting right into the part, apparently channelling some previously unknown schooling in method acting: 'As you back out, lads, keep your eyes peeled and get those elbows out feeling for those saloon doors behind you. You know the ones that are made of wood and swing open and shut. When you feel the doors, don't turn around and walk out, you keep on backing, all the way through the doors, keeping those guns pointed.'

By this point he has shuffled backwards to the dressing-room door himself. 'When you get out of the door and round the corner, then – and only then – do you put those guns back in your holsters and turn to get on your horse.' There is a dramatic pause and then he, with utter seriousness adds, 'And that, lads, is what it is like at a short corner.' Turning, he moseys on out like John Wayne, closing the door behind him.

He could have just said, 'Watch out for short corners, boys,' but where was the fun in that? John King is no longer with us, but to this day none of us know how much of this was his humour, how much affectation or how much was just his idiosyncratic outlook. I like to think it was mostly an unaffected natural eccentricity, though some of the boys just thought he was a bit loopy.

In another pre-match pep talk he turned to our full-back Tony Thomas, and with a grave voice said, 'Wingers are like machine-gun turrets. They supply the ammunition. So, you've got to blow them up. Take some dynamite out there in your boots today.'

A personal favourite was to Ged Brannan: 'You can sense danger, lad. You've got a Geiger counter up your arse.' How lyrical – but you mostly kind of got the point . . . eventually.

I was playing the best football of my career having learned a great deal over the years as a professional. That experience, added to the joy of being given the freedom to create at will by the manager, was everything I needed. It was also the most conventional period in my life thus far, but I was fine with that: I loved the job and I loved the time spent inside our little family unit and the quieter life I was settling into.

I scored again in my next game for my country against Malta up at Ibrox Park, so it wasn't an entirely quiet little suburban life. With just a few months of the season to go every day started with me leaping out of bed carefree and happy.

But then one day, it all changed with one simple phone call from my older brother.

'Hi, Pat, Tommy here. How are you?'

It was the usual introduction but, without the positive air he habitually had in his voice, I didn't like the sound of it. Instead of saying, 'Fine,' I said, 'What's wrong?'

He took a moment and said it straight but with compassion: 'It's mum's cancer, it's back and . . . the prognosis is not good.'

I knew exactly what this meant. We were a positive bunch in our family, but as anyone who has been there knows, there is only one question to ask at that point.

'How much time does she have?'

Tommy was hesitant. 'It's likely to be months rather than years, but the doctors can't be precise.' There was silence down the line for a while, then he eventually carried on. 'I've been looking into new experimental ideas. I read something about yew trees providing special cancer treatments, so we shouldn't give up totally.'

I loved his positivity but suspected he was just trying to soften the blow – or maybe, like many in the same situation, he was willing to try anything. She was only 65 at this point and had given her entire adult life to taking care of her children. She had just reached the time in her life when she could relax a bit and enjoy herself. Her children and grandchildren were blossoming. This was the time to finally, indulgently, consider herself for once, but it was all being taken away before she really had a chance to live it. It felt so wrong, as she and my dad deserved that special period.

This felt like reality, a reality I had never faced in my life before. I knew I had been living a blessed life but, right then, holding that phone and staring ahead into space, I fully understood how fortunate I had been up until that precise moment. I also quickly realised that every single second left with her would have to be savoured.

This news punctured the little idyllic bubble of fun in my work life, and my home life, nestled in that sweet little house in Chester. Annabel and I adored having our young son around while spending an inordinate amount of time with him at Chester Zoo, which fascinated him. We were even getting out most weeks at least once, to go for dinner or watch a movie together. A young neighbour, Ann, was perfect with Simon and was always available as a babysitter. Sure, I hadn't been getting to many gigs, but that was OK. I was perfectly happy spending nights in with Annabel and Simon. There would still be great music when we had more time in the future.*

---

* From my previous life before Tranmere, you might have expected me to be into the new 'Madchester' scene at the Haçienda Club. I did nip over to the Haçienda one night after a New Order gig at the G-MEX and ended up, along with my little sister Kathleen, in the club's VIP area as Tony Wilson's guest. It soon became clear that this was nothing more than a drug den, the last place I wanted to be caught in – even though I was assured there was a special chute in the corner to dump the 'gear' if there was a raid, I didn't fancy being there at all. I got out very quickly and, anyway, it wasn't showing a great example of moral rectitude in front of my 'wee' sister.

There are times when you must make choices: what kind of husband and what kind of parent are you going to be? I loved the idea of being the dotingly devoted type, as much as the work allowed me to be, because now I had to provide for them.

Our neighbours were angelically good people. Chris and David across the road let us use their swimming pool through the summer, which was fabulous for a family with a youngster. It also helped my aching and now slightly ageing legs the day after games. Pat and David next door were always welcoming and were fabulously helpful with kind and intelligent advice for a young couple.

Some afternoons I would pop over to my friends Brian McClair of Manchester United or Vini Reilly of Durutti Column and Factory Records fame. Sitting in Vini's flat listening to him play his latest beautiful music on his guitar was still endlessly magical. In hindsight I should have gone over more often: it was the best and most beautiful way I could clear my head at a time when worries about my mum were growing daily. The emotions produced by his music allowed me to accept my own deep feelings about what was going on with her at the time. He never knew how much he helped me.

Then, within days, there was another blow. Jacqui Geddes, one of Annabel's best friends from university in Glasgow, was diagnosed with terminal cancer too. This put concerns about winning promotion or missing a few gigs into perspective; it also gave me another reason for being pleased about those Friday night games at Tranmere. As soon as the match was finished we would often drive up to see my parents and the rest of the family four hours away in Glasgow. Not having to be down again for training until the Monday morning meant I had good amount of time at home in Glasgow to spend talking to – or, more importantly, listening to – my mum. I remember asking her much more about her childhood than I had ever done before; her teenage years and the early days of her married life. I wanted to ask all the questions that I might regret not having asked later. I got a much fuller picture of why she became the woman she was now. One afternoon she told me about a friend trying to lead her astray as a teenager, a story I'd never heard before: 'She was a bit more forward than me and she said we were going to meet some friends. When we arrived, it wasn't the sort of place I would go to – there were soldiers and sleazy-looking men all around. When I understood what kind of place it was and what kind of girls went to those places, I gave my "ex"-friend a piece of my mind and left right away, even though I had to walk home across the city alone. I wasn't that type of girl. I was a wee bit frightened, but I was even more angry.'

These conversations made me realise that even though I had mostly looked to my dad as an inspiration, there was plenty of my mum in me. Certainly, most of the earnestness came from her, but also the strength of character never to be bullied into doing something I didn't want to do, whatever the circumstances or the expectations.

While life off the pitch was getting more complicated, the football was joyously simple at this point. Near the end of the season, we went on a ten-game unbeaten run and after a 2–1 win against Derby I felt sure we were going to make the play-offs. I was up front again that night alongside Tommy Coyne, and this time I bagged both goals, including a towering striker's header . . . honestly.

This was a magical period at the club; we could see the goal ahead of us and the fans could feel it too. Apart from winning and loving the celebrations there still didn't seem to be any pressures on the field. The confidence that was growing wasn't offset by any fear. From Johnny (Moggsy) Morrissey's arrogance on the ball on the opposite wing, to Tony (the Tank) Thomas's power, skill and scarcely hidden menace at full-back, I could see the entire group believing they could beat anyone.

As the grass returned to the pitches in the spring after a harsh winter, those lush green fields meant we could show how skilful we were. There was a clear echo of my early days at Chelsea with that invincible attitude and supreme confidence. That Chelsea team had won the same league when I was a callow 20-year-old, getting promotion to the top division. I had been here before, and it didn't feel any different or any less glorious this time as the season built towards its crescendo.

There are certain times when the games seem to flow by, almost effortlessly, maybe even fatefully. Creation is easy, and during the games you spend an inordinate amount of time smiling or even laughing with your mates, because you all know how good it is and how much fun it is in that moment. These periods don't last forever, or even a long time, usually – but right then they feel like they will. If you have any sense at all, or maybe just some experience, you should stop now and again to enjoy these times in life – they have usually gone before you realise how special they are. I was old enough and had been through enough by then to know how special it was and, despite some things in my personal life feeling painful, on the pitch I was loving it.

And so, we reached the play-offs after finishing in fourth place. We faced Swindon Town, managed and captained by Glenn Hoddle, in the two-legged semi-final. Now within touching distance of the Premier League, we had stayed with the likes of Newcastle, Leicester City and West Ham for most of the season – enormous, wealthy clubs compared to Tranmere Rovers. During the season Swindon had beaten us 2–0 down in Wiltshire, but we had shredded them 3–1 at Prenton Park with a hat-trick from Kenny Irons.*

This one was too close to call, but we were confident without being complacent – or at least I thought we were. In the first leg we lost 3–1, conceding two goals in the first three minutes, so maybe just a little complacency there! It was bad but not a disaster. We could easily get three goals against them at Prenton – in fact, as Kingy reminded us, we had already done so this season.

---

* Kenny was a very decent player, good enough to go on to a higher level, but I think he was happy where he was. Ironsy didn't officially have Tourette's syndrome, but it was a rare sentence that didn't have an expletive or three in it. After his hat-trick the local Radio City correspondent asked for a live interview. The shock on everyone's face at the very idea confused the reporter. He had no idea that Kenny probably wouldn't manage a live broadcast without inadvertently slipping out a few Fs and Cs.

The home tie was at a crammed Prenton Park, with an absolute belief in the stadium that we could score the three goals we needed. We did indeed score those three goals – I scored one of them and made another for Mark Proctor – but sadly we shipped two at the other end, losing 5–4 on aggregate. After all the effort of an entire season, Tranmere Rovers missed the chance of a Wembley play-off final by a single goal. Not for the first time in my career, I was incredibly close to glory, but those tiny margins are all important. Swindon went on to get promoted instead of us, those two goals in the first three minutes of the tie proving to be our downfall.

Obviously, I was disappointed but there was perspective, of course. We had done incredibly well to get so close. We would be even stronger next season with some more youngsters coming through the youth system. Tommy Coyne would have settled into the team alongside, Aldo, Johnny Morrissey, Ian Muir, myself and Chris Malkin, so we were still going to score lots of goals. There would definitely be other opportunities for us to get to the Premier League.

Because of the play-offs and an up-and-coming World Cup group match against Estonia, there was no chance of a foreign holiday for Annabel and me that year. That was OK though, because I wanted to spend as much time as I could with my ailing mum, and for her to spend time with her grandson, Simon, to whom she was devoted.

The Scotland–Estonia game was at Pittodrie, Aberdeen, as Hampden Park was undergoing reconstruction. Andy Roxburgh had noted my recent performances as a central striker and decided to give me a go through the middle alongside Kevin Gallacher.* Kevin was another

---

* Andy Roxburgh, who went on to head up UEFA's technical committee, said in the build-up, 'I'm looking for Pat Nevin to demonstrate his skills. The reason he hasn't had more caps is that the modern game has knocked the stuffing out of his sort. He is a great entertainer, quite inspirational.' Andy seemed to agree with me that ugly power plays had grown to dominate the game.

lightning-quick forward who would create space for me with his selfless running beyond the defence. Finally, I had a real chance for my country, in my favourite position, though it did seem to perplex some of the Scottish journalists who had no idea why this 'tricky winger' was up front for the national team.

I didn't want to let myself, my family or indeed Andy Roxburgh and his assistant, my old Clyde manager Craig Brown, down. I don't think I did. I made the first goal for Brian McClair, scored the second with a cute chip following a pass from John Collins, and then scored the third with a penalty after I had been brought down in the box.

It was my best performance for my country, but everything was set up to make it just perfect. Paul McStay of Celtic was in midfield alongside my mate McClair. I finally got to link up with John Collins of Celtic and we immediately had an incredible understanding on the field. He and Tom Boyd were unstoppable on the left-hand side and were fabulous to play with. Most importantly I had the freedom to roam and the trust of the manager. It underlined my suspicion that I was in the best form of my career, at the peak of my powers. I had wasted the previous season at Everton through no fault of my own, but I was making up for it now.

Running back to the halfway line after my first goal, Celtic's Paul McStay grabbed me during the celebrations and, while laughing, said, 'You are coming to play for us next season, that's an order.' I wondered if he knew how often his club had already tried to buy me.

In the previous 12 months I had scored 15 goals for Tranmere, making me second top scorer after the unstoppable Aldo, and four more for Scotland. I was creating just as many if not more goals than in any other season in my career. I had started more games than any other outfield player at the Rovers and was runner up in the Player of the Year voting at the club. It was by any standards a good season.

I was, however, playing in the second tier, so for most people in the game, it meant next to nothing. For me that didn't matter: generally, I was as happy as at any point in my career, notwithstanding the concerns about my mum and Jacqui. In every other way there was so much to look forward to, so much to be savoured and enjoyed. I had never wanted to be a footballer, but Prenton Park finally felt like home for me, and, indeed, a relief compared to some of the things happening off the pitch. I couldn't wait for the next season, after the short summer break.

3/
APOCALYPSE

I was stopped for speeding on the M56 as I headed in for the first day of pre-season training. Fortunately the copper must have been an Evertonian as he let me off with a warning. So it is pretty safe to say I was excited about getting on with our next crack at the land of milk and honey and the countless millions of pounds that would pour in from the Premier League if we could get promoted this time. It was my second season at Tranmere but I was acutely aware that my 30th birthday was only a month away. Every footballer knows that this is an important milestone, or at least it is seen as one by others. In short, you are now considered elderly, on the way down and, indeed, on the way out of the game. Your time is short and you better make the most of it while you can.

Personally, I felt great, still incredibly fit, and I was still holding onto my boyish enthusiasm for a new season while blithely ignoring the ravages of the ageing process. There were a couple of friendly warm-up games before the season kicked off and it was not only me, but the whole team that was clearly ready for another cavaliering campaign.

The morning after one of these bounce games, my home phone rang at about 5am. I wasn't sure of the precise time, but it was an ungodly hour so it was unlikely to be good news. I sprang awake. It was Norman Wilson, the secretary at Tranmere. A lovely gentleman to the core, and he hesitated before explaining, 'There is no way to say this nicely, so I will just tell you straight. Tommy Coyne's wife has, er, died during the night. Tommy is at the hospital on the Wirral now. Can you go and see what you can do to help, you two seemed to get on well. Is there anyone else from the team who can go along with you?'

It was a traumatising thing to hear and to try to get my head around as I headed to the hospital moments later after jumping out of bed. Norman was right: I had grown to like Tommy a great deal in a very short time. I'd found Tommy to be a considerate man, who could be belligerent when he felt unfairly treated. He was a big character. His wife had recently had another child, he was new in town, and I did my usual: anytime anyone came down from Scotland to any club I was at, I had tried to make myself helpful in any way, even if it was just showing them the ropes. It is a Caledonian Celtic kindness that is expected, so Tommy had quickly become more than just a teammate whose ability I admired and could relate to. It was a grotesque tragedy that had happened to his family, a heartbreaking, unfair chain of events that can happen to anyone struck by the effects of post-natal depression.

Tommy was also close to Mark Proctor, who was exactly the type of kind, caring, sensible and intelligent man you would want in a crisis. I called him and we met in the hospital car park before going in together. It was a traumatic, harrowing day, the details of which are not mine to tell. But by that evening, having spent the entire day trying to talk to him, console him, listen to him and share even some tiny bit of the burden of the trauma he was going through, it became clear that Tommy needed to be taken away from there. I eventually took him, distraught, to Manchester airport to fly to Scotland, leaving behind an area he would understandably never want to return to.

That journey in the car was awful and I have never in my life felt so inadequate or useless. I had no idea what to say; anything I thought of seemed trite and nonsensical. What Tommy had just gone through was bigger than any words could help. Still, I would have driven him the four hours all the way to Glasgow if that's what it took; the most important thing was to get him back home, to where his children were waiting, as quickly as possible by whatever means. They needed him and doubtless he needed them. In Glasgow he would have to try to come to terms with bringing up his young children, suddenly without their mother, and him without his loving wife. Even having spent that time with him, I couldn't come close to understanding the depths of despair he was facing that day and for the weeks, months and years to follow.

The club was shattered; it was such a small close-knit group that it had an incredible effect on everyone. Tommy hadn't been there long, but he had been accepted as 'one of the lads' by the players, the staff and the fans. I felt stunned by the whole episode. I not only liked Tommy, but had thought highly of Alison the few times we had met. As a senior player, however, I felt I should be spending my time helping other players by listening and talking to them as they dealt with it, pushing my own feelings away as much as possible. After all, what was I suffering in comparison to Tommy?

A few weeks later, I flew to Scotland to attend Alison's funeral and then went on to see my mum afterwards in Glasgow. She was visibly getting more unwell by the week. It was a difficult time, and not one I'd properly seen coming, even though I knew in my head that Mum was ill. But perhaps I was protecting myself. I can now see in hindsight that it was football that was giving me an escape, or at least a refuge, just when I needed it most. For the first time in my life I was embracing the football world to help my mental health, instead of being focused on keeping my distance from the game.

I knew football helped some players in this way, but it had never been something I'd needed. I was too distrustful of the game and its foibles to rely on it, but this time I did. In the simplest way, I was thankful for how much kicking a ball about with a bunch of mates helped me take my mind off the surrounding traumas, even if only for brief periods.

Our son Simon was a strikingly beautiful little boy, angelic in his looks and just as angelic in his sleeping patterns. From his earliest days he always seemed to be on the verge of laughing at any silly games we played with him – from giggling uncontrollably when we made plane noises as food went into his mouth, to loving being 'accidently' buried in the back garden when I was raking huge bunches of leaves together. Annabel and I had simply loved being in his company just as much as he seemed to love ours from day one. Both sides of our extended families were clearly besotted with him; he was the perfect child and toddler.

During this difficult time, however, some slightly unusual things started happening with Simon. We took him for a walk in the beautiful grounds at Tatton Park near Manchester. There was an extremely complicated hedgerow maze which we went right into the middle of. We said to Simon, 'Do you think you could find your way out of here?' He giggled and ran off ahead with Annabel and me in hot pursuit. We had walked the intricate route only minutes before but there was no way I could have remembered 10 per cent of those turns, they all looked the same. Simon did not forget a single turn on the way out, the route seemed imprinted. What an incredible memory.

There were a few disquieting changes we started to notice after that: he began to sleep less well, and when he was with other toddlers his progression seemed delayed in certain areas. He suddenly started to become more easily frustrated. It was even more concerning when he then lost some of his language skills and would get angry when any of his routines were adapted, such as the route into Chester town centre, be it in his buggy, walking or even in the car. The ability to socialise seemed less developed with him than with others his age, though we told ourselves that, at two and a half, it could be shyness or any number of things. Something was vaguely on our minds, but Annabel and I didn't speak about it too much initially.

Again, football was a blessed distraction, not least because there was some very good form at Tranmere. Our habitual stuttering start had been followed by a run of wins that had us right at the top of the league for the first time since I arrived – indeed, this was the highest league position the club had ever reached in its entire 108-year history. There had been a 400 per cent increase in the match-day fan base in six short years. On the

Prenton Park pitch itself, things felt as good as they could have been at that precise moment, and an outsider might have concluded my life was bathed in golden sunlight. The problem was that there were dark menacing clouds circling around everywhere else outside of the football.

Early in the season I was back in the Scotland squad and, as usual, I was holed up in a hotel on my birthday. The 6th of September is almost always a UEFA international date, so for most of my life, from the age of 18 onwards, I've had few chances of celebrating the day with my friends and family. If I thought that was less than perfect for a birthday, it was about to get much worse.

The trip to Scotland gave me a chance to see my mum, who was by now almost totally bedridden. After leading such a healthy life and caring for everyone around her before herself, this disease was as unfair to her as it could be to anyone who has suffered it. She had managed a trip to Lourdes in the summer, via our place in Chester, with my dad and her twin sister, my auntie Josie, but I could tell now that there was no likelihood of her ever going very far again. The doctors had been honest and not at all hopeful.

Those visits home were as beautiful as they were painful, and I cherished every moment, every word she said, every second I had left in her company. She was surrounded in that bed at our Glasgow home with a great deal of love from all her family, including most of her six sisters and her younger brother, Thomas. She gloried in the fading time with her very young grandchildren – Michael, Simon, Lorna, Daniel and Camilla – as well as her own six, now grown-up kids.

I was also popping round to see Tommy Coyne, to see how he was doing. Of course, being a caring, dutiful father, he was finding things indescribably difficult. It was good to talk to him now. I had studied up a bit on bereavement counselling just in case I said the wrong thing but, in all honesty, the thing to do was to talk little and listen a lot. I liked him anyway, but I liked and respected his spirit and bravery even more as I watched him battle through those bleak forlorn days. We built up a trust and nobody knew of my visits except Annabel, my folks and the manager John King, who considerately gave me an extra day here and there at that time for trips back up to Scotland.

There was one day when Tommy came to my parents' house in Glasgow and spent time with my family, as I had shared what I had been going through with my mum. His kindness and thoughtfulness amazed both Annabel and me when he turned up with a present he had bought for our Simon. Considering the dangerous depths he had fallen to at some points, and the level of pain he was suffering himself, his consideration at that moment was beyond my comprehension. Few people I have ever known would have been capable of that thoughtfulness while suffering such recent trauma.

I had joined up with the Scottish national squad that birthday weekend after visiting Mum and Tommy yet again. I admit to being on edge already, but I was awoken from my bed in the team hotel in the morning by two phone calls. First Annabel rang to say that her young friend Jacqui had died in the night from her cancer. It was horrible and heartbreaking that such a lovely young person had gone, and Annabel was distraught. I was guilt ridden that I wasn't there to console Annabel, but she selflessly said that I should stay on with the Scotland squad. Seconds after I put the phone down another call came through to let me know that one of the red top newspapers had splashed a headline across their front page: 'Nevin on Mercy Dash Mission.' Somehow, they had found out I had been seeing Tommy Coyne on my trips north. Clearly I would never have dreamed of talking to a newspaper, or indeed anyone, about our meetings. All the private time I had spent with Tommy, doing my best to help him through this terrible period, was now splashed across the papers and all the trust and closeness that we'd built up was blown apart – all for the sake of selling a few copies of a newspaper.

I knew instinctively that Tommy would be furious and would almost certainly feel massively used and let down by this public humiliation. For my part, it was the angriest I had ever been in my entire life. I knew Tommy would think he had been set up, that I had been talking to him to 'look good' for a headline. I knew that bond of trust was shattered there and then.

What was far more important, though, was the effect it would have on him. I was straight onto their newsdesk (it was 'News' not 'Sport', obviously) and started roaring at them: 'Why didn't your arseholes pick up the phone and ask me about it? I don't hide my number; all your sports people have it! I know exactly why, because you know I wouldn't have allowed you to run that story. Can I speak to the reptiles that wrote it? In fact, I want to meet them in person. How did they get that story? How the hell is it any of your business? How could you be such heartless vile hollowed-out excuses for human beings to publish that shit?'

I ranted on for quite some time and, yes, it was also liberally sprinkled with expletives, but I was getting nowhere. I think I ended with a threat that I would be coming down to search for these lowlifes and would not be responsible for my actions. This was no idle threat at that moment. I am not proud to say it, but I'll be straight: if confronted by any of the people who had written that story at that moment, I would have physically assaulted them and would have found it difficult to stop. I pride myself in rarely, if ever, losing control in any stressful situation, but right then I had gone. It is not in my character, but that level of anger was something I had never come close to feeling before in my entire life.

I went down to training, eventually, with the rest of the Scotland squad and the other players instinctively knew just to stay away from me. I think if anyone had said the wrong thing, I might have lashed out at them with a two-footed tackle. It took a few weeks, and, in the meantime, I tried to call Tommy numerous times; Tommy, understandably, broke off all contact – but I eventually tracked down who leaked the story to the newspaper by pulling every string and asking every journalist I knew in Scotland. To my amazement it turned out that the 'leak' was closer to home than I thought. It was the Tranmere manager John King, although he had no idea that he was being tricked into giving anyone a tabloid story. I didn't blame him at all in the end – they had set him up and he was completely unaware of the consequences.

In time Tommy got a message through to me via his sister to say he now knew what had really happened, but the damage was done and the bond that was there had been broken. Fortunately, he had great friends and family back home, and I know one or two old Celtic teammates of his were towers of strength at the time. How he rebuilt his life from that period is one of the most impressive things I have ever seen from anyone in my life.

Mum was gravely ill, and a couple of weeks later I got the call I had been dreading. I dashed up to Glasgow immediately. I got there at 9pm and mum slipped away two hours later with Dad and all of us, her now grown-up children, around the bed at the Royal Infirmary in Glasgow.

The only possible crumb of comfort was that her faith was so strong that she was absolutely convinced she was going to meet her maker, her own family members she had already lost, and that we would all join her in good time anyway. What I would give to have 1 per cent of her certainty or her faith.

The last words I heard her say while she was still lucid, with us all holding her hands and arms, were with a tearful voice, 'Oh, my babies.' Anyone who loses a beloved parent knows the feelings of desolation we all felt.

It would seem fitting to end this chapter here. The death of a parent is a terrible and defining moment when it happens, whatever their age and whatever the circumstances. But life isn't always so neat and, the next day, what had been a dreadful week, unbelievably got much, much worse.

My mum's twin sister Josie had three fabulous daughters who grew up through the wall to us in the tenements in Easterhouse. I adored Catherine, Jocelyn and Theresa like big sisters when we were kids. They were the kindest, loveliest creatures I had ever met, and still are. There was a phone call the next morning to say Jocelyn's beautiful eight-year-old daughter had taken ill and died suddenly of meningitis. We didn't think our family could be crushed more than it already was, but we were wrong. The joyous, beautiful family dreamscape that Annabel and I and our wider family had was being replaced by what felt like nothing short of an apocalyptic nightmare.

By now I was existing in a fog. Within it I could still peer through and see the shadow of even more bad news in the offing regarding Simon, but I couldn't bring myself to fully face it quite yet. Annabel and I supported each other and, for a while, I had no real idea that she had the same deep gnawing concerns.

There was still the small matter of a World Cup qualifying group game against Switzerland at Pittodrie to deal with – one we needed to win to stand a decent chance of qualifying for the tournament in the United States. I started, still willing to play in this terrible period. We were the better side, but after we went 1–0 up they equalised from a penalty. I feel I played well, and we created a few good chances in a late onslaught, but the damage was done. A point wasn't good enough and this would be another World Cup that got away, one that I would not have been dropped from.

The period around my 30th birthday is still up there with the very worst times of my entire life. Before then I still felt like a boy, to some degree, even though I was a married working man with a son of my own and had had many adventures in a varied life. A part of that carefree life leaves us when these traumas hit. Living the life of a footballer can be fun and frivolous, and it had been for me just a month or so earlier. As a player you get to spend a lot of time acting like a kid, even if I was an earnest one. Now, however, there was little more to be said, other than it was time to grow up.

4/
HIGH & DRY

Having been scammed into being the union rep at Everton before I joined Tranmere, I had since been dragged onto the PFA management committee. This job stole some of my time, as it needed a good deal of study to make sure we did the right things within the organisation.

After my mum's funeral I had to drive back down to Chester but, on the way, there was one stop to make. There was a PFA management committee meeting, and the final point of the agenda was the election of a new chairman now that Brian Marwood had left the post.

I thought it was important that, as a committee member, I should use my vote, so I made my way directly from Scotland in time for the second half of the meeting in a large room in the plush Midland Hotel in Manchester. I think Gordon Taylor liked it there because many important historical union decisions, not just ours at the PFA, had been made in that particular, slightly too ostentatious, hotel. We sat around a huge oak table that could seat at least 30 people and their notes if needed, with plenty of space to spare.

I had no idea and, to be frank, couldn't care less how the candidates had been selling themselves, if indeed they had been. In fact, I didn't even know how the voting process would work. I was, however, willing to listen to each of the 12 committee members who might want the job and what they felt were their key attributes for the role. Actually, I knew there could only be 11 candidates, because I had absolutely no interest in doing the job myself. Losing my mum was still the only thing inside my head – that, and getting back to the solace of Annabel and Simon as soon as possible after the meeting.

Chief executive Gordon Taylor solemnly went round the table asking each member if they would like to throw their hats in the ring and why. I was sitting next to Gordon and would be the last to be asked. I nudged Brian McClair, next to me on the other side, and whispered, 'Do you fancy it?' The answer was an unrepeatable negative. Six players were asked but all politely declined before Lawrie Sanchez said he would be up for it, giving a passionate monologue as to why he would be a good leader – and very impressive he was too. Gordon continued his rounds, but at the same time started kicking me under the table and then stage whispered to me, 'Somebody else must at least make it a contest, Pat.'

I thought, 'Surely someone else will say, "Aye."' But no – Gary Mabbutt, Barry Horne, Iain Dowie and all the others declined. And so, before it even reached McClair, I already knew that I was the only one left in the room who could make it a semblance of a democratic stand-off.

When Gordon eventually asked me, in turn, with what looked like pleading eyes, I answered with some solemnity. 'I have no interest in being chairman, but there should at least be a vote, so, yes, I'll put my name in too. But for no other reason – and I would like to make this perfectly clear – than that there should be a vote to uphold a sense of fair play.' Never was there a more uninterested or, to be honest, totally unwilling candidate in any electoral process in history. It was now up to the committee to have a secret vote and elect Lawrie.

Ten minutes later I was chairman of the PFA. Bugger!

The PFA surprise had been on the Wednesday and I didn't know if I could face the home game against Peterborough on the Friday night so soon after losing Mum. My oldest brother Tommy, home from Singapore, called and suggested that if he brought my dad down for the game from Glasgow it might just give him a little respite from his grief. That made the decision for me: it would give my dad something to do, but would also briefly take my mind to a different place. It was a good decision, we won 2–1 against Peterborough, Aldo scoring as usual and me getting the other. I was delighted I played and it felt like the right thing to do, afterwards.

One memorable thing did happen in the game, though. The opposition's young full-back appeared quite distraught at me not only having a fairly decent game but also scoring against him. Midway through the second half he made possibly the second worst tackle on me that I ever had in my career.* And that is saying something considering the assaults that had been committed over the years. The offence happened right in front of the main stand, on the touchline, yards away from my dad, brother Tommy and brother-in-law Liam. It was a full force, thigh high, leg breaker of a tackle with the ball not even in the vague vicinity. I managed to get my leg off the ground a millisecond before the contact – a skill I had fortunately learned and perfected over the years. I was left with 'only' stud marks the length of my thigh and a leg's length of bruises to boot. I keep a 'video' of that tackle on my phone, and if anyone ever asks if the game was really rougher back then, I just show them it. The usual reaction is to shout, '*Whoa!*', then wince before averting their eyes and then sometimes crossing their legs.

The referee ushered the lad off the pitch before my teammates could get to him, though I reckon he was in far more danger from Tommy and Liam as he trudged up the tunnel. Dad played it cool – he had watched me often enough to know that I had got my leg off the ground just in time to

---

* The worst tackle? Kevin Ball, Tranmere v Sunderland. I had no chance, he caught me with his studs in my chest and I catapulted over the top of him, somersaulting before landing six feet away flat on my back. It was like a move from *The Matrix* film. Amazingly, I wasn't badly hurt, so I turned round while still on the ground, only to see that Kevin had used his momentum wisely and kept on running straight up the tunnel not waiting for the referee to reach for his red card.

prevent a really serious injury such as a broken leg, which would have been a certainty had it been planted on the turf.

After the Peterborough game I was being interviewed on the local north-west TV and had ample opportunity to have a dig at my assailant, but I didn't, for a whole raft of reasons. First, I was now PFA chairman and wanted to behave accordingly to my members, even if one of them had just lost it briefly and committed GBH on me. (In fairness, he had sent in a sincere apology to our dressing room after the game, as did their manager.) Much more importantly I now understood that I might not be fully aware of the reasons behind these moments of madness from my opponents. After all, I was going through an extremely difficult time, and he might be going through something similar. Just a few weeks before, had I been in their company, I would have gladly assaulted the hacks who wrote the tabloid story about me, even if it had been in a busy city centre street never mind a tense football game. That is what extreme stress can do to any of us.

I let it lie, but it wasn't a great advert for our campaign, started earlier that very same day, to stop violence on the field.

Somewhat surprisingly football was back to being the unimportant joyous thing that I needed it to be. In fact, I was flying, we were flying. I scored ten goals in my next 15 games for the club, and I was creating goals and chances at more than my usual rate. We were halfway through the season and each week we were either in first or second place and looking very likely to get to the Premier League this time, without needing to go down the play-off route.

Training was still fun, I still enjoyed the characters around me but, just as importantly, I loved watching those young lads grow as players and as personalities. Earlier in the season I had scored a hat-trick against Oxford and another goal against them in a cup game four days later, which was maybe a little cruel. I remember the lads subtly winding Aldo up afterwards because he had only scored two against his former club in that 5–1 win. He did seem slightly miffed, but maybe that was because they were trying to wind him up more than his nose actually being out of joint with me.

For all that I was now one of the elder statesmen, it was not like I was being treated with too much respect by all of the players. The humour was always there, if sometimes a bit on the base side! If you are under 18 or of a delicate disposition, just miss out the footnote below!*

As I passed the grand old age of 30, I immediately started to get the word 'veteran' casually slung before my name in the press, even though just one week earlier it had rarely if ever been mentioned. My career was beginning its latter stages and, although it was natural to rail against the dying of the light, it was impossible to ignore the reality when every other description of me, however positive, bandied the words 'mature', 'veteran' or, if they were being just a little kinder, 'the highly experienced' before or after it.

Obviously, you don't feel that different over the space of a few weeks, but it quickly starts to make you think differently about yourself whether you like it or not.

With the harsh realities of life just then beginning to close in on me and Annabel for the first time, it was impossible to be quite as carefree

---

* One of the players, who shall remain nameless, had a particular prank. If the gaffer had to get a point across then everyone would be gathered in a circle around him. As he droned on, usually longer than was absolutely necessary, you would be standing there with your hands on your hips, or arms folded or, as many did, with your hands clasped together behind your back, not unlike the stance the then Prince Charles was famous for back then. This one mischievous player would be on the lookout for that stance. He would sneak unnoticed, with the brilliant movement of an international striker, go behind you and then place a certain part of his anatomy into your clasped hands. '*Arrgghhh!!!!*' It was the second most revolting prank regularly played on the players.

The most revolting prank? These were still the days of the team baths. Sitting in this big communal bath after a freezing training session, trying to warm up, mad Higgy or Moggsy would stand behind me. As I was chatting to someone sensible like Mark Proctor, one would then moan, 'Oh baby, Oh baby.' As I turned, he would squirt lathered soap straight into my face, from the 'middle of his body'. I mean, really, how gross can you get? I have to say it was very funny and inventive, and, after all, it was only soap!

and relaxed about the future as we had been. Turning 30, you do not change overnight. However, when it's compounded by traumatic events and you start being treated differently too, the message rings out loud and clear – this isn't going to last forever and you'd better start planning for the next phase.

In the middle of this run of great form, as well as officially becoming an old man, Scotland had another qualifier, this time against the mighty Italy in Rome. The previous week I had scored the winner for Tranmere against our great rivals Bolton Wanderers to take us clear at the top of the league again, once more looking longingly at possible promotion to the Premier League. It was particularly pleasant for our fans because Bolton seemed to be just about the only club that the resolutely sweet Tranmere fans couldn't stand.

Andy Roxburgh gave me the nod early; I would be starting up front again in this one after playing well and scoring a couple as a striker against Estonia. Now, let us be absolutely clear here: Italy were not a bad side, certainly a bit better than Estonia. Gianfranco Zola could only make the subs' bench; there were world-renowned names such as Roberto Baggio, Pierluigi Casiraghi, Roberto Donadoni, Dino Baggio and Stefano Erranio in the team. I would be directly up against Franco Baresi and Allessandro Costacurta with Antonio Benarrivo to help them contain little old me if those two were struggling. I myself would probably have very little help up front from my teammates, who might just have to do a little defending in the eternal city on the night.

Here is the mad thing: as usual, I fancied my chances against these world superstars. It was still among the oddest things about me playing football: I never once went onto a field and thought anyone was better than me or that anyone could get the better of me. Yes, Baresi might arguably be the best defender in the world at that moment, but on the actual pitch I would have thought, 'Let's see what you have got then; see if you can get the ball off me, matey!' It does sound arrogant, bordering on delusional, but I absolutely felt it on the pitch, whoever the opponent. To this day, I am not overconfident and certainly not arrogant in any other parts of my life – it was just on that piece of grass, for those specific moments, when I was there with my boots on.

I had rarely felt so excited about a game in my entire life, playing against the best, and playing in my favourite position – bring it on. We trained at the Olympic Stadium the night before and I felt great. My touch was perfect, I was carrying no injuries and felt brilliantly fit. We went back to the hotel, had some pasta, and went to bed, looking forward to waking up bright and early the next morning, raring to go.

I did wake up bright and early, at about 3am, projectile vomiting across the room. Without going into the rest of the gruesome details, I had food poisoning. Obviously, the Italians were scared to death of the stand-in striker from Tranmere Rovers and had spiked my pasta! Or maybe not. Sadly, it meant there was no chance of me playing. Their plan backfired badly as my replacement Kevin Gallacher scored for Scotland, although admittedly they had scored two by then and made it 3–1 by full time.

Keen to try new things and shake off a bit of the pervading gloom, I immediately said yes when I was asked to write an article for the *Observer* newspaper. Having the 'veteran' moniker just about welded to my name by now, these possible 'next career opportunities' had to be checked out.

Going back to finish my degree had always been the plan, but with every year that passed it floated further and further away as a reasonable course of action. I could catch up with the changes in economics, accounts and law, but the computer programming module might just have moved on a bit more. Maybe journalism would work? I had been writing now and again for music papers and various other magazines, but the *Observer* . . . this was the real deal. Happily, they liked the copy about the state of football on Merseyside, and it was a decent confidence booster that they printed it almost unedited. I then wrote another article for the *Daily Post*, the biggest daily newspaper in Liverpool, so my brain was being engaged and, to some degree, sidetracked momentarily from some painful realities.

The season kept going well. I scored a couple more, including one of the most imaginative of my career, a running scoop from 25 yards against Sunderland which, rather pleasingly, even the referee applauded.

Crucially, we hadn't had the Christmas party yet, which could trash the guys for weeks if they weren't careful, and little old Tranmere were once again seeing off a whole bunch of bigger clubs.

We sold our centre-back Steve Vickers to Premier League club Middlesbrough for just under £1 million and, apart from leaving Higgy, his partner at the back and in the mickey-taking corner distraught for a little while, it was money the club needed to strengthen, and we felt we could cope. Kingy could acquire half a team with that sort of cash, and though we would miss Steve's classy, pacy defending, it was an understandable decision.

The manager had a few plans for his replacement. Yosser Hughes still hadn't been released, however much he sang his heart out every morning. Shaun Garnett was a big raw imposing youngster whose ultra-positive temperament could crush any negativity around him with his force of personality alone. John McGreal was another kid coming through who looked like he could be the next Alan Hansen, given time, and we had Ged Brannan. Ged was frequently one of our best players every week, and it didn't matter a jot whether he played full-back, centre-midfield or, crucially, centre-back.*

After the New Year there was the obligatory slump all the way down to ninth position. It was the usual problems: limited strength in depth compared to our wealthier opponents, and maybe even some recovery time from the Christmas party, but it was mostly because we got sidetracked and exhausted on an incredible League Cup run.

We had beaten Oxford United, Grimsby Town, Oldham and then saw off Nottingham Forest after a replay when I scored with another header.

---

* Players that can play a number of positions are less valued than they should be. In a squad, it's like having three players instead of one, and if you have limited funds these players are like gold dust. I remembered this about Ged and used it years later.

I could feel the incensed eyes of my old adversary Stuart Pearce boring into me, doubtless because of the utter indignity of that one.

We now had a two-legged semi-final against Aston Villa, and the chance of a real major domestic trophy. They were an established Premier League side packed with top international players: Ireland's Ray Houghton, Paul McGrath, Steve Staunton and Andy Townsend; along with other household names at the time like Tony Daley, Dean Saunders and Dalian Atkinson. This was a serious step up in class and a test of whether we could survive at the top level if we ever got there.

Prenton Park was sold out. The affectionately and fittingly named 'Cowsheds' were crammed to bursting point with standing fans. In all, over 17,000 squeezed in on that brisk February evening to watch us dismantle this team of stars put together by 'Big Ron' Atkinson. It was a spine-tingling night – it still is, having lately watched the goals again on YouTube and relived that extraordinary atmosphere. I go to a lot of Premier League football these days and can honestly say, outside Liverpool, Leeds or Newcastle, you will rarely see, feel and hear a noise and atmosphere to beat that night.

I am often told that sophisticated tactical football in England apparently hadn't been invented before the Premier League was born, but that's tosh. John King had a dilemma and had to adapt our formation. He had two of his four defenders missing and came up with a 3–4–3 formation (Antonio Conte and Thomas Tuchel weren't the pioneers of that one!) that completely suited the players he had available.*

I laid on the first for the overlapping Ian Nolan, then Yosser Hughes, part of the new-look back three, got a delightful second following my corner and, incredibly, we went 3–0 up in the second half as Aldo broke away to score.

---

* I recall the fuss around Pep Guardiola playing a 'false nine' in the Premier League, aficionados being amazed at such a radical modern idea. Andy Roxburgh used Gary Mackay as a false nine in the European Youth Championships in 1982. So not exactly novel, and the idea certainly predates that tournament as well.

We could smell a major cup final at Wembley, with Manchester United waiting there. They had the likes of Eric Cantona, Roy Keane, Ryan Giggs, Mark Hughes and Paul Ince, but, at that precise moment, we would all have thought the same thing: 'Bring them on!'

In injury time the referee gave Villa a free-kick that in those days would have never generally been considered a foul. It felt like a sop to the big boys, and I certainly wasn't getting free-kicks for those sorts of challenges on me! They did, they crossed it, and Dalian Atkinson scored with a volley: 3–1, and you just knew that goal could be crucial. It was still an incredible evening. Afterwards my dad was outside waiting, smiling that beaming smile that I hadn't seen for many months, since long before Mum died. The occasion was more memorable for that moment than the incredible excitement of what happened inside the ground that night.

At Villa Park in the second leg, this time with 40,000 fans, most of them howling against us, we lost 3–1, Villa getting their third with a whole three minutes to go. Not unlike most of the sob stories throughout my career, it was extraordinarily close to glory but not quite enough. Our midfielder Liam O'Brien hit the inside of the post with a brilliant free-kick six seconds from full time and I still can't quite figure out how it didn't go in. That goal would have got us to Wembley; we were millimetres from glory yet again. Three of us were playing with something close to flu, and others were coping with injuries, but, with a limited squad, we had no choice: each of us had to play through it. Their keeper Mark Bosnich should have been sent off, but the referee was incredibly lenient in the moment, 'only' giving a penalty.

This time it was an agonising 5–4 defeat on penalties after extra-time. We got as close as you can get without winning, but it doesn't matter how close it is, nobody remembers the losing semi-finalists. Our dressing room was disconsolate, with young players inconsolable and in tears. When Big Ron came in to commiserate with the plucky losers, he got a volley of abuse from the Scouse kids, but he took it well. Villa went on to win the cup and we did our best to recover, but it wasn't easy.

We struggled for a while after that but there was only enough left in the tank to make it to the play-offs once again. This time we would face Leicester City. I felt we were a far better side: we had played them twice already in the league having won at home and drawn at Filbert Street. I felt confident we just had to play at our best, and in the first leg we absolutely did play our finest, most thrilling football.

Unfortunately for us their goalkeeper Gavin Ward produced one of the greatest displays of miraculous goalkeeping I have ever witnessed. We did everything right, but he was unbeatable. Still, there was no panic because going into the second leg at 0–0 was not an insurmountable challenge.

They scored just before half-time, then I equalised right at the start of the second half from a Ged Brannan cut back. From then on the classic play-off tension just grew and grew towards incendiary levels. As if I hadn't been tortured enough, with four minutes to go somebody up there with a real line for gratuitous irony in my life story decided to let the ball drop two yards from our goal to their substitute, David Speedie. This was my old teammate from Chelsea and the player I had most trouble dealing with in my entire career. Obviously, he scored and destroyed our dreams.

The reason he got the ball in the first place was that our keeper Eric Nixon had misjudged a cross, mostly because he was still woozy after Speedie had volleyed him, almost certainly unintentionally, in the head moments earlier. These days David would have been ordered off, banned and probably reported to the police for aggravated assault. Back then he got a finger wagged at him very vigorously.

We couldn't get the goal back in the remaining minutes, though Nixon did get his own back by smashing Speedie during a mêlée that broke out in injury-time. A single goal yet again was the difference between us and possible glory at Wembley. Leicester beat Derby in the final and went up, so, realistically, we could have made it. On the other hand, Leicester were battered week in week out in the next season's Premier League, finishing a full 15 points from safety by the end.

David Speedie and I didn't have a hug at the end of the game, but then I suspect he was hiding from Nicko, who absolutely would have come close to killing him had he got the chance. For us it was another desperate end to the season.

We had lost out again and this time I wondered if this was our last real chance to break into the big time. At that moment, that's exactly how it felt. We knew we would try again next season, but you only get so many chances as a group, and those painful losses can take their toll, they can become the club's and the players' internal narrative. Many people thought it would be a fairytale if Tranmere made it to the Premier League.

Maybe that is precisely what it was.

5/
DON'T LET GO

The second part of that second season with Tranmere must have looked fantastic for me from the outside. We had been relatively successful, twice missing glory by a whisker. I'd played 56 games for the club, more than anyone else, something I was always proud of. The willowy, fragile-looking winger turned out to be pretty robust and resilient over the years. I had scored a very respectable 13 goals, while still being considered more of a creator than a finisher by everyone, including me. The 19 assists underlined the point. I was regularly in the Scotland team and still at the top of my game.

Nevertheless, seeing all the signs, I had initiated the plan for my next career. Having written for the *Observer* and then a series of eight columns for the *Sunday Times* in their Scottish edition – they loved the story that featured meeting Saddam Hussein, and even had it splashed on the back page with a huge colour cartoon – this was certainly one possible direction. I had always loved writing so refused to have these articles ghosted the way the other players did 99 per cent of the time – those long since retired players-turned-scribes included some big names who might surprise you. You would think they would have had a go at it themselves, having found a little more spare time.

The way it works is that they generally speak to a journo, usually over the phone for about 20 minutes, and then he or she crafts it. Even some of the biggest news organisations call the ex-players 'columnists', when they haven't written a single word themselves. I couldn't hack that, probably because I was hoping to become a hack myself. These were hopefully the first steps towards a new career.*

I was also learning the ropes as PFA chairman, and although it was a huge increase in (still unpaid) work – some of it extraordinarily complex, especially morally – one problem was more troublesome for me than all the others. Gordon Taylor and I got on famously. I hugely admired his abilities and trusted in his desire to do the best for the union and its members. The one major sticking point was his new contract. It had been agreed with the former chairman Brian Marwood and I felt it was generous, to an absolute fault! In fact, I refused to ratify the contract because of its huge figures, specifically the possible cost of the final salary pension. I worried that the agreement could be in danger of bringing real financial hardship to the PFA, particularly if things didn't play out well in future TV negotiations.

I was unwilling to allow it through in the form that it was presented to me by the outgoing chairman, which led to the unusual situation of lawyers from both sides being brought in to help thrash it out. This might sound like an inauspicious start to my working relationship with the sitting chief executive, but my earnest side had to be at the fore when doing union work. Other than those negotiations, Gordon and I parked the dispute and worked very well together. It is worth underlining that as chairman I had limited day-to-day involvement or power, but as a backstop and a check, the chair and his management committee were, and are, vital.

---

* I also did a little bit of co-commentating on the radio, covering Everton's nerve-jangling relegation-decider against Wimbledon, just when it seemed like the Toffees might be relegated and Tranmere could replace them in the Premier League. I loved doing it and immediately thought this co-commentating lark could be another possible string to some future bow.

It was, however, still stressful and, if I am honest, not a great deal of fun most of the time.

Life was simply getting too busy – enjoying my passions, particularly live music and theatre, was still having to take a back seat, as many busy parents of young children find out, some of us to our shock and amazement. The truth was, we had bigger things to deal with for the time being.

As well as dealing with several tragedies in the previous nine months, one thing above anything else had begun to shape our lives at home.

Simon had been a perfect baby, sleeping contentedly for the first 20 months and he had generally been a joy to be around. He always got upset when I had to go anywhere but was equally excited on my return. He looked angelic – and while, of course, every parent thinks that of their child – he was especially beautiful as a toddler. Little things started to change however, first almost imperceptibly and then more obviously.

For no real reason that we could fathom, Simon now started having tantrums. 'Fine,' we thought, 'that will be the "terrible twos", then.' By March 1994 both Annabel and I were concerned enough to visit the GP, asking if he might need speech and language therapy, as he seemed a little behind the other kids in playgroup. Being our first child, it was hard to gauge, and the opinion was mixed, with most friends, relatives and, indeed, specialists suggesting, 'He's probably OK, they all just develop at different rates.' But the tantrums were becoming more frequent, however, and Simon's ability to communicate was not like other kids' – if anything, it felt as if he was regressing slightly.

Things he used to love doing became challenging. He'd practically lived in Chester Zoo he loved it so much, particularly watching the repetitive back and forth movements of the clown trigger fish for what seemed like hours. Suddenly, from loving travelling in the overhead train at the zoo, Simon developed a pathological fear of it. Some of his other behaviours became markedly repetitive, but on the positive side, those rituals seemed to comfort him and make him feel happier and safer.

There were other odd fears he had which multiplied quickly, such as a panic when the microwave was switched on – or similar electronic sounds, such as a vacuum cleaner, washing machines, hand-dryers and even certain types of aeroplane, though what he had against 'Britannia' planes in particular we never found out. We guessed he must have got a fright from something electrical being switched on unexpectedly at some point and it had stuck. Then there was a fear of thunderstorms which could make him twitchy even when it was just raining.

From coping with going to the football alongside Annabel, suddenly the unexpected crowd noises would send him into a panic and more meltdowns. The people at Tranmere where fabulously helpful to Annabel, but her opportunities to come to games became limited; it was a trial with Simon in tow, though she bravely soldiered on for a little while. In a short time, however, she had to admit defeat and could no longer come to the games. There wasn't even a chance of Simon coping with a babysitter by that time: he would have gone through the roof had he been left during the day.

Annabel and I having any time alone also became problematic, as there would be an uncontrollable tantrum if we left him at any hour. We loved going to see movies, but getting out of the house was now becoming an incredible rigmarole. With Simon in bed and the babysitter taking care of him we would creep out the back door for a rare dinner out or movie, but if he heard the slightest sound, such as a door latch or the car leaving, he would lose it and often we would have to come straight back in, the night ended before it began.

Annabel couldn't leave him that distraught: this was different level stuff, not what you would usually see in an upset child – and, anyway, it was unfair on the babysitter to leave her with Simon in that state. We tried everything, like leaving the car down the street and round the corner so he couldn't hear the engine start. The back door would be left open so he couldn't hear it being shut when we sneaked out. He wasn't lacking in intelligence, though: he realised that if the babysitter was there then we might just be going out, so he was unsettled. Most parts of life were becoming more stressful and at the beginning we thought, or just hoped, 'Yes, this is just what having children is like.' But as time went by the nagging doubt became a serious concern – this wasn't normal.

Simon's random wild tantrums in shops or cafés made life even more difficult when we took him out. Sadly, it often happened when Annabel was out with him alone in Chester while I was at work. She was made to feel that she had some inadequacies as a mother, even though she was always, in every respect and at all times, the most loving, doting, caring, dedicated and completely committed mother that you could imagine. The sneering stares or snarky comments in shops from other women about her 'inability to control that child' were crushing.

I have always been a voracious reader and, before the days of the internet being able to tell you everything at the click of a button, I started searching medical articles looking for some clues. I came across a story about something I had never heard of called autism. It might amaze the modern reader to know, but back then it was a little known and certainly an extremely little understood condition in the general population. I felt there were too many lightbulbs going off in my head at the same time after reading it.

I asked my sister Mary, who often worked with differently abled adults, and she agreed that there were a few similarities when she thought of Simon and we shouldn't ignore it. Annabel had spoken to her dad at the same time about Simon's behaviours and we finally shared our mutual concerns that we hadn't fully vocalised to each other before. As a mother, at every stage, she was well ahead of me in understanding that there was a difficulty, and this all happened over the period of only a few months when other worries were closing in.

A day that really hurt me was when Simon went to a local nursery. I arrived to pick him up, only to find him standing in the corner of the field at the back of the nursery, alone, ignored, frightened and confused with no one around taking care of him. The lack of care and understanding infuriated me – and Simon would never darken their doorstep again – but it underlined that he was incapable of joining in with his peers and he needed help.

You do not want to accept anything is amiss with your perfect child, as you know there is a decent chance it will break your heart when you find out. But, in the end, you don't have a choice. The little voice in your head eventually becomes a constant nagging, and you simply can't ignore it any longer. We spoke to our next-door neighbour, the lovely Pat Powell, who worked in speech and language therapy. I reckon she had been waiting a while for us to bring it up, as she knowingly but sensitively said, 'You really ought to get a specialist diagnosis.'

And so it was that as all the excitement was going on at Tranmere during another fantastic season, Annabel and I were entering the hell that was the special needs paediatric healthcare system. We were trying to get a diagnosis, some information, some advice, some direction and even just a little help. We wanted to speak to experts, but they were few and far between and always extraordinarily busy. We wanted to know what we should be doing, but the information was incredibly limited, and no one even wanted to make an informed guess. We needed someone to throw us some sort of lifeline as we were drowning in a sea of confusion and ignorance, but there was next to nothing of use in the early days and months.

There was, finally, a diagnosis of sorts from a wonderful specialist in the Scottish Borders, a Dr Margerison. He treated us like intelligent adults and used the phrase 'Semantic Pragmatic Disorder'. These days that would translate as 'somewhere on the autistic spectrum', though even this language seems to change annually. Dr Margerison was the first person to try to explain the spectrum idea to us. It was as helpful as it was painful to hear, and it did explain that there were no specific categories, certainties or boxes we could or should put Simon into.

Suddenly, from having a perfect son, we now had one with a disability (or, as it would now be described, 'different ability'), and we had no idea of the severity or how much it would affect his life from now on. In regards to how much it would affect our lives together in the long term . . . we would have to wait and see, but that was going to be a massive, if secondary, consideration. Some people talk about this type of discovery as not unlike suffering a bereavement. The child you thought you had has gone and you now have to deal with the new reality. I never felt this way, but I totally respect and understand why people would feel that desperate and that disconsolate.

Superficially I had been coping well, but there was one evening when it finally hit me hard. Annabel was downstairs making supper while I was sitting on our bathroom floor, back against the wall, head on my knees. As Simon was splashing about happily in the bath, which he always loved, I could no longer keep those dark thoughts that were nagging at the back of my mind at bay. Suddenly all the things that I might not do together with him, that a father expects to do with his son, flashed before me one by one. 'Will we ever go to a football game together? Will he ride a bike? Will he ever drive a car? Bring a girlfriend home? Have a job? Be able to communicate with us at all to any complex, meaningful level? Will he have any friends? Will we be able to go on holidays together? Will he ever have a brother or a sister?' We had been told autism could be hereditary and that the next child's difficulties could be the same or possibly much more profound. The questions kept crowding in, with an intensity that I had beaten off before but couldn't now. Up until that moment I had outwardly coped fairly well, affecting an air of quiet control. But right then my head was crammed with too much to deal with.

My old friend, the actor Gerard Kelly, had once asked how I always remained so calm in extremely stressful situations, even when people were trying to assault me on a football field – and sometimes off it too. My answer was, 'Oh, I just store it inside myself and never let it out, in a very British stiff upper-lip way. Eventually in time, the tension just seeps away unnoticed.' His answer was classic Kelly: 'Tic . . . tic . . . tic . . . tic . . .' That evening, in our bathroom, that ticking time bomb finally went off and I broke down. I was distraught and oddly very lonely, something I had never really felt before. I also felt the pain of Simon's loneliness: how would he be able to take part in this world? The latter thought is one that has never disappeared and is the constant concern for anyone taking care of those who are (as would have been described then, but not always today) on the spectrum.

Simon, splashing away in the bath, looked over at me with a confused air. Another question concerned his ability to care about others as well as understand them. We were constantly told that autistic people had difficulty understanding the complexity of other people's point of view or that they just had a lack of empathy. Could or would our Simon ever have any understanding of what Annabel and I felt about him?*

Then I thought about it all from a different angle: 'What do I feel about my son?' The rest of us gauge everything through the prism of our neurotypical perception, but it was already obvious that more complex consideration would be needed with Simon. As I glanced over, I realised the answer was that I felt a pure love of who he was, whatever that was going to be, and, yes, it was up to us to try as much as we could to empathetically understand how he would view the world and help him in that way. As he stared over directly at me, I could see in his eyes that there was care and consideration for me in that moment. I could see it and feel it, even if he couldn't verbalise it then and might never be able to do so. He looked confused but also concerned. I got myself together and, by the time I had got him out of the bath, dried him and got his pyjamas on, I was ready once again to be the strong and steady support I believed Annabel needed me to be.

It was a complete turning point for me, or at least a moment of true understanding. This was not going to be easy, there were going to be difficult times, but I knew that he had been born to two people who would be totally dedicated to him. We would give him every opportunity, and we would do everything that we could to help him make the best out of whatever life and talents he had. This lovely lad could have been born into much tougher circumstances – indeed, millions are – but we would make sure he would be allowed to flourish with support, just as any child should be. It was not his fault he had these differences, so I decided it was simply time to get on and play the hand I was dealt.

There was no doubt that although the difficulties to come would test us as a couple, it would always be 'us' and these problems would not destroy our relationship. I was determined the stresses of coping with an

---

* Later, this was all explained brilliantly by Uta Frith and Professor Simon Baron-Cohen, among others, in the 'theory of mind' concept.

autistic child would never drive us apart. I also instinctively knew it would be harder for Annabel to cope with than it would for me.

Over the next few months life changed for our perfect little family unit – we went from ambling along nicely, on to a grinding seemingly never-ending treadmill of trying to find the right help and more information. Visits to child psychologists, audiologists and language therapists – and subsequent assessments – took us from the Borders to Birmingham. There were brain scans, blood tests, reviews, questions over which nursery; will it be a special needs school? Or a mainstream school with help? Trying to get a 'Statement of Needs' proved to be the most Kafka-esque thing we have ever had to do. It became another life, one that was totally alien to the one we had lived or had envisaged living. We also didn't share the burden much, even with groups of friends. Yes, our families knew, and they were as helpful as possible, but they mostly lived 200 miles away in Scotland, so most of the time we coped alone, or tried to.

We also had a decision to make on whether we should talk publicly about Simon's condition. From the start we agreed it wasn't the right thing to broadcast our circumstances – maybe for us, but certainly for Simon. Eventually he would be the best person to decide if his autism was something to be discussed by others totally unrelated to him. We had no idea if he would ever even understand that he was, as we say now, not neurotypical. We wanted to give him the chance to make that decision, so it was never something we discussed with the press, or in my public life. I had spent a lifetime keeping the two worlds separate anyway.

As the years went by some journalists would meet Simon and then ask if they could do 'the story' on his autism and its effect on us. Each time I said, 'We would rather you didn't, out of respect for him as an individual, but we can't stop you.' Not one outlet ever mentioned it. Only here and now can I thank those particular journalists for their honourable behaviour.

That we didn't even talk all that much to friends about Simon's complications, and how they were affecting us, might sound surprising. I just felt that I didn't want to burden anyone else with our problems, so, however difficult things were, I kept an upbeat disposition and a cheery smile on my face, helped by the invisible scaffolding of that British stiff upper lip. So even though I have written about and talked about my life a great deal over the years, I have never until now discussed the one thing that affected our lives more than anything else.

Although it is not the style in the modern world, I would react the same way now, though I understand why many decide to publicly air their difficulties and let the world share their suffering. For me, I thought that in time the best way to be of service would be to help in the understanding of autism, but back then I didn't understand it enough or indeed its effects. Nobody did at the time, so we just got on with it.

We took Simon to the Isle of Arran every year and there was always utter panic from him and the inevitable full-scale meltdown while we were boarding the ferry, with the usual disparaging looks from some of the other passengers. The noises and the sensory overload were just too extreme, but he loved the island so much when we got there that the short-term trauma was worth it. We even managed to get on a plane to Rhodes for a two-week holiday, where three-year-old Simon excelled in coping with an incredible heatwave in Lindos. The phobia of getting onto planes, however, was to influence our ability to go abroad for a while after that. We thought we had dodged that bullet – we hadn't!

But there was a moment by a pool we visited in Rhodes that had a profound effect on my understanding of Simon's personality. Annabel had taken him swimming every week since birth, so he was confident in the water, even if following instructions, like the other children, was beyond him. The other youngsters in Rhodes were jumping in from a little height off a fake well by the side of the pool. Simon went up on top of the well on the first day but couldn't bring himself to make the 'huge' leap into the water. It took nearly a week of trying for him to pluck up the courage to finally do it, with no involvement from Mum or Dad other than a watching brief. He had a steely determination to overcome his fears and a desperation to prove his own independence. Just as importantly, he was trying to be like the other kids, something that we thought would be alien to him – or at least that is what we had been told. In that moment I was as proud of him as I had been of myself for anything that I had done in my entire life. Like every version of autism, Simon's was going to be different and very interesting.

Discovering Simon's autism had a major effect on my outlook on life. That carefree love and joy for football didn't leave me; in fact, conversely and surprisingly, it became more important to my sanity. It did, however, mean that for the first time in my life I knew a different pressure. I had to think about the future more seriously, about money, about taking care of someone who would need our care for the rest of our lives and, indeed, his life after we were gone. Most parents try to prepare their children for when we ourselves die, but those who have children with different needs are in a different category. It can be all-consuming if you aren't careful.

It was clear to me that, at the age of 30, and 13 years into my career, one way or another, football finally had to become my real job. It was a job that I didn't want to lose, and now maybe I couldn't really afford to lose. My life was now so different from that teenager at Chelsea who had floated along with a carefree attitude to his existence. The trick was still to retain that feeling of freedom on the field, but it wasn't as easy to be that way all the time now.

It had been an incredible season, but off the field in real life it had been harrowing. Some of my lightness of spirit had certainly been crushed for a while, but this made me no different from any human being: we all have our troubles, and I refused to be self-pitying. Whatever happens, you are dealt those cards and you just play them the best way you can. In my life I still felt I had a brilliant hand, and Simon was going to be a major part of it.

6/
RACE FOR THE PRIZE

At most professional football clubs you have a separate players' bar, to keep the fans and players apart. That wasn't even a consideration at Tranmere. Under the main stand there was a large room, almost the length of the stand, where the players and the fans would mingle after the home games. We all mixed, chatted and enjoyed each other's company, win, lose or draw. Our supporters seemed to love what we had achieved as a team and never took the success for granted; everything positive that happened was a bonus to be celebrated. It was a golden era for the club, if not *the* golden era in its history.

Those fans didn't like getting beat any more than I did, but there was an innate positivity and respect from them towards the players – and the reverse was usually the same. That 'mutual respect' line is a well-worn cliché at most football clubs; it's also often a blatant lie – but it wasn't here. There was an enduring family feel to the entire organisation. I can honestly say that I never met a single Tranmere Rovers follower that I didn't actively like.*

---

* Half Man Half Biscuit were a band I'd liked since my Chelsea days. The one thing everyone knew about them, apart from their great songs and brilliantly funny lyrics,

At the centre of it all still was the manager Johnny King, supported by Ronnie Moore and the always impeccably turned-out Ray Mathias. Kingy may have been eccentric, but you underestimated him at your peril – and many did. Somehow, he managed to keep the team competitive even though we had a much smaller budget than all the other teams around us. A classic example of his fiscal smarts involved Ian Nolan, our young left-back, bought a few seasons earlier for peanuts. I loved playing with him, with more than one TV commentator describing our understanding as 'unstoppable'. Premier League Sheffield Wednesday were similarly impressed and, as already mentioned, bought him for £1.7 million.

John King eventually replaced him for £350,000 with the experienced Gary Stevens, who had played with Everton, Glasgow Rangers and nearly 50 times for England. The manager had acquired a top-class international as a replacement for a young developing player and come out of it with a £1.35 million profit! Brilliant business; classic Kingy.

There was no reason to suppose we would be anything other than serious challengers for a third season after the gloomy, crushing end to the last one. Could we do it this time? Could we go the extra mile – or should that be inch? – seeing as we had come so close before?

To make sure we had the best start for our next assault on the big time, and to lift spirits, we flew to Ireland for a pre-season tour. On the flight over there was a drop-dead gorgeous, full-figured female flight attendant, who many of the lads were intent on impressing. She seemed to lift the team's spirits just by existing, but appeared to have captivated them more than they were enthralling her. Having clearly heard every line countless times before, she effortlessly batted off their advances with breezy disdain and a few well-rehearsed one-liners. We arrived, went to the hotel, trained in the afternoon and were given a few hours off before reconvening at the hotel for a team briefing.

---

was that they were Tranmere Rovers nuts. They even refused to go on *The Tube*, the best TV music show at the time, because that was broadcast live on a Friday and the Rovers played that night.

As we sat in the foyer, waiting to find a room for the meeting, the stewardess walked in fully clad in a skintight black leather outfit, only a smidge off the full dominatrix look. On her arm was one of the lads who had obviously impressed her more than we had realised. This would normally be declared open season to give both some, shall we say, merry banter, tinged with a bit of acerbic jealousy and suggestive language from most of the lads. But no, she was that impressive and his achievement so remarkable that the entire team just stood up as one and solemnly applauded, nodding sagely to each other with deep respect, not unlike a cricket crowd at the MCC in Victorian times following another century by W.G. Grace. The only comments were, 'Good show, old boy!' and 'Well played there, young man.' Even a nice Dan Maskell impersonation of, 'Oh, I say!' The only downside was that I found out minutes later that I was sharing a room with him. I would be getting limited sleep unless I found another room and fast.*

In the opener at Prenton Park we beat our old rivals Swindon, who had been summarily dispatched back down to our division. Aldo got a couple and I got the winner with a 20-yarder. We didn't lose at home until December, so the team spirit was obviously fine.

We were battling with Middlesbrough, Derby, Wolves, Sheffield United and Watford, among others, all of whom were substantially bigger and wealthier than us. There was still that antipathy with Bolton Wanderers, which went back way before I arrived at the club. Bolton aren't the nearest rivals geographically but, clearly, they were still considered

---

* I impressed the lads with a new trick of my own. Training below the flight path at Dublin airport, Ged Brannan asked, 'What kind of plane is that?' 'A 737 100,' I answered, without turning round. 'OK, smart arse, see if you know the next one without looking.' 'Aer Lingus 747. Too easy. Try again.' An airbus. Followed by a turboprop ATP. I didn't have a particular interest in planes, but had taken Simon to the viewing area at Manchester airport every weekend for many months. I had spent so many hours reading while he called out the plane types. I could soon reel them off, just by the noise of the different engines.

something close to the evil empire by Tranmere fans. In December we had a double-header – two games in two days – which is bordering on unthinkable now. (Actually, scratch the 'bordering' from that sentence.) With Aldridge injured and me named captain* we beat Derby County at home 3–1, but Bolton beat us 1–0 at Burnden Park the following day to leave us in fourth.

What I probably needed at this point was a quiet time after the busy festive period, but that was trashed when, watching TV on 25 January 1995, Eric Cantona decided to launch his infamous kung-fu kick at a Crystal Palace fan. Like most people I was stunned at the insanity, before it suddenly dawned on me: 'Annabel, this is going to make my life a bloody nightmare over the coming days, weeks and probably months.' And it did!

For a period, it was the biggest story on the planet, and I had to deal with some of the fallout. This is why no one wants to be PFA chairman: it's unpaid but you are still in the firing line when 'it' hits the fan. The press were quick on the phone with the perfectly reasonable question, 'What are you going to do about your PFA Player of the Year assaulting a paying customer?!' In these situations, as a 'representative' I was made to feel I was personally responsible for Cantona's actions, as the bold Eric† was unlikely to say anything, other than some tosh eventually about seagulls and

---

* When the manager asked me to be skipper, I reacted the same way I did when I was asked to be chairman of the union: 'Why me? I don't want this and I am not suited for the role. But I'll do it if you think I am the best man for the job.' The first time leading them out I said, 'C'mon, team, let's go.' It had all the brute force and machismo of Kenneth Williams on one of his camper days. Higgy never let me forget it; he got the effete, 'C'mon, team, let's go,' line in every time before I said it. I liked the effect it had. We always laughed and then went out relaxed, any nerves left in the tunnel. It probably wasn't the manager's original intention when he gave me the armband, though.

† I'd never met Eric, or thought I hadn't. Recently I spotted an ancient cotton French international top in my loft, but I couldn't recall playing them. I Googled Scotland 'B' games, and there it was: Scotland v France, Pittodrie, 1987. I'd swapped shirts with their striker, the enigmatic Cantona himself. I have no memory of this

trawlers. Gordon Taylor and I had an emergency telephone conversation and our holding position was agreed.

As the lawyers flew into action the next day and the entire nation went wild at Eric's wild side, Gordon and I finally got a chance to meet up in person. I was fairly confident I knew what had happened: Eric had cracked after some abuse from the fan. Every player has felt that furious welling at one time or another. The abuse can be vile, and back then it was accepted that opposing fans could scream whatever they liked with total impunity. Say the same thing in the street and you could be arrested, but at football grounds players were considered fair game. It is interesting now that abuse, particularly racially motivated slurs, is absolutely not accepted by players when they hear it, even during games. So maybe Gordon was ahead of his time on that one.

The PFA media line was: 'Eric was provoked, despicable things were said about his close family. And although his actions could not be condoned, it was the "so-called fan" and his offensiveness that incited the robust response from Eric. In fact, it just goes to show how controlled our members are, that this is such an extraordinarily isolated and unusual occurrence. Instead of suggesting our members are mindless thugs, maybe you should consider how they are treated and how they generally react with fortitude and dignity.' A final line to the newspaper interrogators was: 'Would you put up with those types of insults at your work?'

I wasn't totally convinced. 'How about we also mention that Eric was out of order too? Apologise to the fan and to young, impressionable fans who were watching and might be shocked – or, worse still, might consider copying his antics?' Gordon felt attack was the best form of defence, though not quite as literally as Eric did.

So we backed our member as that was the union's job. I understood that, but people aren't stupid, they know when it just sounds ridiculous. I braced myself for a few days of firefighting for our French firebrand.

---

then unknown French kid still at Auxerre, but the shirt's probably worth a few quid now seeing as he wore it, and the collar still turns up nicely.

After all the interviews had been done (none ducked), I slumped back on the sofa at home, and said to Annabel, 'Do you know what? That actually went pretty well. They mostly bought it, and the show is already moving down the road to the next big story.' It felt like a good result, and I didn't sound quite as ridiculous as I thought I would, even though I was defending a man who had just manufactured a makeshift martial arts move on an unsuspecting member of the public in front of 20 TV cameras and a live international audience of billions of viewers around the world. I didn't have a leg to stand on, but here I was still standing.

Then the telephone rang one more time: 'Hello, is that Pat Nevin, chairman of the PFA?'

'Yes, can I help?'

'This is *Newsnight*. I wonder if you could come on this evening and discuss the Eric Cantona situation.'

'Er, erm, oh well, I . . . I am a bit busy tonight. I am supposed to be at an eh . . . a boy scouts' meeting! That's it. I have to present their prizes.' It was the best excuse I could come up with at a moment's notice.

'We will pay the scouts a fee for you not turning up.'

'I can't get to a studio. I've had a glass of wine.'

'We'll send a car.'

I was running out of ideas. I stalled again, asking, 'Out of interest, who would be interviewing me?'

'Jeremy Paxman.'

'I'm sorry, I'm training in the morning and need my rest. I will do it next week, if you like. Goodnight.'

The phone was down before I could hear his reply. Don't debate with Paxman when you're on ground as solid as quicksand. Next week would never happen, news moves fast, but I never wanted to make an argument I did not fully believe in again. For all my efforts, I never did hear from Eric or his team!

There were other big newspaper splashes to deal with, as well as inquisitions on TV and radio. Stories suggesting bungs had been taken by Brian Clough and George Graham smouldered away, while the John

Fashanu and Bruce Grobbelaar match-fixing allegations were still hanging around from an earlier time. From the outside, the game looked like it was swimming in a cesspit of sleaze, especially when you added the kiss and tell stories that were regular features in the red tops. Gordon Taylor himself had apparently been 'stung' by one of the 'dailies' in a front-page story. That story, and the phone-hacking that preceded it, would eventually lead to huge changes in the newspaper industry. This is when some of the first evidence of industrial-scale phone-hacking was discovered by Gordon and others.*

Gordon's contract negotiations rumbled on. I couldn't accept the possible cost to the union, especially that final salary pension cost and the effect the overall package might have on the union's finances in the future. It was all dealt with separately, but Gordon is the most dogged negotiator I have ever come across, and it led to a constant low-grade pressure and, by mid-February, even clear-the-air talks. I wanted it over with but couldn't allow myself to yield. If I got this wrong, then I would deserve the blame years down the line. It carried on for months but, in the end, I learned how to cope by observing Gordon closely and taking notes, knowing that he was the best in the business and that I might be able to use those skills one day myself.

Back on the pitch I had a football career to consider, one that was still going very well, whatever was happening in the outside world. Tranmere wanted me to sign a new three-year contract that would see me to the end

---

* It was reported that Gordon received £700,000 in damages from the *News of the World* some years later. It eventually got out that illegal phone-hacking was why Gordon won the case, and the red tops were on the back foot for the first time in their history. As noted, a quarter of a century later the police finally informed me that Glenn Mulcaire had my number too – poor man, listening to my dull messages hoping for sleaze. He was probably trying to intercept discussions between Gordon and me. The police said it wasn't worth taking the matter further regarding compensation. In retrospect, maybe I shouldn't have been taking financial advice from Plod – lots of other people made a fortune!

of my playing days, or very close to that anyway. I still had a hankering to do a year or two back in Scotland, but things were so good on the Wirral that it was a no-brainer to put pen to paper. It took some of the financial pressure off our young family, so I was as happy about that contract as any I had ever signed and, for once, not only because it gave me the chance to play more football at a club I liked.

John Aldridge had been missing from December 1994 to early March 1995, but we battled through with Ian Muir and Chrissy Malkin up front. A couple of 1–0 wins, against Reading and then Charlton where I got a scrambled winner, put us on top of the table again, the Premier League well within our sights for the third season in a row.

We got Aldo back and scoring for the run-in and by April we were in second spot with only six games to go, but this time only one team would be promoted directly as champions, with second to fifth going into the play-offs. The first of these half-dozen games was against the reviled adversaries Bolton Wanderers, who were vying with us for the title. Unusually it would be shown live on terrestrial TV, and the feeling was that if we could win this one then promotion was not only possible, but very likely.

It was a tight match, but we got the 1–0 win and I got the crucial goal with a great volley from . . . one yard. We'd had chances before but surely this was our best opportunity yet to get to the Premier League. It was in our own hands with only five games to go; we were on good form, we just had to keep our nerve and our belief. We managed a grand total of two points from the final 15 available. Surprise, surprise, we were back in the play-offs again for the third time in a row.

Everything was coming to a head in May yet again. Just to add a little more tension, Annabel was pregnant and expecting our second child at any moment as the day of the first play-off arrived. Simon had decided to make his entrance at 3.20am on the morning of an Everton v Chelsea game four years earlier; Lucy decided not to be upstaged and arrived at 3am on the morning of the first leg against Reading. I have a clearer memory of driving away from the hospital that morning at 6am than I have of the game that day, maybe unsurprisingly. I left the hospital car park, turned on the radio with dawn ready to break and, like an over-obvious piece of scripting, the very first bass beats of 'Protection' by Massive Attack came on, every word sung by Tracey Thorn feeling like it was written for me and my new girl.

Of course, like many people at the time with autistic children, we'd had that warning of the increased likelihood that subsequent children may have similar and possibly even more profound tendencies. This was a lot to take on board and there were fears from both Annabel and me, but we had decided to try to have another child as we had both always wanted more than one. Although it was worrying, we accepted that 'whatever will be, will be'. We would cope with the next child and give it all our time and love, whatever the circumstances.

Considering Simon's autism was not obvious immediately, there were concerns even after Lucy's birth for some significant time. Her development was so quick and her reactions so impressive on any scale, we had lost those worries before her first birthday. Having said that, I shouldn't gloss over it thoughtlessly: a year is a long time to have those uncertainties always crawling around in the back of your consciousness as she crawled around in front of us. Fortunately, she was a lovely baby, and apart from refusing to sleep for the first two years, she was a constant joy and gave us very few if any concerns from there on, or indeed in her entire life to date.

We lost 3–1 at home in the Reading game I have absolutely no memory of. I have clearly expunged it from my mind completely; it was either that bad or I was totally zonked following Lucy's birth. The second leg was a dull 0–0 draw and once again the Rovers had stumbled with the finishing line in sight. At least this time it wasn't a single solitary goal that killed us off – a very small mercy. It had been a dreadful denouement to the season after that warm sunny afternoon when we beat Bolton back in mid-April, topped the league and began to hope. That was a big mistake. To rub salt into the wound, Bolton, our great rivals and sworn enemies, won the play-offs and made it to the Premier League Promised Land instead of us.

The bare statistics for me were: games played, 54; goals scored, 5; assists, 19; children, 2. I was back in the Scotland squad, winning a couple of games and drawing others. There was another season to look forward to, and at the end of it would be Euro '96 in England. Now this was one tournament I really wanted to be involved in. Even though I was getting on a bit in everyone else's eyes, I still had the most appearances at the club that season. Two more wins at the end of the campaign and we would have been in the Premier League, so surely the good times at Tranmere would continue again after the summer?

7 /
I DIDN'T SEE IT COMING

John King was at it again. The manager continued with his madcap but successful team talks, which helped the general feeling of fun at the football club. His ideas for defending corners were often the subject of his eccentric thinking and were usually sprung on us moments before kick-off: 'OK, lads, we will leave two up the field for "corners against" today. Pat, you and Moggsy, pin three of them back.' He thought for a moment then, 'Better still, leave three up, they'll have to leave four back. Aldo, you stay up with those two.'

This was foolhardy to a fault, especially away from home and, anyway, Aldo was great in the air and useful in defending those balls whipped into the near post. Aldo wasn't convinced: 'Are you sure, boss?'

Kingy thought again on the hoof: 'Now that you say it like that, I've got a better idea. Let's leave four up. Ironsy, you stay up there as well. They'll have to leave five back to mark you four.'

There were incredulous looks all around as the gaffer walked towards the dressing-room door, before he stopped turned on his heel and said, 'Actually, the sensible thing here would be not to do that.' Thank goodness he had seen sense. 'We'll leave five up and they'll have to leave six back and their keeper. That'll work.'

And off he breezed out of the dressing room.

We just couldn't do it, and when he was gone we agreed that we would just leave two up and another on the edge of the box. He came up with some crazy ideas, but this was beyond the pale. About 25 years later I was covering a game and, lo and behold, one of the coaches appeared to leave five players outside his own box, edging up the field at a corner, asking the question, 'Are you brave enough not to mark those players up field?'

That coach was Pep Guardiola. I'm still not sure if Kingy was years ahead of his time or just eccentric.

Surprises came from all angles at Prenton Park. There was a game organised between the first team and the reserves around then. These are almost always horrible affairs and, with the 'stiffs' allowed and even encouraged to hammer into every tackle to show how desperate they are to be in the first team, the second string usually win!

A young centre-back from the fringes of the squad was given a start with the first team. We got a throw-in down near our own penalty area and, as the kid was nearest the ball, he picked it up. We went towards him, only for him to throw it almost to the far 18-yard line, more than half the length of the entire pitch! The game stopped dead. After the laughing had died down, everyone turned round to stare at this youngster who didn't seem to think this astonishing ability to throw a ball like Superman was particularly unusual.

Young Dave Challinor was asked, 'Don't you think it might have been worth mentioning that you can throw a ball further than any player we have ever seen or heard of? Or as far as some of us can bleedin' kick the thing?' He just shrugged his shoulders, but we had discovered a new weapon, entirely by chance. He would go on to set the world record for a throw-in, of 152 feet!

Because the usual success was likely to carry on for yet another season, all the blatant silliness was happily still going strong. Standing beside our physio Les Parry when a player walked into the physio's room one morning, I overheard their conversation, along with everyone else.

'Les, I don't think I will be fit for Wednesday; I strained my groin in the bath last night.'

Les sensibly answered, 'How did you do that?'

'Well, my missus and I were . . .' He then went into a graphic X-certificate description of what he and his wife were doing in the bath when the strain occurred. Anyone else would have stuck with the obligatory 'I slipped on the enamel getting out' explanation, but he thought it entirely necessary to share the intimate and frankly disturbing details . . .

I had three seasons left on my contract, but with so much going on in my life I had enough self-awareness to know that it would all be over soon enough. And, unlike modern players, I couldn't earn enough money from football to be financially secure afterwards. I had left the top flight the season the Premier League had started, so I had just missed out on the extraordinary wages that had come into the game.

I accepted that I now wanted to stay in the first team and keep playing – for all the 'right' reasons, as I saw it, but also for the money and the security it afforded. The filthy lucre became important for the first time: not for anything I could get for myself – I still didn't have any material desires, so you could keep your Porsches and Rolexes – but only for what I could give to the family to be comfortable and safe. Maximising my earning potential in these last few years was vital.

The first pre-season game of 1995–96 augured well: we beat my old club Everton at Prenton Park in the annual friendly. I scored one of the goals, so there was a brief guilty little moment of self-satisfaction. It was only a friendly, so the smugness was gone as quickly as it arrived. There was the standard sluggish start in the league, but we soon got into our usual rhythm and, by November, we had lost only two of those first 16 games. After wins against Derby, Leicester and Port Vale we were as nicely positioned as ever, this time in third place. Little old Tranmere Rovers vying for a Premier League place was now the norm; this would be the fourth season in a row and we had all got very comfortable with that.

Then, from out of the blue, I got a surprise phone call from an old friend. Fellow Scot Ian McNeill had been assistant manager at Chelsea in my time there – he was the man who'd put his job on the line for me with Ken Bates, when I originally went to Stamford Bridge. Batesy could only see a scrawny, malnourished weird little teenager, but Ian said he knew I would be a success and would stake his job on it. We had a great relationship and I loved having the chance to speak to Ian again. He was now scouting for a Premier League club and, after the pleasantries, got to the point: 'We want tae buy ye; ah've told the manager that ye would be the perfect man tae create for us and he agrees. I know enough about ye tae know that money isnae the big issue, but it'll be a considerably improved contract in comparison tae what you're on noo, probably four or five times what you're makin'. But we need tae know if you'd would be willing tae come before we waste oor time wae the bid.'

This was a tricky decision: no doubt they would pay a whole lot more and it was a chance of Premier League football, but I was so happy at Tranmere. I didn't want to put him off, but I needed time to think, and, as ever, I also had to talk to Annabel. Was this a good time to move home? She would have as much say in the decision as me. I plied him for some more information. 'Ian, you haven't actually told me which club your working for. That might make a difference.'

'It's Bolton Wanderers.'

The arch-rivals. The only team where a potential move would infuriate the Tranmere fans who had been so good to me. Could I do that to them? It isn't quite like a Celtic player signing directly for Rangers, but it would have felt like that to the Rovers faithful. I needed time, I needed to stall.

'I am chairman of the PFA, Ian. It would look bad if I was seen to be doing this illegally. I'm not supposed to talk to any other clubs directly, so we should do it the right way: just get Bolton to contact Tranmere, and we'll take it from there.'

'But yer no dismissin' it, then?'

'No,' I replied, with more than a little guilt to those unwitting Tranmere fans.

Annabel and I sat down to discuss it. She reminded me once again, just as she did when I almost signed for Paris Saint-Germain instead of Everton, 'Why would you go there? Would it be for the right reasons? Would you be going just for the money? Would you be as happy there? Would you enjoy your football there as much as you do at Tranmere? Would their style suit you? I'll support you, but don't do it just for the money. That's not who you are.'

It isn't who Annabel is either, and it is one of the multitude of reasons I married her. It would be a huge benefit to our financial security and that couldn't be ignored at this point in my career and indeed life. The length of the contract wouldn't even be important because the wages would be so much bigger at Bolton. After just a few hours' chatting, however, we knew the answer that we suspected after two minutes. I loved Tranmere and I was going to stay.*

About a week later John King called me into his office for a chat. I slipped on my best 'taken aback' face. 'What is it, gaffer?'

'There has been a bid for you, lad, and I want to be fair with you. I always promised that I would tell you if a club came in and, although I don't want you to go, I'll fully understand if you want to talk to them. It is a top-level club.'

I had my soliloquy at the ready. 'Unless Tranmere really needs the money then I am not interested. I love it here, I love the way we play and the freedom I've got to do my own thing.' I thought I should add a little flourish, as he loved a sprinkling of hyperbole himself. 'When I came here, I promised I would try to get us to the Premier League and I still want to do that. It has been a great journey, but we haven't reached the destination yet.' Kingy seemed moved by me talking his metaphoric language. 'If that's all, gaffer, I'll get outside and get on with training.'

He said he was delighted with my honourable attitude and, as I was shutting the door, said, 'Out of interest, don't you want to know which club it was?'

---

* I should make one other thing clear from way up here on my moral high horse. Bolton hadn't started well in the top flight and there was every chance they would be relegated and Tranmere could get promoted. That might not have been a great scenario to find myself in.

I looked over my shoulder with the door closing to a crack and replied with as much naïvety as I could muster, 'Oh yeah, who was it?'

'Celtic!'

The door was shut and I was outside by the time I had processed it. Oh my God, what had I done? Celtic were the team I supported, and I had just turned them down without realising it. This was the fourth time they had shown an interest in signing me, but this time I had killed the deal myself, even if I had thought it was Bolton. Standing in the corridor stunned, I thought about what to do. There was no way back after my spiel to Kingy, but it served me right for being such a smart Alec. I should have just shut up and let him speak.

Although conflicted, I told myself, 'This is simple. I have a contract with Tranmere. I have always been honourable and loyal that way, and, yes, it is still fun, and there is still even the possibility of being very successful here.' In the back of my mind, however, I wasn't sure it was an entirely sensible decision to have turned down both the mighty Celtic* and Premier League Bolton Wanderers in the same week. If I was going to feel any regret, that would have to wait until after my career; there was little I could do about it then. I decided not to tell my dad what I had turned down. He might have struggled to forgive me for that one.

I tried to put Bolton and Celtic to the back of my mind. It was an odd time, though, and anything but simple. I wanted to pursue this journalism idea and, having been a student and a footballer when I was young, I thought, 'Why shouldn't I be a footballer and a journalist at the same time now? Well, that and the PFA chairman, father of two and a sometime DJ to boot.'

I was asked to take over a radio show in Merseyside for a while and loved it. Friends Graeme Le Saux, then at Blackburn, Brian McClair from Manchester United, Barry Horne from Everton, Simon Raymonde from the Cocteau Twins, and others, joined my little weekly show, talking

---

* Celtic didn't win any silverware that year and Bolton were indeed relegated but went straight back up to the Premier League again the following season.

football and music. Broadcaster Janice Long and Pete Wylie from Wah! were involved in setting up the station. I thought then that they were great shows, though I am not convinced I would feel the same if I could hear them back now. It was a possible direction and, at the time, BBC Radio were also making overtures about me fronting some afternoon shows, but there wasn't the time to do that justice while I was still playing.*

Tranmere's good run continued and in November I started for Scotland against San Marino, scoring one and providing three assists. I scored another goal that night but it was disallowed for offside even though footage clearly showed it wasn't. Where was VAR when I needed it?! With Euro '96 in England only seven months away, I was in the squad with a very good chance of being in the starting XI. I was thoroughly enjoying this successful late summer, or possibly early autumn, to my career. The problem is, the moment you have such thoughts in football the weather changes abruptly.

Suddenly, from that clear blue sky, games that Tranmere would normally have won, we started narrowly losing, usually by the odd goal. We weren't playing particularly badly, but what started as a blip turned into a slump and, before we knew it, we were in freefall. I'd witnessed this before in my last season at Chelsea, and I recognised the signs again. There were only four wins in the next 24 league games between late November 1995 and early April 1996, but 15 of those 19 were either draws or single-goal defeats. The margins were gossamer thin between easy-going, upward success and a sickening downward spiral. At Chelsea we had been relegated and, as we plummeted, it began to feel like the same unthinkable thing could happen here at Tranmere. The speed of the descent after nearly four years of effortless success was dizzying.

Everyone would have had their own ideas of where the problems lay, and obviously no one ever thinks they themselves could be part of the

---

* They got Simon Mayo to do it eventually, and, to be fair, that was the right decision with bells on.

problem. Was it the ever-changing centre-backs that never quite gelled? Were we not getting the ball to Aldridge quickly enough? He seemed to think so, but then strikers always do. Aldo had groaned about that the previous season, and we did perfectly well, nonetheless. Had we sold too many of the core quality players? I was not convinced of that either. I certainly felt we had become a bit more direct down the middle with our attacks. Everything in midfield was now going straight towards the strikers – not lumped up there, but passed, threaded or clipped over the centre-backs.

This idea is fine, but if it becomes your only major outlet, you become predictable, and I thought we had gone down that route far too eagerly. But, then again, I would think that because, as a wide attacker, I was now being starved of service for the first time since I joined the club. New players had come in, but they were all technically good enough at this level. Shaun Teale had played for Aston Villa in the top flight for four years; Gary Stevens, signed the previous year, was an England international; Liam O'Brien was an Irish international; and Paul Cook was a combative but classy midfielder. Whatever the reason, the swashbuckling side was no longer buckling its swash to quite the same level.

John King had a quote at the time which I thought was just another of his fanciful florid metaphors: 'Building a football team is like baking a cake. If you get the ingredients right, it rises perfectly in the oven and tastes great. But if you get the mix wrong, it will go flat and stodgy and will be inedible.' In the end he was right: the ingredients were all still there, but the mix was wrong.

After taking Tranmere to the brink of the Premier League from the bottom of the lowest tier, where they'd been when he took over ten years previously, surely he would be given time to tinker with the mix?

Sadly not.

After a heavy defeat against Derby County away from home, and sitting only four points above relegation with six games to go, the board blinked and sacked the man who had been the heart and soul of the club – a stalwart of the team as a player in the sixties, manager in the seventies, as well as the core of its success during this era. Well, they 'moved him upstairs', which was a typical kindness from such a lovely club. But he was gone, and there would be a new manager brought in to salvage something from those last few games and secure our survival. There was a horrible feeling around the club that week and a real concern that everything we had constructed was in danger of being washed away over a few short months.

I understood well enough by now that a new manager wasn't necessarily going to be a positive thing for me, personally – it hadn't been at either Chelsea or Everton. I was, however, willing to do just about anything to help us out of this predicament, just about anything.

The chairman Frank Corfe asked me to come and see him in his office. I was intrigued. As an experienced player I thought he might want to ask for my thoughts on who he was considering to replace Kingy. Maybe he wanted to know if assistant manager Ronnie Moore had the respect of the lads and would be worth a try. Whatever it was, I was going into that room to do my best for the club and its future. I would be honest to a fault. Frank was blunt and to the point: 'Do you want to be the new manager?'

'What?!' I hadn't seen that coming at all. If I am honest, I was as flattered as I was flabbergasted. I considered it seriously for all of three seconds, so the speed of my reply doubtless surprised him: 'I've never wanted to be a manager. There are too many other things I want to do with my life. Thanks for considering me, but I don't think that would be a great idea. I wouldn't be right.'

He shot back quickly: 'Would you consider doing it short term until the end of the season?'

I thought it best to make myself very clear. 'Look, Frank . . . sorry, Mr Chairman.' I never could get used to the formality of that football convention. 'I love tactics and all that sort of stuff, but, honestly, I don't think I've got the right personality. I haven't got that hard edge, the willingness to hurt people and let them down without feeling the pain of what that does to them and their families. I'd be worrying about that stuff all the time. I wouldn't be able to sleep, so I wouldn't be any good at it.'

Not to mention, of course, I had a huge amount going on in my head at that point too. I knew in my heart that this level of extra responsibility could well be beyond me at this time.

Frank was gracious and, although he was a go-getting businessman, he did understand my lack of hard-nosed ambition that, many years before, Ken Bates at Chelsea had singularly failed to fathom.

'Fine, the other man we are considering is John Aldridge. What do you think of him for the job, would he be any good?'

'I honestly have no idea. But he does have some of the attributes you need. He's got the drive, the ambition and the self-belief. And he wouldn't flinch from making painful decisions.'

There are some occasions in life when a long-involved period of consideration, introspection and self-analysis is necessary, but this wasn't one. Typical for me, though: jobs I had no interest in were being offered to me on a plate seemingly on a regular basis. From being a professional footballer in the first place, to becoming chairman of the PFA, an organisation that I hadn't even so much as asked to become a club delegate for. Now I was being offered the possibility of a good level manager's job while still in my early thirties. Back then you didn't even need to have the coaching licences if you were a player, just a promise that you would go on the courses.

But I couldn't let the folly go any further: this sport was making every effort to envelop my entire life, and I still didn't want that to happen. I was happy to play football for as long as possible, but going into the game at a management or coaching level afterwards held zero interest. I didn't love the football industry enough to give it all that time and make all those sacrifices. I knew that when I was 17, and I had never budged on it for a second in the intervening years.

It may well have been that Aldo was always Frank Corfe's first choice. I offered my best wishes when he took over, knowing that it would be tough for him. The team was struggling and, on top of that, he was going to continue playing as well, so he would be treading that always difficult and fine line between teammate and boss. It is a complex but not impossible task – in the short term, at least. 'But another good reason for me turning the position down,' I thought.

The last six games under Aldo saw two wins, four draws and a comfortable mid-table finish. We might well have got those results with Johnny King still at the helm, but we all know that football owners get jumpy at the slightest whiff of relegation.

With the luxury of being safe with a couple of games to go, I was able to concentrate on my role at the PFA awards dinner. As chairman I would sit beside our special guests during dinner and spend most of the evening taking care of them before and after donning the nosebags. I initially couldn't catch Gordon's drift when he'd said to me a few months before, 'We should go for a really special guest this year, Pat.'

'Were our previous special guests not special enough?' I thought. Terry Venables, Kenny Dalglish and Denis Law had been impressive, and I had been honoured to spend the evening as their host.

Gordon enlightened me: 'It might be your final year as chairman, so how about Pelé?'

There was a slight pause, while I attempted to remain outwardly cool about the conversation.

'That would be . . . quite good. Can we get him?'

Gordon smiled. 'We can try.'

Gordon was suggesting this was partly a thank you to me, for the last few years' hard work, that we should try to get the great man now, before I left the post. Much to my amazement we did get Pelé, and the evening was a huge success when it eventually happened. Les Ferdinand won the Player of the Year Award, only the third player of colour to do so, and he was given it by one of the greatest players ever to play the game. Pelé was a stunning individual to spend time with and, as chairman it was my 'job' to hang out with him for the evening. Being in his presence and observing how everyone reacted around him was astonishing. We had previously welcomed many huge stars but the reaction to Pelé was like being in the presence of the Pope, the King and a national treasure such as David Attenborough combined. The queue in front of the top table for his autograph seemed endless. It was filled with world famous current players, huge captains of industry, Lords of the realm, MPs, and all manifestations of the great and the good who would never dream in any other circumstances of demeaning themselves by asking for an autograph from anyone. Even when I announced that, during dinner, 'We should leave the great man alone and allow him time to eat,' the queue didn't sit back down but waited respectfully at a small distance until he was ready to flourish his pen once more. For his part, Pelé never looked in any way put out by the constant intrusion, which he had doubtlessly dealt with his entire life. He was the perfect gentleman.

We chatted for hours, and, apart from his sincere and obviously misplaced humility, he was attentive, interested and quite clearly seriously intelligent. He had been sports minister in Brazil and was certainly sharp enough to do the job, even if he hadn't been the most famous footballer on the planet as well as being a living legend in his own country. Maybe even more impressively he understood my Glaswegian accent perfectly well, which was a huge surprise, although I did use my Radio 4 voice.

In between numerous efforts to make each other laugh, he was desperately keen to know more about the PFA, what it did and how it could afford to put on such a lavish event. He was amazed by the union's reach, power and the scope of its good work in the game and beyond. Just before I stood up to introduce him – like he needed an introduction to the fawning throng – he leaned over to me and said a line I will never forget, 'Patrick, why don't you come over to Brazil and stay with me for a while and help me set up a players' union over there? We have nothing close to this in our country, even though for many people the game is the most important thing above religion, politics and sometimes even their family.'

It is not an offer you get every day, but I had to be honest in my reply. If anyone was to go over there and advise him on how to set up a union, it would have to be Gordon Taylor himself, or one of the others who worked alongside him at the time, such as Brendon Batson, Mick McGuire or Micky Burns.

When Pelé spoke to the assembly, which he did exceptionally well, you could have heard the proverbial pin drop. It was a magical evening that nobody wanted to end, particularly not me, sitting beside him throughout. I concentrated on being the perfect host, and even though I promised myself I wouldn't impose, I couldn't resist it in the end. Just before coffee I asked him, 'Would you mind signing your place name card for me, as a memento of the evening?'

He said he would love to, but explained first, 'You know, I do not really like the name Pelé. My friends call me Edson, so I want you to call me Edson.' That was good enough for me – I would happily dine out on that line for years – but he explained further: 'My father named me after Thomas Edison, the inventor of the lightbulb, because I was the light of his life. He just didn't manage to spell Edison correctly.'

He wrote on the card: 'To P. Neven. Thanks very much, Edson = Pelé.'

Well, if his dad could misspell his name, I was OK with him getting mine slightly wrong. As we went out, he asked if we would meet again and, suddenly, I remembered: 'Actually, Scotland are playing England in the upcoming Euros. I am in the Scotland squad. I heard there was a chance you might be at the game, so we might see each other there.'

He smiled that famous smile and said, 'I am the guest of honour that day and will be meeting the teams before the game for handshakes on the field. When I come to you, we shall have a big hug to show how good friends we are.'

What an incredible thought. Within seconds I had it all planned in my head. I will not mention this to anyone, and when the moment comes it will stun not only all my teammates but also everyone around the country and the world watching on TV.

Pretty soon I had to come back to reality. The next day at training I didn't bring up the subject of my new 'besty' mate either – the Tranmere lads would find out soon enough. The fact was that the season had gone pear shaped for the Rovers, and in these circumstances it didn't feel right to gloat. We avoided relegation, but for us and our own higher expectations, that wasn't something to overly celebrate.

Just as upsetting as the poor domestic season, my old Scotland nightmare of getting dumped just before a major tournament came back to haunt me, even though my personal form hadn't dipped at all. From starting in the national team in November, creating goals and scoring, I was suddenly dropped to the bench, then all the way to the Scotland 'B' squad for a game against Denmark. Maybe Tranmere's recent fall from their usual heights was part of the reason, but it was just the same old story for me, whatever the cause.

The 'B' game was a classic Catch-22. If I played brilliantly, then it was only a 'B' game and it would count for nothing. If I didn't play well, it was a perfect excuse to drop me, and one or two others picked alongside me. I played in the game, knowing that I had a damaged vertebra from a recent injury, just to show willing, but in my gut I knew well that, just like the 1986 Mexico World Cup and the 1990 Italian adventure, I was going to be jettisoned once again. It was bad enough losing out on that experience, but – worse! – I wouldn't even be able to show off my new mate Pelé!

But even putting that aside, somewhere in the back of my head another nagging voice was growing louder . . . 'You've been here before, haven't you, and not just with Scotland? You were having a great time at a club, then the manager who bought you gets sacked and, when the new one comes in, suddenly the fun, the good times and soon enough the regular starts are history. Do you think this could this happen with Aldo? It happened at Chelsea and at Everton, why should it be any different this time?' As the summer drew to a close I gave it some thought and came up with the considered rational answer to my own questions: 'It's not just likely, it is a racing bloody certainty!'

8/
SETTING SUN

From the beginning of my fifth season at Tranmere, I thought John Aldridge, the new manager, didn't sound as if he was completely sold on having me around. At first it was nothing explicit, but soon my antenna started picking up all the same signals I had heard before. Aldo was a teammate and somebody I had made a considerable number of goals and chances for, but I was convinced that it was more than paranoia or plain old *déjà vu*.

There are usually clues like lack of eye contact or body language to start with, but I couldn't put my finger on exactly what it was about Aldo's demeanour other than that. It didn't take long for my suspicions to be proved right. On the pre-season tour I was fined for not being drunk with the rest of the lads. It was meant to be funny, I think, but it was a direct mirror of what had happened with Howard Kendall at Everton five years earlier.

Even more obviously, just like at Everton with Polish international Robert Warzycha, Aldo bought a player who would play in my precise position. By the time the opening game of the season arrived, I was already relegated to the bench, something that would have been unthinkable under John King a few months earlier. The odd thing was that I didn't get particularly annoyed with the new manager. I knew this could happen. I had been there before so would have been a bit thick not to spot it and realise I would have to deal with it.

I still had two years left on my contract and would honour it if the situation demanded. I would also give everything when I was picked and would do the same in training. If Aldo wanted me to leave, he would have to tell me so. Then we could sort something out, or maybe I would just retire if they paid me all that I was owed to the end of my contract. I was fairly sanguine in the end because of the security of the contract, even if, as ever, I felt I still had plenty to offer. I had survived this far in football and if this was to be my final club, and even my final season, I could cope, and I had certainly begun preparing for the end anyway.

To think I had turned down lucrative moves just months before to Bolton in the Premier League and the mighty Celtic, even if the Celtic debacle was undeliberate.

It turned out to be a completely wasted season for me after the previous enjoyable and successful ones, which was a bit of a shame because all I really wanted to do was play some football. Some of the joy of the game faded away once more without the excitement of match days, but it didn't stop me looking for it wherever I could.

One place I did find the fun was with the man taking my position, Ivano Bonetti. On his first outing he was handed the number 11 shirt (my shirt almost every week up until then) and he proceeded to grab a giant pair of scissors and cut it almost in half along the midriff. I wasn't sure what look he was aiming for, but it had a whiff of the early Madonna belly-button bearing 'Like a Virgin' stylee to it. We all watched with astonishment; there wasn't a replacement shirt, so whoever was wearing that number next week would have to rock that style too. This was before the time of domestic squad numbers and names on shirts, or indeed a whole lot of money to afford buying new strips each week.

Our funny and talented physio Les Parry couldn't believe the gall of the man. Les is a brilliant mixture of old-school ideals and ethics with ultra-modern knowledge in his field. He also happened to be a very talented writer for the club programme, and the only man I have known to go from physio to manager with a club at that level, which was obviously at Tranmere some years later. He also had a penchant for wearing only shorts and a T-shirt on the bench, which is hardcore in the middle of February in Birkenhead with the wind whipping off the Irish Sea, up the Mersey, straight into Prenton Park and up those skimpy wee shorts. Les took it as a personal slight that Ivano had partially destroyed one of our brand-new shirts.

Maybe at Ivano's previous clubs Juventus, where he won the Serie A title, or Sampdoria, where he did the same – as well starting on the losing team to Barcelona in the European Cup final in 1992 – redesigning your shirt would have been perfectly normal behaviour, but it wasn't at Tranmere Rovers. I liked his rebellious outlook from the start. Within days of our first training session we became great friends and admirers of each other's skills. In training if we played together we were close to unstoppable, but there was no chance the manager would use us at the same time on match day, which I thought was a huge pity and a big mistake. Admittedly, we maybe overdid it a bit by setting each other up to score overhead kicks in training just for the sheer exhilaration and the creativity.

Ivano was an international-class footballer with world-class skills, and he knew it. He loved playing but, like me, the beauty of those skills seemed just as important as the end product, and this did not always go down well with the more prosaic British football attitudes. He was also fabulously truculent and would not sit there quietly accepting being told to do something that he felt was wrong. I could see that he and the new manager were on a collision course long before either of them even considered it.

At one point Ivano and I were injured at the same time with the same ailment, plantar fasciitis. Well, he said that's what his injury was, but he wasn't in any great hurry to get back out there to help the manager. It was still early days at Tranmere for him, but the expected communication breakdown had already happened with the manager. Ivano often used the old 'I cannot understand your English very well' line when Aldo was either shouting at him or trying to get him to do something that he didn't want to do. It was classic behaviour that I have seen used by a number of foreign imports when their understanding of English was, in fact, perfectly good enough to get the message.

Physio Les would work every injured player to exhaustion, often on the indoor rowing machine, or any other means of torture he could get his hands on. But whereas most of us would do the work, get fit and get out of there as soon as possible, Ivano could not to be manipulated so easily. Most of the injured players wanted to recover as quickly as possible so that they could get back into the team and play, but just as importantly they wanted to get away from Les's exhausting, painful and borderline sadistic regime. It was a smart if brutal way of Les shifting any shirkers from his treatment room.

Ivano, on the other hand, would mysteriously acquire another 'niggle' to his trapezius that didn't allow him to row, or he would just do as much as he thought was the right amount of work with the physio and then stop when he felt like it. If he had respected his manager, he would have been as committed as anyone. He didn't respect Aldo, so the boss getting my Italian mate to do what he wanted was like explaining the delights of a fine wine to a devout teetotaller. It was ignored with a uninterested shrug.

Ivano and I had a discussion one day about the best derbies, and while he regaled me about the merits of Juventus v Torino and Sampdoria v Genoa, I countered with my Everton v Liverpool and Chelsea v Spurs (or Arsenal) and even Scotland v England experiences. I then said, 'Of course they all pale when compared to Celtic versus Rangers, if you are talking about atmosphere.' He thought this was nonsense, so I promised to take him to an Old Firm game so he could judge for himself.

Fortunately, Ivano was mates with Paolo Di Canio, who was then at Celtic, so getting the three tickets – for him, me and his mate Mario – wasn't a problem, even if they were right up the back of the 'Celtic End' at Ibrox. I was a Celtic fan anyway back then, so felt at home, even though it was −2° – which was a heartless −5° with the windchill on top – in the middle of a biting Scottish winter's evening. I knew how passionate he was about passion, so I suspected he would be impressed by the usual mayhem up there, and he was.

After about 20 minutes Ivano turned round and said over the deafening noise of the constant roaring and singing, 'Pat, the man beside me, I think he might be unwell. We should call for help.'

I looked at the Celtic fan, who was dressed in his short-sleeved green and white hooped shirt.

'I don't think so, Ivano. He looks all right to me.'

'But, Pat, it is minus-two degrees, there is wind and snow in the air. I am cold wearing thermals, two jumpers and a coat, and the man is only wearing a little shirt with no sleeves.'

I looked over again. 'Yes, I know, but still, he seems fine to me.'

He paused for a moment, studied the Hoops fan again then turned back to me. 'But, Pat, he is sweating.'

'Yes, I know, but in the circumstances, this is still considered normal behaviour. I reckon he is fine. It's just the level of passion you get up here!'

As a confused smile spread across his face, you could tell that Ivano was impressed.

There was no point in going into a stroppy huff with the Tranmere manager or even the Scotland manager because I hadn't been called up for Euro '96.* Obviously, I wanted Scotland to beat England, but the Gary McAllister penalty miss followed by Gazza's glorious goal seconds later meant that, as usual, Scotland didn't make it out of the group stage.

There had been plenty of media work available during the tournament, so I went into full journalist mode and ended up not only doing work for BBC Radio 5 Live and some for *Match of the Day* with Gary Lineker and co., but, to my mind far more importantly, I was writing a series of columns for the *Independent* and even a regular

---

* OK, there was a little painful twinge when I wasn't there to show off my mate Pelé before the game. But then, as I watched the line-up pre-match, Pelé hadn't made it either, which was an odd small relief.

humorous TV skit for the *Daily Record* in Scotland. The opportunities being presented to me underlined that this was the direction I would most likely be going when my career finished. The articles were barely being edited by then, so I began to hope I might be getting close to the required standard as a wordsmith.

For the entire first half of the new season, I was relegated to the subs' bench, and sometimes not even that. I loved my dad's company, but sitting in the stands beside him, after he had pointlessly travelled all the way from Glasgow by train, was by far the most painful part, just as it had been in my final season at Everton.

I was ordered to play for the reserves, which was something that I had rarely been subjected to before, even when out of favour at Everton. I had probably only played a handful of reserve games in my entire career, and that was usually only for fitness purposes after coming back from injury.*

It was all a bit predictable. From being a key player loved by the fans and playing well, to within a matter of months being treated like the proverbial leper. Halfway through the season the manager got me into his office and asked, 'Do you want to put in a transfer request, Paddy? It might be the best for everyone.'

That was code for, 'Rip up your contract and give up your rights to your lump sums of signing-on fees and I can get you out of here.'

I replied in kind, 'If you or the club wants to sell me, just carry on, but I always honour my contracts, so I won't be handing in a transfer request.'

That is footballer code for, 'Pay me all, or most of the money owed for the rest of my contract, and I will go, otherwise you are stuck with me unless we find a club I fancy.'

It didn't go down too well, understandably. Aldo would have wanted to use my wages to get another player in, or maybe even two. I understood

---

* There was a Manchester United reserves game at Old Trafford that included Roy Keane, Andy Cole and Brian McClair, among others, so that one was fun and a good test, but most were dull, unmemorable affairs.

his position, but now I had to think about what was best for my family financially. Something would be sorted out in the end, I knew that, but I had to go through this long tedious dance first.

Other attempts to needle me backfired. After coming on as substitute, I was booked for bouncing a ball in anger when the referee didn't give me a foul. There was a little frustration, but also an attempt to put pressure on the referee if he had to make a similar decision next time I was fouled – basic psychology. Whatever the case, I was fined £200 by the manager during a post-match rant. It felt small-minded, but I accepted it and promised to play from then on with no visible reactions whatsoever, positive or negative. I was never the most demonstrative on the pitch but, even so, this must have looked a little odd.

To give Aldo his due, though, when he was sent off the very next week for remonstrating with the referee, he fined himself £400. I have no idea if he ever paid it, but I suppose it was the thought that counted. It was quite satisfying, although you wouldn't have known from me as I was now showing no visible emotion! The most I allowed myself was a Paddington Bear-like hard stare.

I was getting the odd substitute appearance and had created a few goals, mostly for Aldo, who was still playing and still scoring regularly even while he was manager. I finally started my first game of the season at Prenton Park in mid-January following a terrible run for the team over the festive period. An entire half a season had been wasted for me, but I was always ready to give my best, so I was trying everything on my rare outing. We beat Swindon 2–1 and I scored both goals – the first an overhead kick that Ivano said he enjoyed from the stands – giving us a vital win to help stop the rot.

The manager was fuming with me after the game, though. Having already scored two, we got a late penalty. I had taken it and the keeper saved well diving to his right and flicking it round the post. Aldo, not only the manager but also designated penalty taker, had subbed himself by this point, so it was unclear who should have taken the spot kick. I had scored two, had played well and later got man of the match. I fancied the idea of a hat-trick, and my confidence was high, so why not me if there was no designated taker?

This logic didn't cut it with Aldo, and he aimed a sustained tirade at me in the dressing room after the match. It felt as if he was furious that I had proved him wrong by playing so well, with the crowd clearly on my side and, indeed, wanting me back in the side. For my part, I had learned from Ivano, and I simply ignored the gaffer's negativity, while enjoying the fans' positivity. The fans were forever asking me why I wasn't playing anyway, but they were a polite bunch and were not at this point going to turn on club legend Aldo – even for me. On this occasion, it was obvious a few of the players were on my side too.

Just as with an almost identical time at Everton under Howard Kendall, after scoring a late goal that won us the game, the manager couldn't bring himself to say those two simple words, 'Well done.' I wasn't surprised, but, in fairness, he kept me in the team for a little while after that even if I knew it was on sufferance.

A variety of agents called to alert me that the manager was trying to offload me, to which I always reacted with the phrase, 'Fine, I'll listen to any offers when they come in.' I still didn't have an agent myself, but it was odd to think I was being hawked around the football world without having given my permission. I comforted myself with the thought that they would need my approval eventually!

The season petered out with us in mid-table and by then Annabel and I had decided it was the time to finally move back home to Scotland. She had followed me throughout my career, and the deal was always clear: we would go back to live near where she came from in the Scottish Borders, or possibly Edinburgh, when it was all over.

Even more importantly, we wanted to raise our children in Scotland. We wanted this for many reasons, but none of them were anti-English. I don't feel any anti-Englishness, though some of my countrymen and women allegedly do! We love Scotland and its beauty, and we wanted to be close to our families, but the schooling for Simon was paramount. Kids with special educational needs were treated very differently in different regions of the UK back then. Scotland was more proactively integrating kids on the autistic spectrum into mainstream schooling, whereas in Chester the direction of travel was special school with no mainstream integration. That wouldn't suit Simon or his needs, and neither would it maximise his talents and opportunities.

If I stayed at Tranmere for that final year of my contract, at least we would have time to sort everything out regarding Simon, as well as other small considerations like buying a new home and me finding another job! But, in reality, I thought there was little chance I was going to see that final year out; neither side wanted it and, one way or another, I was sure we would reach an agreement.

I couldn't have faced the idea of my final season as a player being an utterly joyless one. The joy was why I played the game; the possible lack of it, the reason why I never wanted to be a professional in the first place – and it might now be the time to be true to my convictions and just walk away as the fun was being extinguished.

If it meant retiring as a professional and then just kicking a ball about with mates, as I always promised myself I would, then so be it. I still felt fit enough to play at a high standard and believed I was good enough to carry on, but that was secondary. I was approaching my 34th birthday, time was not on my side, and I acknowledged to myself that I'd had a decent innings. I had very few regrets, no anger either, even at John Aldridge. I had accepted that it was now just about time for me to start my real life, post-football.

The PFA had gone through another protracted argument with the leagues, which was keeping me busy. As ever, it was about the monies due to us from the TV deals. These TV deals were now becoming very lucrative, and the pressure was building on the union and those of us leading it. It didn't exactly help – in terms of desirability from other clubs – to be sending out strike ballot papers to all our members with my name and signature on the bottom of every single one of them!

The union had also dealt with the Bosman case, which was extremely complicated.* It wasn't clear whether we should support it or stand back. The Bosman ruling would help the wealthy players get much wealthier, but there was a good chance that others further down the food chain might find it harder. Both groups were our members and deserved to be best served by us, but what was good for one might disadvantage the other. In the end the decision was made mostly on moral grounds regarding freedom of movement, but it was an uncomfortable dichotomy and dilemma. The threat of industrial action over the issue just made that whole season all the more stressful.

Then there were the legal cases following the alleged 'bungs for throwing games' by PFA members John Fashanu, Bruce Grobbelaar and Hans Segers, which became huge after a sting by the *Sun*. They were on the front and the back pages for what felt like an eternity and, of course, the union was forever being asked for its position.

It wasn't an easy stance, as the case went to the very heart of the integrity of the sport. Our line sounded simple and logical: 'We cannot comment, the rule of law must run its course, and giving ignorant opinion in the meantime is unhelpful and possibly even prejudicial.'

Sadly, this position sounded like a cop-out when given to the media. Remember, if the players were found guilty, they would have been cheating our own members as well as the fans and the game in its widest sense. Understandably, the media, the fans, the general public and many politicians wanted a bolder reaction from us. In the most personal sense,

---

* Jean-Marc Bosman wanted to move clubs. The buying club, Dunkerque, wouldn't pay the fee, so his former club, RFC Liège, held his registration even though his contract had expired, reducing his pay by 70 per cent into the bargain. He took his case to the European Court of Justice and won, meaning players could now move to a new club at the end of their contracts without their former club receiving a fee. This radically changed the power and financial balance in football for the players. The Bosman ruling also then prohibited quotas on foreign players from EU states playing for other clubs in the union, also changing the face of the game forever for the top clubs.

I disliked being dragged into that ugly world and actively hated the idea of trying to argue their case if any of them were eventually to be found guilty.*

For all that this sounds stressful I can honestly say that the work the union was doing in other areas, like providing and paying for checks for heart problems such as cardiomyopathy, kept me upbeat when I went into the Manchester offices. That particular decision about delivering better heart monitoring was one I was passionate about. I had first come across it when a very young player had died, suddenly and for no apparent reason, before I arrived at Everton. His case and the hidden dangers were initially highlighted to me by the Everton chaplain Harry Ross, but I also knew of other tragic cases such as Terry Yorath's son Daniel. The press might have been all over the bungs, scams and strikes, but I believed the cardio screening was far more important.

One of my final appearances in a Tranmere shirt was to be for Dave Higgins's testimonial at Prenton Park. Dave wanted me on from the start, so as I was playing, suddenly Ivano Bonetti piped up, 'In that case I will play as well. I am fit for tonight.'

The fans liked both of us – and although the manager had frozen us out by this point, that didn't matter: it was a good sales pitch for the game and, of course, it was only a friendly to raise money for a club stalwart. Ivano and I would finally get to play on the same team together. But when Ivano said to the manager that he was suddenly fit, the boss replied, 'In that case, you start and, Pat, you're on the bench.' Ivano's face dropped. 'In that case, I'm unfit again.' And off he trotted, with his slight limp, suddenly making another unexpected guest appearance halfway down the corridor.

It was sad, as it would have been good to let us play together in a friendly to see how it worked, and I am sure it would have been very entertaining. But the manager obviously had his reasons.

---

* Ultimately they weren't, but that was concluded just as I left the post. After two criminal trials they were both cleared. Grobbelaar then sued the *Sun* for libel and in the end won £1 of damages.

So was it personal from John Aldridge? I never thought it was at any point. The easiest thing to suggest was that I was a threat – after all, I had been considered for the manager's post at the same time as him. It is never easy having someone in your dressing room who could be perceived as a threat, someone who you think will step into your shoes the moment things go wrong. He couldn't have known that I was truly uninterested in being a manager but, even so, I still don't think that was the deal.

I reckon he thought he could get players that were better suited to his style than me. He was always going on about getting the ball into the middle quicker, but my assist numbers had been extremely good throughout my career, so I knew when an attempted cross would be blocked and when I could get it in. That was my speciality, and I certainly wasn't for stupidly trying to cross or pass it when I knew it wasn't on.

I knew exactly when it wasn't worth trying a specific pass – the timing is in milliseconds – but some strikers never understood that. They could be one dimensional in their thinking – but, of course, that's exactly why they are successful. I still rated Aldo as one of the best finishers of his generation, and it had been an education playing with him. I could also appreciate his single-mindedness and his drive. Traits I didn't share. In my first season at Tranmere I had asked him how he scored so many goals. Was there one trick above all the others I could use to increase my own numbers?

'It's simple,' he replied. 'When the ball is played into the box, go where the defenders aren't. That's it. Players always go where they think the ball will go. But what is the point if the defender is already there? You will get a lot of tap-ins that way.'

With that infuriatingly simple piece of advice I had the best scoring season of my career, getting 19 for club and country. As with many relationships there was plenty of good before the short bad period at the end. I always like to focus on the good times more, especially if they are a better and more honest reflection of the entire period. Too many players leave clubs, and people leave jobs, only thinking of the last difficult part. I choose not to.

I was saddened, knowing that my time at Tranmere was over. I had suspected as much when the new manager was announced, but being forewarned is to be forearmed – that's why there was no real bitterness or surprise. It wasn't me, it wasn't personal, it was just the circumstances – and just about every single player goes through this at some point, usually more than once in their career. There was nothing to be gained by sitting and stewing about it. It didn't make me happy, obviously, but my world view was that others would love to have had my career, and few things annoyed me more than other well-paid professional footballers mumping and moaning about their lot, just because they couldn't get exactly what they wanted. I was far too grounded to take that line. I would have despised myself if I thought that way and, anyway, Annabel wouldn't have allowed it.

Over the next two or three years under Aldo, Tranmere slowly slid down the table before eventually being relegated, and the glory years were finally gone. There is, however, one thing I still feel immense pride about regarding those Tranmere days. When Rovers fans put together their greatest combined XI in the club's history, I am usually included, as is Aldo, obviously. I am not sure that is the case for me with any other club I played for. It was definitely a special time.

After I left, they made it to Wembley in 2000, the year before the relegation. They faced Leicester City in the League Cup final, and I was lucky enough to cover it for the BBC. It was a wonderful sight to see so many Rovers fans at Wembley for a national final that Aldo had steered them to, even though they lost narrowly, just as they always seemed to at the biggest moments, whether I was there or not.

PART TWO
RUGBY PARK

9/
DIFFERENT STARS

During the summer I was promoting my first book, *In Ma Head, Son!*, co-written with psychologist George Sik. I had wanted the title *Football and How to Survive It* but was overruled. My suggestion was a nod to *Life and How to Survive it*, by Professor Robin Skynner and John Cleese, written many years before, which had been my initial inspiration for the idea. But I always thought the original title was a good one and I hoped I'd be able to use it one day.

I wanted to write the original book because I was interested in the psychology of sport and felt it would be good to get my thoughts out there on the subject. I had studied some psychology while on my degree course way back when the discipline was still in its infancy in football, so the timing seemed right.

There was a small-scale launch, with most of the publicity done in a single day down in London. The set-up is that you sit in a studio where dozens of five-to-fifteen-minute interviews are arranged one after the other, each with national and regional broadcasters around the country. The big sell was at the end: an hour-long interview on Capital Radio to go out mid-afternoon. The presenter was a big fan from my Chelsea days, he had read the book and wanted to go into some depth about it to a very good-sized audience. I got a taxi round to their studios but, five minutes before going air, I was given the news that the presenter was ill and wouldn't make it. They needed a stand-in. Hopefully it would be someone steeped in football, with a good knowledge of my career as well as the book.

When ballet dancer Wayne Sleep all but pirouetted into the room, he was not exactly who or what I had in mind. I thought I'd better find out how *au fait* he was with my world before we went on air: 'Oh . . . hello, Wayne . . . nice to meet you.' I left a suitable pause. 'I'm guessing you haven't read the book?'

He deadpanned back, 'No.'

'Do you like football?'

'No.'

I desperately tried another direction, with as much hope as I could muster: 'Have you ever been to a football match?'

'No.' He might have actually said, 'No, Sweetie,' at this point, as it felt like he might have found the question bordering on an insult.

It was more pleading than questioning from me by now. This could be a long, long hour of radio. He then thought for a moment and, with a barely perceptible tone of annoyance, asked, 'Well, have you ever been to the ballet and do you like ballet?'

'I have been to many ballets and, yes, I love classical dance. In fact, two of my best friends are Antony Dowson and Fiona Chadwick, principles at the Royal Ballet. I'm a regular at Covent Garden.'

When he recovered from the surprise, what followed was one of the most enjoyable hours of radio I've ever had. There are so many things that ballet dancers and footballers have in common and, to everyone's surprise, we began to hit it off immediately – well, we did after that slightly shaky start.

Footballers and dancers get the same injuries: mostly foot, ankle, knee and back problems. We have to perform irregardless of how we are feeling, fully fit or not, and are always judged as though we are 100 per cent. We are only ever considered as good as our most recent appearance – what you did in the past means little in terms of your next show or game.

Both professions have a limited career span, although Wayne bucked that trend impressively.

It goes further. There is always someone in the company or in the team who openly wants to take your place. You are an individual performer but also part of a team that must work together or else the whole thing falls apart. Both the stage and the football field are incredibly competitive, with few opportunities to 'phone in' performances; you are expected to give everything every time you walk out there, the audiences demand it. There are also the highs from the audience reaction; and, as we agreed, the delights of creating 'art' at the top level can give you the highest high imaginable. It was an hour of entertaining and enlightening radio, but sadly I forgot to talk about the book!

I was also writing regular columns for each issue of the BBC's *Match of the Day* magazine around then about whatever current football issue took my fancy. And I was writing for *Goal* magazine, providing long-form interviews and articles on the likes of Stuart Pearce, Gazza and many others. I was accepting that I may well have played my last game of professional football, and these other interests should now be taken seriously. I knew where I was going, or at least I thought I did.

Much to my surprise, after the summer I was back in pre-season training at Tranmere and even went on the tour to Ireland with the team, but there was a call from the Tranmere secretary while I was over there: 'Kilmarnock want to sign you. Could you go straight back to Scotland and talk to their manager, now?' Within a couple of hours I was on a flight to Glasgow.

Like with almost every move for every footballer, there was precious little time to say goodbye to a bunch of people I had grown to like and had shared so much with. There was no chance to say goodbye to the fans with an emotional swansong appearance either – though I had never fancied that sort of thing anyway, even if I understand why some players do enjoy those moments. It is an incredible whirlwind at times like these; your entire life changes in a matter of hours, sometimes minutes. I had just about enough time to phone home and tell Annabel the news before I caught the flight from Dublin to Glasgow airport.

On the flight, which was on a rather bedraggled-looking propeller affair, I considered some of the pros and cons of the possible move. On the negative side Annabel and I would have to spend some time apart, and there would be less time for me with the children for a little while. Leaving Tranmere wasn't a problem – I had loved the place and the club, but that was in the past. If Aldo was manager, I wasn't getting a game, so staying when there were other options wasn't a serious consideration. Leaving our home in Chester would be a wrench in some respects: the children had started their lives there, we had many fond memories of our early married life; but, then again, they would want to be Scottish in the end, so the move would happen soon enough, whether I signed for Killie or not. An added bonus would be that Simon would also be joining the integrated Scottish education system just when he was capable of doing so. Leaving the PFA wasn't difficult either: I'd never wanted that job and considered I'd done my bit by then.

On the positive side, being back in Scotland at last and getting an extra few years' playing was sorely tempting, even if it might not be that lucrative financially. I tried to get my head round whether I should make this move, but it was impossible to know for sure before I met the people who I would be working with. Deep down, though, over and above everything else, the simple idea of getting a game of football back home, had me just about sold before the wheels were off the Irish tarmac.

From Glasgow airport down to Kilmarnock's Rugby Park stadium in Ayrshire is only 30 minutes along the M77. I had time to think about the club on that drive. In the nineties they were usually to be found in the top division, but had won the 1997 Scottish Cup final earlier that summer, an exceptional feat for what was still a mid- to small-sized club at the top level in Scotland. Home gates against the bigger clubs were around 15,000 and, having trained there for some Scotland squads, I knew and liked the stadium. The pitch itself was one of the biggest and best in Scotland, which is why we regularly used it with the national team for practice.

I went straight to see their manager Bobby Williamson in his office at the ground, and I liked him from the moment I met him. He had been brought up in the Easterhouse scheme in the east end of Glasgow just like me, so we had plenty in common. He was straight-talking, had the classic dour arid-dry Glaswegian humour I liked, and came straight to the point in our first meeting: 'I didnae think you'd even consider us; I feel I've won a watch even gettin' you this far. I don't deal wi' the money, but if the board can offer you enough to sign, then you'll make us a better side. We need tae add a bit a' creativity tae the team. They're a good bunch; we've just won the Scottish Cup, but we cannae stand still.'

I knew Bobby had played as a striker for Rangers, but I had never actually seen him play, as almost my entire career had been spent down south. I tried to find out if we had similar outlooks on the beautiful game. 'Were you into the creative side of the game yourself, Bobby?' I ventured (I didn't need to call him gaffer yet).

'Nah, I jist liked tae kick people.'

He wasn't totally joking. He might have been the same height as me but that is where the physical similarity ended. He appeared to be made of solid rock, if a little more rounded post-career, and the death stare was not that of a soft striker. Just then he was called out of his office for a private phone call. I settled down on a chair to wait. Thirty seconds later he came running into the room grabbed me by the collar and physically hauled me out of his office.

'Wait, what . . . what the hell is going on?'

'Ah've jist remembered. I read your book last night, Nevin, and I know exactly whit ye dae when you're left in people's offices!'

He was referring to me rifling through Ken Bates's drawers at Chelsea during contract negotiations when I was 20, trying to find all the other players' contracts. I would never have considered doing that in these circumstances in Bobby's room, but I could see his point of view. I also gauged from his cheeky grin, it was just a joke from Bobby – well, mostly.

I was sold on the club, but like every other footballer making a move to another country, I still had to be sold by another club, and there were logistical problems yet to be resolved along with the contractual ones. Tranmere and chairman Frank Corfe fully understood that the most Killie could afford to pay me was about a third of what I was on at Tranmere. Money had never been the driving factor, but I couldn't afford to take that sort of hit. We did the sums, and the Rovers' board were generous to a fault. I then talked to the board member at Killie assigned to agree the deal and explained the figure I needed to make it work – it wouldn't bankrupt them!

The only other stipulation was that I needed a loan of a second-hand car for a season to get me up and down from Chester, as the family would still be based there for the first year of the three-year deal. We couldn't move Simon that quickly from the routine of his life: autism doesn't allow those sorts of spur-of-the-moment changes and time for planning his education was needed; these, over and above everything else, were the main things that stopped us from moving up right away.

It was all agreed quickly and painlessly, or so I thought. I had got used to trusting people in the game a bit by then and, as PFA chairman, I didn't think Kilmarnock would welch on a deal we had shaken hands on. The car never materialised. It wasn't that important, really, but it did grate. I suppose I should have known: the man who promised it was a used car salesman by trade, so I accept there was a bit of naïvety from me on this occasion. He had plenty of cars but, like the hoary old cliché about people in that business, he wasn't to be trusted on his word. I wouldn't be getting even the oldest jalopy on his lot.

My travelling up north would, however, make life extremely difficult for Annabel. The plan was that I would drive the 250 miles to Scotland very early on a Monday morning, train with the team, then stay until after training on the Tuesday before heading back to Chester. I would then go back up on Thursday morning for training and stay until the match on Saturday, before heading south after the game. That way, in theory, I could spend Saturday, Sunday, Tuesday and Wednesday nights at home with the family. It wouldn't always work out when we had midweek games, but Bobby promised that he would let me train alone at home some weeks.

He had done his research and knew I was a fanatical trainer, even without supervision. I didn't need to be harried into working; it was far more likely that I would need to be told when to stop or slow down, as a player of my age needed to be careful about overdoing it.

It left Annabel alone coping with Lucy, who was now three, and Simon aged seven. He still had the ever-challenging and ever-changing difficulties due to his autism, and now Annabel would have to care for both on her own for longer periods. The idea was that when opportunities arose over the season, we could start looking for a home up north to finally settle down. This difficult, painful period of nine months just had to be dealt with. It was terribly unfair on Annabel and, even though I could meet friends and family when back in my hometown, I still felt awful every night I was away from my family, who needed me back down south.

From being on the verge of retiring, I was now back in Scotland, in the top league, with a three-year contract, and our transition to our new life back home was starting. It was a fabulous opportunity for me, but I cannot underline enough just how immense those strains and sacrifices were on Annabel. I judged it would be worth it in the long term, as within the year she would be back living close to her mum and dad and her siblings, but then I wasn't the one doing the metaphorical and literal heavy lifting at home.

The season started quickly but it didn't start well. In fact, it was awful. Kilmarnock had qualified for Europe, so it was a packed schedule but, weirdly, nine of the first twelve games were away from home. I hadn't played in European competition throughout my career with Everton and Chelsea, due to the ban on English teams. I did play in the Anglo-Italian Cup with Tranmere, but now, with Kilmarnock, there was the joy of the European Cup-Winners' Cup to look forward to; a real major European tournament. We saw off Ireland's Shelbourne in the first round but faced Nice, the French Ligue 1 side, next.

We were well and truly hammered in the away leg and I personally couldn't seem to build any understandings with my new teammates.

Subbed after an hour in Nice, I sat beside Bobby Williamson surveying the wreckage for the final 30 minutes. Somehow, we only lost 3–1, but it should have been by many more. It did, however, give me the chance to see the new manager at work from close quarters. The entire time I sat there, Bobby shouted at our left-back Martin Baker, 'Bakesy, Bakesy, stay oan yer feet! Stoap the crosses and don't get fuckin' booked!'

Bakesy didn't stay on his feet, didn't stop the crosses and did get booked.

'Bakesy, stoap those fuckin' crosses and don't dive in an' get sent aff!' They scored two of their goals via crosses from our left-hand side. And Bakesy did indeed get 'sent aff' in the end.

We flew home that night and were ordered back the next day for training. Bobby assembled the team around him inside the centre-circle on the training pitch beside the stadium and shared his thoughts in a menacing sotto voce, pointing at each player one by one.

'You looked like a rabbit in the headlights . . . And you didnae make a tackle aw night . . . You, you were jist pish . . . You were shite . . . You [at me] played like an auld man.' And so on, until he came to Bakesy. 'And you. Ah telt ye no tae get booked and ye gote booked. Ah told ye no tae get sent aff and ye gote sent aff. That's a 100 quid fine and if ye dae it again, I'll kick yer fuckin' c*** in.' And off he walked calmy back to his office.

As a very recent chairman of the PFA,* I honestly hadn't heard players been talked to like that for over a decade. For a moment I felt like a vicar at a Billy Connolly concert. I looked around. 'Is that for real, can he really say that?'

One of the lads turned to me and whispered, 'Bloody hell, you have gone soft since you went down south. I thought you were from Easterhouse. That is perfectly normal patter up here!' He was absolutely right, that was just Bobby's straight-talking style, ensuring he was getting his point across directly.

---

* I had in the end given up the role when I left English football. The position of chairman of the PFA in England was meant to be a role solely for a current player who plays in the English leagues.

I am sure the manager wouldn't have kicked Bakesy's . . . well, assaulted him in any way, even though he was hard enough to do so. This was just a more grounded earthiness than I had witnessed for many years. In truth, I didn't mind it at all. Rather that, than the inability to voice what was bothering you that I had come across with some people in the English game. Letting the bad feeling fester and allowing it to kill the team spirit was not uncommon in my previous 14 years down south. Doubtless some players today would need counselling after that sort of rhetoric, but Bakesy and the others handled it well. When Bobby had finished his tirade, it was over and forgotten about, with no bad feeling lingering from him or towards him.

The grass training pitch adjacent to the stadium was very handy. The problem was that you could only really train on it once every week or it would be destroyed. So, to my amazement, we would often arrive for training to discover we had nowhere to play and had to wait until the management found a local park with a piece of suitable grass to work on. Preferably one where 'the parkie' wasn't likely to appear out of nowhere and chase us off. After years of having a regular home training ground it was shocking to find that at the elite level in Scottish football not all the clubs had even the most basic facilities.

We could have trained on the actual pitch at Rugby Park, of course, but there is a special idiosyncratic breed of man that becomes a groundsman in Scotland. These men will try to physically assault you (when they can catch you) if you deign to walk on their beloved grass outside a match day. Even standing too close to their treasured turf gets them twitchy.

Gus was in charge of the playing surface at Killie, and I liked his rough uncompromising shtick, though it seemed to annoy the hell out of everyone else. The pitch was kept in pristine condition, unlike many of the other grounds in the Scottish Premier League (SPL), and that was important to my game, so I was on his side.* He once confided in me in

---

* They eventually tore up that beautiful playing surface years later and replaced it with a plastic pitch. Sacrilege.

his broad Ayrshire accent, with more than a hint of disappointment: 'Dye ken, ah reckon ah shid be allowed tae have a gun – no a big yin, jist a wee yin. Wan wi pellets. An ah shid bae allowed tae shoot any yin, players an' aw, who walks ower the gress, right in the arse. Ah said it tae Boaby, bit he wullnae let me.'

The first few weeks of the season came and went, but I just couldn't get to the pace of the games. Everyone seemed to be running at 100mph, 100 per cent of the time, but not in the directions I expected them to run, which was baffling. The perfect example came in an early home game against Hearts at Rugby Park. I had suggested to Bobby that if he played me in the number 10 position, I might be able to have more of an effect than I'd had so far. Until then I had been stuck out on the wing watching the ball sail long and high in the vague direction of the strikers. Ten minutes in, I found a little space between the midfield and forward line when someone actually passed the ball to me. I turned, drew three opponents towards me and glanced up to make sure my teammates had run into the space I had just created. Instead, they were standing stationary, appreciating my little moment of skill. I was thumped, crunched and smashed by the opponents I had been drawing in, because now I had nowhere to go and no one to release it to. At all my previous clubs, players knew, understood and had the game awareness to figure out what was going on when I drew defenders towards me – but not here, not yet.

I was subbed at half-time and sat alone on the dressing-room floor, now thinking that signing for Killie could be the worst mistake I had ever made in my career. From the stands I must have looked like the most useless football player in the league – less like a committed former international and more like an old man turning up for a last payday but no longer willing or able to do it at that level.

I knew I could play at that standard even if I was nearly 34, but how could I make my teammates understand what to do when I had the ball? After having finally got back home to finish my career in Scotland, having always wanted to do just that . . . in those moments I seriously considered getting out before it got too embarrassing. By the time I had driven the four hours back to Chester after the game, however, I'd had time to think and had come up with a plan. There were decent players at Killie, they just needed a crash course in exactly what to do when I got on the ball.

The strikers Paul Wright, Jerome Vareille and Mark Roberts were fine, the movement was intelligent, and I could work with them. I asked both full-backs, Gus MacPherson and Dylan Kerr, to do what all my previous full-backs had done: 'When I get the ball, start dribbling and drawing opponents, you just get on your bike and sprint into the space I develop on the flanks. We'll worry about underlapping later. The ball will arrive and if it doesn't then it's my problem, not yours. If I lose it, I'll hold my hand up and take responsibility.' It had worked at Tranmere, so why shouldn't it work here?

In the midfield Gary Holt had the unstoppable engine of a squaddie on the battlefield. Possibly because he had been in the army, although I think he was more of a chef than a full-on green-beret type while he was serving Her Majesty. He was, however, among the most energetic and powerful players I had played with in my career. He got the message quickly and would take off like a thoroughbred racehorse every time I got possession, making a bee-line towards the opposition goal in the hope and expectation I would play him in.

Over the space of about six or seven games it began to improve, for me and for the team. There were defeats against Rangers, Celtic, Hearts and St Johnstone but there were also a few narrow wins against Motherwell and then Hibernian, where I got the winner from 20 yards.

Eventually, against Dunfermline in November, it all suddenly clicked into place. Dylan Kerr and I tore them apart down the left now that I had got the overlapping and underlapping message across. He had played at the top level with Leeds United and was now playing left-back behind me when I switched wings over to his side. Over a few short months he became a close friend and has remained so ever since. He was an eighties music fanatic, though more Human League and Heaven 17 to my Joy Division and New Order, but there was a bond and an understanding on and off the

Getting to Tranmere Rovers and being allowed to play with freedom
was a release, as was scoring for the club, clearly.

Tranmere secretary Norman Wilson on the right, then me as usual in a biker jacket instead of the expected suit. Manager John King is on the left, finessing his next off-the-cuff remark.

Celebrating the good times with John Aldridge after scoring against Sunderland for Tranmere Rovers.

Me and my mate Edson at the PFA awards dinner. I have never felt so
honoured to have a hand on my shoulder, being wound up for not speaking
comprehensible English by a Portuguese-speaking Brazilian.

Simon, Annabel and me in Chester in very happy times.

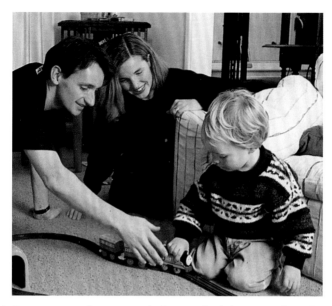

Simon's fascination with trains and planes, which has carried on throughout his life was, in retrospect, a huge clue to his eventual diagnosis.

Simon, Annabel, Lucy and me in a team photo in our home in Chester.

The football on Merseyside was fine, but it was just a front for my real passion – DJing. Here I am presenting a weekly radio show in Liverpool.

A complete stitch-up that left me as Chairman of the PFA, stuffed inside a suit and having to learn all those notes and more. Brian McClair, Gary Mabbutt, Barry Horne et al. are pleased to have me as the new flak-catcher in chief. (Secretly, it was an honour.)

Playing for Scotland and scoring my second goal of the night against Estonia. I was entrusted as penalty taker; thank goodness YouTube didn't exist back then, as people would have definitely checked out one of my previous efforts for Chelsea versus Manchester City.

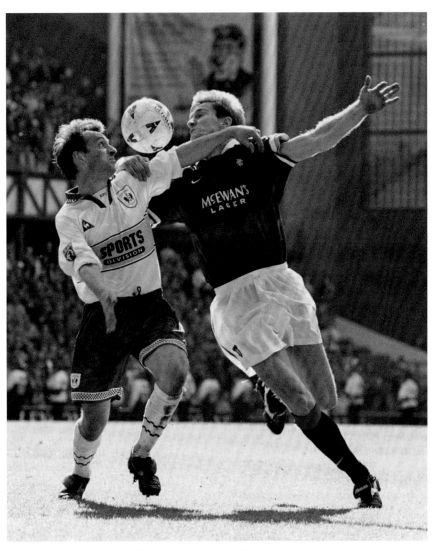

Tussling with my old Scotland and Chelsea teammate Gordon Durie,
for Kilmarnock at Ibrox against Rangers.

field. I loved his boundless irrepressible enthusiasm for everything in life, not just his willingness to learn.

The team had been improving but that day against the Pars the game was glorious to play in and to watch. I scored both goals in the win and played well enough to show the fans that I was not a lazy has-been, far from it. The entire team gelled, and we could easily have scored six or seven. Mark Reilly, Gary Holt, Dylan and I really 'got' each other on and off the field. With Paul Wright, Ally Mitchell and Jerome Vareille we were suddenly a potent attacking force.

The most important thing apart from playing well was that I felt completely at home in the dressing room – not a turn of phrase I'd ever used before in my career. The humour was very Scottish, the attitudes earthy but honest, and I went on to make more long-term friends in that dressing room than I did at any other club I played for. I liked every single player at Kilmarnock. Just a month or two after thinking this was my worst move yet, I was incredibly happy, enjoying the company, playing well and working with a fast-improving group of already decent players.

Some of the lads stayed behind with me to learn some specific skill ideas that I was happy to pass on. Alex Burke, David Bagan and Ally Mitchell (AKA Burkey, Bagey and Bully) were each very keen to improve their techniques. I was now actually doing some coaching, after a fashion. The nicknames, which everyone had, were a sign of our togetherness, and even I reverted to my old childhood moniker of 'Nifty'. So, we had 'Bunyon' (Paul Wright), 'Wingnut'/'Dafty' (Mark Roberts), 'Bully' (Ally Mitchell), 'Mavis' (Mark Reilly), 'Zippy' (John Henry), 'Magoo' (Kevin McGowne) and 'Ditcher' (skipper Ray Montgomerie).

I always want to find the provenance of people's nicknames, and maybe Ditcher's was the best. In fact, I didn't even have to ask, I figured it out myself after one game. He was our centre-back and a club legend, but he wasn't lightning-quick in his later years, which can be a problem for a defender – hence Ray's penchant for, and indeed fabulous ability to make, last ditch tackles, thus 'Ditcher'. It was brilliant, inventive and accurate, the best type of nickname; the sort that always sticks. Fortunately, attempts to call my mate Dylan Kerr, 'Wan' instead of 'Dylan', didn't stick. He didn't deserve that!

Part of the draw of going back to Scotland was to play against Celtic and Rangers as well as the other big clubs like Hibs, Hearts and Aberdeen. All had big supports and grounds I had visited as a child but had rarely played on in my career until then. What did come as a surprise was that there were one or two players who were nervous, bordering on scared stiff, when we turned up at Celtic Park or Ibrox. The Hoops by then were a very decent team with a truly world-class star in Henrik Larsson up front, but it had been many years since I had played for a team that was jittery against a big club, just because of the name and the history. Usually, whether it was Chelsea, Everton or even Tranmere Rovers, we couldn't wait to have a go at the biggest names in the game. In Scotland there was still that inbuilt fear of the institutions that the Glasgow giants were – well, there was for a few of the players anyway.

Initially the Old Firm were beating us by three or four at the start of the season, but eventually the games became much closer until we finally and crucially beat one of them at the end.

Initially, one of the best games of that campaign came at Tynecastle against Hearts and, even though we lost 5–3, I felt we had plenty to offer and were becoming more entertaining. I scored one, but the other that I helped set up was a brilliant move, showing the capabilities of the team. Bobby and his coaches, Jim Clark and Gerry McCabe, were clearly doing a good job.

Near the start of that game at Tynecastle, I was haring up the right wing over by the Wheatfield Stand. The Hearts fans positioned there are as physically close to you as you will find at any ground, and they aren't slow to wind you up. One guy tried very hard: 'Hey, Nevin, yer too auld.' I ignored him. The next time I went past: 'Hey, Nevin, yer too slow.' Blanked again. 'Hey, Nevin, you've gote a huge nose.' 'Hey, Nevin, yer goin' bald and yer just a wee fuckin' Tim.' (Celtic supporter.) His efforts were still falling on deaf(ish) ears, so he tried his final insult on my next foray up the flank: 'Hey, Nevin, yer book's shite!'

I spun around: 'Steady on, that's taking it too far, but you must have gone out and bought it then, eh?' A decent riposte, I reckoned. On my next pass he was ready with his answer. 'No fuckin' way. I goat it oot the library.' Good answer, and by this time both of us and the rest of the fans nearby were smiling.

A Celtic fan tried a similar tack a little while later as I dribbled down the line in front of what used to be my old stomping ground in the 'Jungle' at Parkhead. 'Hey, Nevin, yer book lacks literary merit.' Top quality abuse from the more cerebral Celt.

Unsurprisingly, football is much more fun when you are getting results. I scored four goals in six games and everything about the club was suddenly enjoyable, particularly the training with such a great bunch of guys. Unfortunately, there was a less enjoyable moment just a little while later.

It was Friday afternoon, and we were having the customary seven-a-side game. Stranraer were waiting in the Scottish Cup the next day, and for us, as holders, there was a great deal of anticipation. At the end of the session a cross was zipped in from the left and I came flying in at the back post. Twisting my neck as I leapt in the air, I powered a header into the net. At least I think it went into the net – I never managed to see it. I hadn't checked behind me and our full-back Gus MacPherson, he of the solid rock head, came in at full speed and slightly too late, trying to stop my header.

The back of his head went into the side of my face at speed and with full force. I hadn't anticipated the hit so couldn't cushion the blow at all. When I came to my senses, sort of, I knew exactly what they meant by the phrase 'sickening' thud. I have had my fair share of head knocks over the years – it is impossible to go through a career of games and training sessions for this not to happen in a contact sport such as football. I knew that head-injury feeling well, but I also knew that the excruciating pain generally went away after a little while, as did the nausea. I sat up, rather groggily and with a considerable wobble. There were half a dozen players already around me staring down intently. 'It's all right, lads, I'll be fine to carry on in a minute. Just got a bit of a dunt there. It'll be OK, honestly. I'll carry on.'

I could see that for once my mate Dylan Kerr was not smiling and Bobby Williamson said, hesitantly, 'Am no sure aboot that.' I went to rub the side of my face where the impact had been, and most of my face wasn't there! 'That's suboptimal! Maybe I'll be OK by tomorrow, then?'

Fifteen minutes later I was carted off in an ambulance to Crosshouse Hospital. I had a compressed fracture to the cheekbone, snapped in three places, with a concussion and a hefty jolt to the skull and jawbone. The surgeon said he would operate in the morning. By this time, I was vomiting, woozy and basically a shambles of a human being. Happily, the drugs helped, but the medic described it as an RTA (Road Traffic Accident)-type injury.

Bobby had to make the dreaded call to Annabel, who was still in Chester, letting her know that I was in hospital and getting prepared for an operation in the morning. He was shocked, but I was delighted to hear later that she was very matter of fact about the information. She found out which hospital I was in, but there was no panic in her voice. Bobby later wanted to know why she was so calm, so logical and not seemingly that bothered: 'Does that wife ae yours actually like you, wee man?'

But I knew that was just the 'medical family' thing. Her dad was a doctor and her mum a nurse. The whole family had been schooled to understand that panic doesn't help anyone in these situations – it doesn't mean they don't care.

The next morning the surgeon poked something down under my cheekbone and clicked the three breaks back out again, like a child would push a snapped chicken wishbone back together. Not that I knew anything about it, as the anaesthetist had done a fine job. When I woke up, the surgeon was waiting there for me: 'Mr Nevin, the operation went well, I think. I am very happy with it. Would you like to ask the question now?'

I gave him a quizzical look and then immediately regretted it as the pain seared across my face. This struck me as an odd time to play a guessing game.

He tried again: 'I know what it is going to be, so just ask it.'

'OK, when I can I play again?'

Before I'd even finished he said, 'Eight to ten weeks if – and only if – all goes well with the recovery. You lot are all the same. You should be asking about your family, about the operation, whether you are facially disfigured. But no, you all ask the same thing. When can I play football again?'*

I hated being so predictable. Even more predictably, I got straight on with the job of talking him down: 'You say eight weeks' – I ignored the ten – 'but if the recovery goes really well it could be seven, maybe even six weeks?'

He sighed the sigh of a man who had heard this all before: 'We'll see about that, but I suppose it is possible, in theory. Just come back next week and we will discuss it further.' All his artistic handiwork to reshape my face could be spoiled by my impatience. The bottom line was: he just wanted me to recover safely; and I just wanted to get back playing as soon as possible, or maybe a bit sooner.

I got out of hospital a few days later, after a very welcome visit from a bunch of my teammates. I had never known teammates doing that at any other club I had been to. I was touched; in fact, I even managed to laugh when they presented me not with a bunch of grapes but with a box of toffees – excellent banter. Considering I was 'eating' through a straw with a face smashed like a windowpane, and even laughing was torture, I thought I took it quite well.

Two weeks later, I was back to see the surgeon for an x-ray and an update. The bones had fused back into place and he seemed pleased with his handiwork.

---

* Brain damage from concussion or repeated heading of the ball is a huge concern in football now. Back then you didn't care about it too much. It was accepted as an occupational hazard, and all you cared about was getting back onto the field. Like many others, I realised that if I was unlucky I might face the consequences later in life, but it was a chance I was willing to take. It wasn't sensible, but it was, in all honesty, just how we felt at the time. One day soon we will hopefully discover if the regular head knocks like the one I had are an important part of the story about the high levels of dementia in football, or if it is simply down to heading thousands of footballs over a long career.

'So Doc, it feels great.' (It absolutely didn't!) 'You said five or six weeks.'

'I actually said eight weeks or more.'

I ignored that line and pressed on: 'Well, five weeks feels right to me, but what about say . . . four weeks? I am a very quick healer.' I regaled him of stories of getting back less than three months after an anterior cruciate injury, and less than two weeks after an appendectomy, as well as playing for Scotland with a cracked fibula.

'Don't be stupid. Four weeks? That's impossible and dangerous. What if you went up to head a ball and bumped it again, even slightly?' To be fair, that thought was horrendous at that moment, but I tried to be upbeat and pleasantly persuasive again: 'I play on the wing, and I rarely head the ball. The injury is on my right side and I am playing wide right just now, so the damaged side is facing away from the play.' He looked unconvinced, and rightly so, it was total tosh.

I was back the next week to see him again. 'It feels great, Doc, good as new.' It didn't, it felt as if the bones were being held together by chewing gum with some grit inside. 'So, how about that four weeks, then, Doc? Could we make it about 30 days, post-injury? We have two big games in four days around then.' Trying to bamboozle him with numbers didn't seem to be working yet.

He was almost worn down and sighed, 'You're mad. OK, who is the first game against?'

'Celtic.'

'You absolutely cannot play. I will not sanction it. It is far too dangerous. Who is the second one against?'

'Rangers.'

'Yeah, no problem. You can play in that one.'

'Thank you, Doc.' I think I figured out who he supported, especially as he had an Irish-sounding surname.

Five minutes into the Rangers game I went up for a header and got an opponent's shoulder straight onto the damaged cheekbone, obviously. Fortunately, it didn't collapse again, and I helped the team to a 1–1 draw. The only important dent was in Rangers' chase for their tenth title in a row. Both the doctor and I had a particular interest in that not happening.

One of the real joys of Kilmarnock was that, at last, after 15 long years, my dad didn't have to make round trips of many hundreds of miles to see me play every week. The journey to Rugby Park was only 40 minutes, and he loved the place. He was a Celtic man to the core, so I didn't ask him or indeed any member of my family who they supported when I played against the Hoops. Dad still wasn't keen on wearing a blue-and-white scarf, particularly in Scotland, and more specifically when we played Celtic – that would be sacrilege. Other than that, he was incredibly happy that season, especially as we went on a brilliant run that took us from tenth all the way to fourth in the league.

I was, however, beginning to acknowledge a growing feeling of discomfort about the whole religious sectarian feeling in the west of Scotland. I had been away for a long time and thought people had started moving beyond it, as society matured. I was out of touch. It all still felt very present now that I was back home, even if Celtic were then using campaigns like 'Bhoys Against Bigotry' to try to root out the more objectionable goings-on.

On the other side of the divide, the blatantly sectarian and offensive 'party' songs were still in full flow. In the past I had blanked it, to a degree, because it had simply always been there when I was growing up – but now, a little older and more widely travelled, I began to feel more personally irritated by it. I didn't aim my annoyance at any single football club; it was just a general dislike of having that hateful 'culture' in the background all the time, specifically in the west of Scotland. It didn't seem to be as much of a problem in the Borders, Edinburgh and the east coast or the Highlands and islands, as far as I could gauge.

I was maybe a little harder on '*my*' club Celtic. We were supposed to be inclusive, liberal-minded and welcoming – and no one should be made to feel uncomfortable turning up to support 'us', whatever their religious or political persuasion. Celtic didn't have the religious apartheid that Rangers had in the past; we signed anyone, they wouldn't sign Catholics for a century, so surely 'we' had the moral high ground. The problem for me was that some of the songs on both sides were uncomfortable and unwelcoming to fans, like me, who didn't think such factionalism should have to be borne at a football game. This hatred then seeped into parts of the rest of cultural life in that section of Scotland.

A perfect example of this came from one individual at the club. He was due to be married in the summer and he did us the great honour of inviting Annabel and me to his wedding – or at least the partial honour: 'Pat, I would love you to come to my wedding, and it would be great if you could bring your wife along too.'

'That sounds lovely.' I had only known him a few months, so I felt humbled and not a little moved.

'There is only one thing,' he continued. 'When we go back to our place after the ceremony, would you mind staying out in the garden? The thing is: my dad doesn't allow Catholics in the house.'

To be fair, he was embarrassed saying it, and I wasn't at all annoyed with him, personally, just saddened at how sectarianism made some people behave in such an outlandishly bigoted way, from whatever side of the divide. I didn't go in the end. I wasn't even a Catholic by then, and hadn't been for nearly 20 years, but I did send a nice present to show that I didn't have negative feelings towards anyone or any religion. (It wasn't a framed picture of the Pope, in case you were wondering. I'm guessing his dad might not have appreciated the ironic humour.)

Being back in Scotland also meant that I was getting to see my family in Glasgow, meeting up with my old friends and, of course, finally seeing some gigs again at last. Glasgow famously has many great venues, from the Barrowland's to King Tut's Wah Wah Hut. Around about then I had discovered a few new favourite bands from the west of Scotland. Belle and Sebastian were releasing classic singles such as 'Lazy Line Painter Jane' and were on the cusp of delivering their classic *The Boy with the Arab Strap* album. The Delgados were also flourishing alongside more established acts like Teenage Fanclub, who sounded like effortlessly brilliant songwriters to my ears. I even went with teammate Dylan Kerr to see Echo and the Bunnymen for the first time in many years – one band where our tastes overlapped.

Although getting back into the live music scene was great, it was also tinged with sadness, not having Annabel there to share it with. She was back down in Chester, four hours and 250 miles away, dealing with the children all day and all night. I told myself, and Annabel, that I would make it up to her by getting us a lovely home, and we would be together constantly in the Scottish Borders very soon. I told myself I wasn't the only partner who had to spend time away earning a living and providing for our children's futures. I told myself a lot of stories, but I was still riven with guilt. There were also the dangers of driving regularly up and down to Scotland, especially in the winter. Keen to spend as much time as possible with the family, I would usually sleep in Chester until 5am and then drive straight to Kilmarnock for Wednesday or Thursday morning's training. I had the John Peel shows I still recorded to keep me entertained and informed on the journeys, so I didn't mind it too much.

One morning, driving through the dark in less than perfect weather, I was passing Carlisle at 70mph on the M6, following the red tail lights ahead, all of them going along in nice straight lines. I was enjoying the music, relaxed, cosy and warm in the car, when suddenly all the tail lights started dancing in different directions up ahead in the darkness. I couldn't figure out what was going on for a couple of seconds: was I hallucinating due to lack of sleep? Then I realised they had hit a sheet of black ice and were spinning wildly out of control all over the carriageway and hard shoulder dead ahead of me.

I knew I couldn't brake, as I would do the same as those other cars, so somehow, with sheer luck and a decent amount of calmness under pressure – and with feet off the pedals – I slalomed between the assorted vehicles strewn across the motorway. It was about the closest I ever came to my end. Happily, everyone survived, though many cars didn't. Incredibly, neither I nor my car emerged with a scratch on us. It was clear to me, though, that this amount of driving held a certain degree of risk, and it couldn't go on forever.

Our team had grown in confidence, and the season was looking like another successful one for Killie. After I scored those two goals against Dunfermline in November, there followed only four league defeats until the end of season, and three of those losses were by the odd goal! We were competitive in every game.

When Celtic visited Rugby Park with six games to go we narrowly lost 2–1 against Henrik Larsson, Craig Burley, Paul Lambert, Tommy Boyd and co., but we then picked up seven points out of nine before a crunch match at Ibrox against Rangers in our second-to-last outing. Rangers needed a win to stay on track for an unheard-of tenth league title in a row. Celtic had managed nine on the bounce in the 1960s and 1970s, with me cheering them on from the terraces, and now their great rivals had a chance to overtake that phenomenal record. Rangers stood on the precipice of a historic triumph in the Scottish game; they could have bragging rights for decades.

With the likes of Richard Gough, Brian Laudrup, Ally McCoist and my old mate Stuart McCall among many other star names in the home side, their fans turned up expecting an easy and triumphant three points on the road to glory. The Killie lads fought tooth and nail for every ball, for many reasons, not least of which was that a win for us would give us European football and a fourth-place finish. There was also the promise of a tidy bonus for that European spot. One or two of us also wanted to stop Rangers winning that tenth title, so we were well up for the battle.

It was still 0–0 and the 90 minutes of almost constant desperate defending were up. We had run ourselves to exhaustion, but it looked like we had managed to salvage a crucial point. I broke down the line, intent on wasting as much of the injury time as possible with a mazy dribble into the corner. Getting tired, however, I fed our centre-back Kevin McGowne, who was even wider on the right wing. What was he doing there while we were supposed to be fielding a backs-to-the-wall defence? Kev crossed after a bit of jinky wing play, and our perpetual motion midfielder Ally Mitchell nipped in at the back post to score the winner in front of a wall of Killie fans.

It was an extraordinary, historic moment. Celtic went on to win the league by two points over Rangers the next week, and the ten in a row would never happen. We celebrated wildly on the pitch after the game and in the dressing room – judging by our reactions and those of our fans, you would have thought that we had just won the league.

At the end of every season, you ask yourself the same question: was it successful? This clearly was success for Kilmarnock. We secured European football, finished fourth in the league above a good few clubs with bigger fan bases and far more resources than us. We also ended the season on a very good run, with this glorious moment against Rangers setting it off nicely. It is up there with one of the favourite moments of my entire career, so much so that I keep a photo of us all celebrating in front of our fans in a corner of my weights room, and the memory never fails to make me smile. As ever in football, the celebrations were fleeting – there were a couple of games still to be played – but it was a magical moment.

I left Ibrox quickly that day to see my family, who had never before celebrated a Kilmarnock win as much. My dad was there and we met my brother at McChuills bar after the game with their cool Andy Warhol lookalike owner, Nicky. He came straight over and promised I would never have to pay for a drink in his Celtic-leaning bar ever again! As still a Celtic fan at heart myself back then, it was a glorious day in every way.

But while I was basking in the glory on that warm sunny evening, the undoubted high-water mark of my time at Kilmarnock, something happened in our dressing room after I had left, something that in time would change the course of my entire future. I found out about it a few hours later. One of our players called to alert me that a Killie director had come into the dressing room, enjoyed the celebrations and then informed the team that they wouldn't be getting the promised European bonus, after all, as it hadn't officially been written into our contracts.

What a surprise that they left it until after we qualified to notify the players of the anomaly!

By the time I got back into training on the Monday for the final week I was still fuming. I demanded a meeting with some of the directors, still wearing my training kit and studded boots, making it perfectly clear how I felt about 'the lie', as I saw it. They were shocked at my attitude but, after being lied to regarding the car, this was a step too far. In every other way I loved the club, and there was certainly no blame attached to the manager Bobby Williamson, who was quietly on our side but whose hands were tied.

They refused to budge, and for a short while I didn't know how to react. Should I go public with it to embarrass them? Should I resign on the spot in a fury, as I wanted to? Or should I wait and see how I felt after the summer? I chose the latter after advice from my dad. He had the usual wise words: 'Act in haste, repent at your leisure.'

There was a last 1–1 draw against Hibernian in the league, followed by an Ayrshire Cup final triumph against local arch-rivals Ayr United. Winning that trophy was a huge deal for our fans, even if I had never heard of the Ayrshire Cup up until the week before the game!

I was awarded Man of the Match in the final, and while driving south afterwards I considered what a great end to the season it had been on the pitch, particularly with the promise of European football to follow after the summer break. In that warm glow I mused, 'This has been great fun. I love it here. Surely we can sort out these little problems between the club and me with some sensible negotiations when I get back after the summer.'

As a local Ayrshire man once said:

> The best laid schemes o' Mice an' Men
> Gang aft agley

When I arrived home in Chester I thought I finally had a chance to help Annabel over the summer. She had done an incredible job under increasing pressure. She had managed to get up to watch only one single Kilmarnock game as Simon, with his complex difficulties, needed constant care, help and understanding. Lucy wasn't sleeping well, waking up at 2am every night and, as any parent will tell you, that is about the most debilitating thing imaginable.*

We had, however, finally found a house in the Scottish Borders, near Annabel's family. It was time to move back and put down our roots. The idea of spending the entire summer together was bliss, but yet another unexpected and unsolicited short-term job offer arrived, one that I didn't want to pass up, and we were pulled apart again. Annabel again gave me the encouragement to take it, even though she would then have to do the lion's share of organising the move from Chester to Scotland. With Lucy being four and Simon eight, it was an extremely stressful time once again, but the hope was that now, at last, I had provided the base, the security and the future home in Scotland.

This little 'side job' was a good one! BBC Radio 5 Live wanted me to be one of their co-commentators at the World Cup in France. This Gallic jaunt might, with a bit of luck, also be the foundations of my next career.

It ended up being a glorious summer in the south of France – apart from Scotland getting knocked out in the group stage. There was brilliant football, in a beautiful country with fabulous food and delicious wine. I enjoyed the company of my BBC team alongside the lashings of culture I was able to squeeze in – mostly phenomenal art galleries and incredible architectural wonders such as the Palais des Papes in Avignon. And they were paying me for it too!

That magical month was like a dream, but reality was waiting back home, even if it wasn't a particularly bad reality. We would probably have

---

* Lucy was such a bad sleeper for those years that, when she was a teenager, I would often wake her up at midnight to remind her what it was like to be disturbed from a deep slumber. She never enjoyed that 'joke'. I only stopped doing this when she became an exhausted NHS front-line doctor, qualifying just months before the start of the Covid-19 pandemic!

bought a place in Edinburgh and settled there but, with Simon's needs and the specific difficulties autism presents, we decided on a more rural life in the Scottish Borders, near Coldstream, where Annabel was from and where her parents still lived. We have been in that same home for more than 30 years now.

Simon, however, was unimpressed at leaving the comfort of his surroundings in Chester, as well as the security and familiarity of his routines. This is hard enough for most kids, but particularly testing for those on the autistic spectrum. As usual, Annabel had my help only briefly through this trauma as, less than a week later, I was off again with Kilmarnock on a pre-season tour of Germany. The new home had to be paid for, after all!

At least there was some security and, for the first time in our lives, there was some sense of a plan on how our future might pan out – for several years anyway. The only fly in the proverbial with Kilmarnock was my continuing annoyance about the two broken promises. I wasn't ready to drop the disappearing bonus as it involved the entire squad and, considering my previous (English!) PFA chairmanship, I simply couldn't accept the immorality of it. Nor could I accept the amateurish, two-bit, hustler attitude I thought Scottish football seemed happy to put up with. Was it really that backward in comparison to England? Certainly, the Scottish players' union (the SPFA),* though keen to help, had nowhere near the power we had in England to force the clubs to do the right thing.

Still, there was much to look forward to: I loved the Killie lads; got on well with the coaching staff; and the fans had warmed to me, and me to them, in equal measure. In terms of the joy of the game, that previous season had been as happy and as gratifying as any of the previous 16. Considering I had been contemplating retirement just nine months

---

* I had tried to link both unions in my time as the chairman down south, through Scottish players' chairman Tony Higgins, but failed. They finally agreed closer ties 15 years after I first tried to arrange it!

before, it was a delicious late summer to my career. The stats were decent too: getting ten assists and scoring five myself, making me third-top scorer in the team.

Killie then acquired a new player, one I rated as among the best Scotland had produced for many years, in terms of vision and pure talent: Ian Durrant. This was a player I could certainly work with and had briefly done so already in the Scottish national side.

At the start of the season there was also the UEFA Cup to prepare for. The trip to Sarajevo for the game against Željezničar was memorable, but mostly for the horrific scenes that peppered the beautiful city. The war had finished only a few years before but the scars were everywhere. On the flight into Sarajevo the evidence was unmissable: there were huge cemeteries with masses of white crosses marking where the recently dead lay. The stadium itself was rumoured to have been the scene of multiple war crimes, as it was used as a prison for a while. The most poignant moment was when a few of us went to look at 'Sniper Alley', with the bullet holes and shell pockmarks on the houses, shops and hotels down there. It was the abnormality of the normality that jarred. Holiday Inn hotels are ubiquitous in every city I visit, but they don't usually have the ordnance damage and the ghosts of those who perished still in the air. War leaves a banal but dark shadow that is hard to make sense of when the guns eventually fall silent.

We drew in Bosnia, but won the tie, and then had the first game of the SPL season against Dundee United to enjoy on a warm sunny afternoon in Ayrshire. I scored what was by some distance my best goal for the club that day, chipping United's giant keeper Sieb Dijkstra from 25 yards in a 2–0 win. Being congratulated by my friends and colleagues, realising the team was even better this year than last, with the knowledge that Ally McCoist would be signing within the week – he was a good player, but also very good fun – it all pointed to another joyous season.

I had settled into thinking that I had survived this career in football relatively unscathed, and although there had been a few negatives along the road, they had been eclipsed by the many positive games, the countless good experiences and the many enjoyable seasons I had managed to stay involved for. The last two years could be treasured: I could concentrate fully on my love of the game, and that usually led to me playing well and being successful.

Except for the small inconvenience that I would be gone from the club within four weeks, and this nice little Indian summer was about to turn into a four-year maelstrom.

PART THREE

FIR PARK

10/
DO YOU REALIZE??

'Don't you think the board should act with a bit more dignity and honour, considering how dishonest you have been with players who got the club into Europe?'

I had finally got a meeting with a few of the Killie directors. Well, I ambushed a couple of them outside on the steps of the main entrance to Rugby Park after training. In answer to my frank statement it was made clear that, although they accepted there was a promise broken regarding the bonuses, they would not be paying up.

My lack of respect seemed to have rattled them, however. It was a warm afternoon, but my intrusion got a very frosty reaction as the speaker fiddled with his club tie: 'You can't speak to directors of the club in that tone. You're basically calling us liars.'

'Well, yes, why shouldn't I? The players have acted correctly. If we have the moral high ground, and we haven't been lying, we can say it like it is.'

'Who do you think you are, talking to us like that? You don't have the right to use that language.'

I might just have swallowed it one more time, but being spoken to like a child, with that arrogance, was unacceptable. There was also the disdainful Victorian-mill-owner-talking-to-the-worthless-workers vibe which I wasn't absolutely delighted with at that point.

Was it the former PFA chairman coming to the surface? Was it my pomposity as an experienced international player? I know they thought that was the case. Was I getting too self-important and maybe even 'above myself'? It certainly must have looked that way to them. They had the threat of fining me, or generally making life difficult if I didn't play by their rules – and I thought they were prepared to do that. I was happy to let them know I couldn't care less if they did. Having bought Ian Durrant, who would fill at least some of if not my entire creative role, maybe my stock was lower in their eyes than it had been.

But that wasn't how I saw the situation. It was most likely that the earnest creature that lived deep inside me had simply been drawn out into the open once again. You could have treated me that way at any point in the previous 18 years and got a similar reaction. If you try to scam me, then I am happy to walk away on a point of principle. I was happy to do that there and then, and told them so.

It was such a shame, because I still had two years left on my Killie contract and, otherwise, I was happy there. If they could just relent and pay those promised bonuses to the lads, it would all be hunky dory from my perspective down at Rugby Park.

I may also just have failed to mention something else at that informal meeting, something rather important that had happened the previous week.

Many years before this encounter, way back when I was playing for Chelsea in the early 1980s, a guy called John Boyle (JB), who was in the holiday industry, had contacted me a few times. It was usually to ask me to turn up at one of his little holiday firms to meet the staff and do a little friendly free PR work. His small group at Sunfare and Falcon Holidays were a nice bunch, and a few had even been students with me in Glasgow when I was a teenager, so the affairs were always very pleasant and convivial.

Roll on more than a decade and JB had been made an offer for his holiday businesses – from memory, over £10 million, I believe. He decided to think about it over the weekend, consider it from all angles, and just 'wait and see' – although, like most people, I would have bitten the hand off anyone offering me that sort of money. But John wasn't being as daft as I thought: another company came in over the weekend and, by the end, the rumour had it that the business was sold for 'north of £80 million' after a bidding war!

Whatever the price he was paid for selling his company, and however much he personally got out of it (I couldn't say), he was now minted and was in the market to buy a football club – not for the first time. But this time he was successful. In mid-July he'd called me and asked if we could meet up to give him some advice about the football industry. We met in a very nice restaurant in Glasgow, as was JB's style, with him insisting he would foot the bill, so I should order whatever I liked. I had witnessed his boundless generosity before in London, and he hadn't changed a jot. John tended to bluster into rooms rather than walk in. He cut a slightly portly but always well kempt dash, while being physically and facially not unlike Terry Jones of *Monty Python* fame. Roughly the same height as me and Scottish, but with a more delicate accent, he was often accompanied by a heavily perfumed aroma, a more florid one than the football players would have been routinely sporting.

'Basically, I've bought the football club, Pat,' he said. 'But there's a lot that needs to be done with it. When I run a company, as you know, I do it the right way and treat people the right way. It isn't a case of them and us between the owners and the staff; it's always an *us and us* situation.'

'It might be worth telling me which club it is, John.'

He had another gulp of the vintage wine: 'Of course, it's Motherwell, the team I favoured as a boy.'

'Oh, really, we're playing them in a few weeks in the league,' I lightly countered. 'Me playing for Kilmarnock and you owning Motherwell, that'll be interesting.'

'What if I owned Motherwell and you were playing for Motherwell too? And maybe even helping me to run the club?'

It did take me by surprise, but it wasn't a complete shock. JB had sounded me out in the past about running a club for him, but this time it was absolutely real and he wanted me on board in his new venture. Motherwell were in the top flight of Scottish football, not dissimilar in size and history to Kilmarnock, but maybe surprisingly I didn't have a great interest in the offer at that precise moment: I still had no desire to stay inside the game after I stopped playing. Instead, I fancied going into the media and, anyway, at the time of our meal I still thought the problems at Kilmarnock could be tidied up. I told John that I would think about it for a few days, but, as we were leaving the restaurant, there was a typically grand, generous, off-the-cuff, JB flourish: 'Whatever job you want at the club, it's yours. From manager to director to player – whatever you want. I need you to oversee the whole thing. It's yours if you want it.' With that he poured himself into the back seat of his car and his driver moved away at a stately pace into the night. I stood there thinking for a moment: 'This could be life changing if I did it – but no, in truth, it doesn't sound like my idea of a good fun time.'

Those few days later, by the time I had finished my chat with some of the Killie board members, JB's admittedly vague offer was sounding a lot more tempting. Killie might have thought I was in a weak position, but they weren't to know that I had been offered a post as a player–director–manager–whatever the hell I liked at Motherwell. I was holding more and better cards than they could possibly have known.

The next few weeks became a weird blur. I was angry at Killie for what I saw as their dishonesty. On top of that they had acquired Durranty, who wasn't cheap, and were now getting Ally McCoist, who doesn't work for free either! This was the club that was apparently too skint to afford me last season, so I had signed for a third of the weekly wage that Tranmere had been paying me. On top of that they couldn't afford those promised European bonuses to the players, as well as an old banger for me – but they were still hoovering up expensive ex-Scottish internationals!

On the credit side, we'd had European football against Željezničar and Sigma Olomouc; on the debit side I was left out of the team for both Czech ties, and given only three minutes at the end of our match against Rangers. I hadn't been sidelined last season, so was this the board getting me back for confronting them? I didn't think Bobby Williamson could be swayed that way, but I couldn't be sure. I was, however, sure that it was very quickly making me less enamoured of the club and my situation there.

John Boyle asked me to come into his central 'Citigate' offices in Glasgow for a serious chat two weeks after the first meeting – a much more sober affair than that original west end dinner and, by now, I was in a very different frame of mind after Killie had irked me.

John was persuasive in that meeting, but it was still a friendly chat with no hard sell. I liked the casual informal attitude we shared, and we talked mostly about his vision and his ideology. I liked his ideas – well, most of them anyway. Although a businessman, I knew that he was big on fairness, on treating his employees well, with integrity and equality. He treated his staff in his holiday business in London just like mates, so I knew it wasn't just a line. He was modern, liberal-minded and a million miles away from some of the old unreconstructed businessmen at some other clubs. We talked as much about a mission statement underlining our beliefs in equality and anti-bigotry as we did about football at that meeting. We still had to figure out what job I was being offered, before I could really consider if I would accept it. He asked me, 'If you came, would you want to be the manager, the player–manager, or what? As well as being general overseer of the football department? Where do you think you could have the best influence?'

I explained, 'First of all, you already have a manager in place. Secondly, I have no interest in being a manager anyway.'

'You could play for the team and be a director on the board.'

'That would make sense. If I'm overseeing the football side of the operation, I would have to know what was happening at the club from top to bottom, from the back four to the boardroom.'

'What about your title? What would you like?'

'You could give me whatever title you want – I'm not fussed. "Director of Football", "Sporting Director", "Board Member", or whatever – I couldn't care less, it's only a name. It isn't about titles or status, it's about looking at the club and giving it a vision, as well as a costing for the future, and doing the mundane things like overseeing the contracts and the budgets.'*

'Exactly, Patrick. I couldn't have put it better myself. So do you want the job?'

'Steady on. I need a little time to think it through. And, gauche though it might sound, we haven't talked about my remuneration yet.'

John made me an offer as a player which was a good deal more than I was on at Kilmarnock. Now that we had agreed what my sphere of influence would be at Fir Park, if I took it, a separate offer for the executive role was also made. The problem was that his offer was totally unacceptable in my eyes: it was to be our first disagreement. The figure he quoted me was about double what I would have expected! He also offered me a package of shares that would make me the second largest shareholder at the club after him.

'First, I don't want part-ownership of the club, even though offering it for free is extremely kind of you. This is your company, not mine, as well as your investment. Secondly, I will agree to the contract if you halve the figure you are offering. If you want me to acquire players, do the contracts and keep the finances within an agreed budget throughout the entire football department, I'll tell you when you are being overcharged. Overcharging is not uncommon in this industry, and this is a perfect example. I will not sting you and will try to make sure no one else does.'

John trusted me anyway. It wasn't proving easy talking me into taking the job, but when it became clear that I was obviously not 'on the make', I reckon it sealed his belief in my honesty in our dealings. I'd had no particular hankering to be a manager or an executive, even though the roles were now there and waiting. I hadn't even considered it seriously before, having never wanted a position of power in any work situation. My first thoughts were that if I did take this job, I wouldn't use the power and status

---

* For all my often tiresome high-minded idealism, the working-class boy who had gone to study business management at degree level also knew the importance of good, dull, solid accounting and budgeting.

the way other people do. JB wasn't that type either, so maybe we could run this club another, more modern way. I hadn't wanted 'that kind of job', but this didn't appear to be 'that kind of job' – this sounded like a whole new egalitarian way of running a football club.

I called Annabel on the car journey back to the Borders and brought her up to date with developments. I then had a three-hour drive at limited speed (bloody Edinburgh bypass traffic) to mull over my options. This was a gigantic fork in the road, metaphorically speaking. In reality, I was still stuck on that bypass. By the time I got home and, after a further discussion over dinner, I had just about made the decision, much to my own surprise, that this Motherwell offer sounded like it could be an amazing adventure.

Annabel and I thought long and hard about it that night. It was a big call, a serious job, and many people would be depending on me. There was also the fact that Motherwell, an industrial town previously dominated by its huge steelworks, was positioned 15 miles east of Glasgow just off the M8 motorway, helpfully 45 minutes closer to our home than Kilmarnock. In taking the role of overseeing an entire club, I would share JB's moral positions towards the staff, but it would undoubtedly test those attitudes to the limit. I wasn't worried about my capabilities, particularly with my background as chairman of the PFA, and that business degree I had been doing before I started out on my pro football career.

Whether or not I had the right personality to be a boss was a bigger concern. When tough decisions had to be made concerning people's livelihoods, would I be able to make them? That was the real concern. I then thought to myself, 'If I am faced with a difficult decision, I should make it easy. I should do the right thing, the honest thing, the morally correct thing. If I can't do that, or am not allowed to do that, then I should resign from the job immediately.'

I thought I could make this work interesting, but I suspected it would be hard, probably the hardest job I had ever done. Did I need this hassle? I didn't – but was that a good enough reason to turn away from it? I generally always did things because I liked them or enjoyed them;

maybe it was time to consider what many other people have to do – jobs that are sometimes a chore, maybe even difficult or possibly not even enjoyable at times! This could be a real test of my character, more than just kicking a ball around. Air-headed nonsense, of course, but those were my thought processes.

I made the call to JB the next day. 'John, to use one of your favourite phrases, I'm minded to take you up on your offer. We should meet and iron out the final details, but I suspect it won't be difficult between the two of us.' There were no power meetings with lawyers or agents on either side, no accountants arguing over the intricacies of pension payments or sophisticated payment schemes, just an agreement on ideologies – and the deal was sorted on trust in 20 minutes, just the way I liked it.

There was still the not insignificant problem of me legally relinquishing my position at Kilmarnock – but we were both confident that could be sorted, even if there would be some bad blood spilt on the way. Unsurprisingly, Kilmarnock suddenly wanted compensation for my leaving, even though I had been close to *persona non grata* just a few days earlier. I wasn't overly concerned: I had been through bigger and far more painful struggles with the PFA; I knew this would sort itself out in time.

The next few weeks were a tiresome tug of war between Motherwell and Kilmarnock, all played out in the press once they got wind of the story. In the meantime I had to go in for training at Kilmarnock for a few days – a silly sham, but it had to be done even though all sides knew it was senseless. One way or another I was moving, it was a just a case of how it was done. There was the rigmarole of should I put a written transfer request in? Should I just retire on the spot and forget about playing? Should Kilmarnock just let me go – I'd cost nothing from Tranmere, after all?

The players at Kilmarnock were fine with me, even though they knew I was going. I had been a 'leper' before at clubs, so it didn't really bother me unduly if I wasn't training with the first team now. When Bobby Williamson left me out of the squad for the 3–0 win against Hearts at the end of August, it became clear this would be sorted sooner rather than later. Kilmarnock felt they could no longer use me, and Motherwell weren't yet getting my services, even though I had agreed to join them as soon as I legally could.

Killie upped the ante by saying they would withhold my player's registration, not allowing me to play for Motherwell unless John paid £100,000. With that line, I knew we were now back in familiar football finance territory and we could get on with getting the deal done. I said to John, 'What a cheek! Don't pay that much. I am 34, I'm not worth it – and I cost them nothing. They don't deserve £100K. If you want me to run the football side of the club, that would be my first piece of advice to you: don't spend that money on me. I don't have to continue playing; they can keep my player's registration and frame it for all I care.' I was a bit miffed with the Killie board at this point. I was angry and not thinking clearly in the moment, but I soon appreciated that they were just trying to get the best business deal they could. It was infuriating but understandable.

As suspected, a deal was soon done, after Roger Mitchell, CEO at the SPL intervened. He later told me he did the deal in the toilets of a city centre hotel, a phone in either ear, finally getting it over the line for £70,000. So John bought me in the john – not exactly a glamorous start. On the upside, I could now carry on playing with Motherwell.

So why did I decide to leave Kilmarnock in the end? What pushed me or lured me over the edge? Was it really the promise of that 'adventure'? That would make me sound very windswept and interesting, but it wouldn't be the full story. There is no doubt that the wages at Motherwell would be a significant increase on what I was earning at Killie and, yes, I admit that was important – but it wasn't the deciding factor, far from it.

The main driving force behind the decision was the false promises. Had they been honest about the car and the bonuses, I would have stayed at Kilmarnock – had they wanted to keep me. There is no question about that in my mind. I loved Killie, the players, the manager, the fans, the football style, the pitch and the stadium. In the simplest terms, I loved playing for a team I liked again, and it was a huge wrench to give it up, whatever exciting job alternatives awaited. I had learned by then that nothing beats just playing football every week as an occupation. It might have looked like I was jumping ship for a lucrative and powerful job, but I absolutely didn't want to go, I just couldn't stomach the attitude I was getting from some members of the Killie board. That was the key reason, over and above everything else.

Because of the drawn-out saga of the last few days and weeks, when I finally left the ground for the last time there were no emotional goodbyes, no tearful leaving parties. The day I left I just walked into the boot room, picked up a couple of pairs of my boots, walked back out, slung them in the back of the car then drove off. There wasn't a fond look back. I needed to get away. Some time would be needed to heal those scars, on both sides.

11/
SOON

The initial brief at Fir Park was simple, even if it would take a bit of work. I would have to study the club – from the players to the coaching staff; the youth development and the structure of the facilities; as well as other things like the acquisitions policy and overall costs – then, after a month, I would come back with a report. I had to bear in mind that John had already promised a decent level of investment even before I arrived, and he was keen to reconsider every part of the club to see where improvements could be made.

The actual role would be fleshed out in time – 'overseeing', which is what he said I should do, is a pretty vague concept. In fact, aside from jinking down the wing for another few years, my future role was so open that John said I would be the best man to choose what it would be! His level of trust in my abilities and knowledge was staggering, but, even so, I informed him that if I couldn't find a suitable role for myself other than playing, then I simply wouldn't take one. From the outside this attitude seemed odd, but we were both cool with it.

John was, and I guess still is, unstintingly generous, often to a fault. Even that early, I thought this might be a problem in football because this generosity could be taken for granted and his kind nature abused. I knew the way a lot of people in the game behaved and, perhaps, I thought I could maybe shield him from that.

The first time I went to the club with John, he proudly gave me the guided tour of his new premises, starting in the bowels of the main stand at Motherwell. As we passed by the dingy canteen and on up to the classically furnished but slightly stuffy old-fashioned boardroom via the directors' box – having gone through a warren of dark corridors – he said, 'You know, Pat, we could make this a better place to work. We could make this club special, different, modern and successful if we do it right, but I do understand it will cost a bit initially.'

I could already see a good deal of money was needed for the upgrade, just from the ancient paint peeling off the walls. I warned him right there and then, with something of a prepared speech, 'John, on my side of the business, kindness and generosity are often seen as signs of weakness. We shouldn't lose our positive hopeful outlooks, but you must understand what a dog-eat-dog world this is, particularly with players, agents, managers and the other clubs. They are ultimately ultra-competitive animals, in it for personal glory and for the winning at just about all costs. That means someone else loses. You have to make sure that you aren't the one who's losing. It may seem glamorous from the outside, but it will more often feel mean spirited than it does kind hearted, especially if you aren't successful, whoever you are and however well-meaning you are.'

He assured me that he had been in some tough business scenarios himself and that he could cope – and, anyway, I didn't want to crush that almost naïve excited exuberance he had. John then jauntily asked me with a little pride as well as some excitement in his voice, 'What do you think about the idea of me buying Motherwell football club in the first place?' I was clear and honest in my reply and maybe didn't give the answer he either wanted or expected: 'You are obviously a very good businessman, but it doesn't matter: owning a football club will cost you a lot of money.'

He sounded confident in his reply: 'I think I can do it differently, in time – at least differently from the way the others in Scottish football do it. I have a more modern outlook.'

But I wasn't for budging: 'You can look at pricing, changing the squad and adapting anything you like, but in the end football clubs are costly businesses. If you are doing this for fame, then it's a mistake, you'd be better off out of it. Fame is not all it's cracked up to be, and there are many downsides that aren't obvious from the outside, and you'll soon get fed up with fame anyway. If it was me in your position, to be brutally honest, I wouldn't have touched it. On the upside, however, if it suits your personality, you will experience highs and lows you won't find anywhere else. The adrenaline hits are incredible, and they are addictive. On top of that this will be an adventure you will never forget, for good and for bad.'

John assured me: 'I want to do this, I am committed.'

I smiled and replied, 'I think you ought to be, but that's your choice.'

Convinced he was doing it chiefly for 'his' community, he did mention one thing that stuck in my mind that day.

'You know, you could be chairman of M&S and virtually no one in Scotland will know your name. If you're chairman of a club like Motherwell, however, you'll be ten times as famous here.'

Fame or indeed infamy can be quite cheap to buy, when looked at through that particular lens.

When John talked about buying Motherwell at press conferences, he liked to sell his vision big, but some of the initial comments were bordering on embarrassing, and sometimes counterproductive.

With the press room at Fir Park bursting at the seams with journalists, all desperate to get a few juicy lines from the new, unknown owner in Scottish football – one who was allegedly a bit flamboyant – they waited with some excitement for his pronouncements, and JB didn't let them down. With me sitting beside him – I admit somewhat uncomfortably at the top table; an array of TV and stills cameras aimed at us, the table lost under a mass of microphones – JB proclaimed among other things, with more than an echo of Tony Blair at his peak, 'This is a new way. We are going to be the third force in Scottish football.'

Happily, the cameras were trained on John, because if they had been on me, you would have spotted my head almost swivel off my neck. '*We don't say things like that in football!*' is what I wanted to scream. OK, so he held back and didn't claim we would overtake Celtic and Rangers, but bigger clubs than Motherwell, such as Hibs, Hearts and Aberdeen to name just three, would have been happy to take umbrage. It's fine to aim high, be positive and proclaim you are a winner, but I was acutely aware that every statement with that level of bravado comes back and haunts you in football. More importantly, in the short term it would also cost JB financially, because he now had to put his money where his mouth was. I quickly changed the phrase 'the third force' to 'the third way' when journalists asked me about it, evoking my own inner Alastair Campbell!

In those early days I did try to gag, or at least temper, JB to a degree for his own safety, as I knew the press would eventually have a ball with those sorts of comments: 'John, if you are going to say things like that in the press, is there any chance you could pass them by me first? The whole idea is for me to help you navigate your way through this industry. I can't do that unless you keep me informed of your more . . . headline-grabbing ideas.'

On the other hand, as I wanted to temper the message, right at that moment the press loved him. He was so different, so much of an outsider in the game, that he made even me look and sound in comparison like the most butch, cliché-driven, grizzled, old one-dimensional soccer pro you've ever seen. And that's not easy! As one journalist said to me at the time, 'He is a breath of fresh air . . . well, scented air, to be more precise.'

Suddenly, out of nowhere, the Scottish Football Association got in touch by phone: 'An SPL club has contacted us to underline that a current player is not allowed to be a director of a club.' I hadn't even got my feet under the desk. 'Why isn't it allowed?' we asked.

'Because it is in the rules. Because it was decided.'

'Why and when was it decided?'

'It was in the previous rules.'

'Can we change those rules? They are bloody archaic.' (Like lots of other things at the SFA were back then.)

'Maybe one day, but they can't be changed just now.' (I read that as, 'Not for you, you oik!')

The SFA were committed to upholding their statutes and explained that it might take years to change them. Committees would have to consider any reforms, then make reports on them and, anyway, somebody had already complained about my proposed role. I asked who, but apparently they weren't at liberty to say who it was that was blackballing me. I could see a ball, black or not, being hoofed into the long grass a mile away, and so could JB. This was a pointless and indeed unimportant battle.

JB had an answer: 'Fine, if those are the rules, then you can be the chief executive and a player. That means you can come to, and be involved in, board meetings, but you are not officially a director, even though it is a stupid and frankly prejudicial rule against the workforce that has an unpleasant but distinct whiff of the 19th century about it.'

So that is what we did. As a result of the SFA's archaic rules, I would be CEO and player. Something I hadn't previously considered, and, it turned out, a first in British football. It was admittedly an odd situation, but probably the person who found this strangest of all was our Finnish manager, Harri Kampman. Or, as he was routinely called in the press, 'the genial Harri Kampman' – which was an accurate if over-simplistic description. Like every manager, he could have a sense-of-humour failure with the best of them when he was annoyed.

We had a few league games in this initial period that would give me a good opportunity to understand the strength of the squad at close quarters. As it happened, it was at very close quarters, as Harri picked me on the bench.

Even though he picked me, he didn't seem to like the idea of his boss, me, the CEO, being in his dressing room. I accepted that it was unusual and, indeed, maybe unique – but, at an early and admittedly awkward talk in his office, after my first game, I explained it to him clearly, and he seemed to get it: 'I want nothing to do with picking the team. That's your responsibility. If I'm in the team, on the bench or in the stands, it makes no difference whatsoever. I am nearing the end of my career, so my position is irrelevant. I'm available on a Saturday if you need me and you think I can help. When I am in the dressing room, however, I am just another player to be treated exactly like the others. You can shout at me as much as you like and there will be no comeback.'

He wasn't the one shouting at me in my second game, which just had to be against my old club Kilmarnock. Their fans, unsurprisingly, gave me the bird. It was the only time I ever got stick from a former club's fans, but they didn't know the whole story. My only reply in the press afterwards was, 'I loved my time at Killie. I was sad to leave and, even though some fans have negative feelings about me, and made them clear today, I have nothing other than respect, thanks and happy memories to hit back with.' The Killie fans soon forgave me, and now I am made to feel as welcome there as anywhere in football.

Harri Kampman had initially seemed satisfied when I explained our situation, but a couple of weeks later he headed for Glasgow airport and was gone. The flying Finn was back in Helsinki before I learned he had resigned, leaving a little press bomb behind him, ready to explode. The next thing I knew was that there was a newspaper report from him claiming I was picking the team! I called him immediately and he counter-claimed that it was lost in translation, a total error. 'No problem,' I replied through gritted teeth. 'I will tell the press that and look forward to you retracting the statement.' Which, to be fair to him, he did – but it got nowhere near the splash of the original story, unsurprisingly.

Things were already moving at an extraordinary pace – so much more so than I had anticipated. Not only was there the issue that, only a few weeks in, we didn't have a manager – but the task of finding a new one fell to me. This was a massive decision that could affect the club in any number of ways. I set to thinking about it, hard.

My mate Brian McClair had come back to Motherwell just before I arrived. The 'dream ticket' of him and me managing was never going to happen, however. I'd considered it momentarily, and it appeared interesting and obvious from the outside, but neither of us wanted to be football managers.

But my understanding of business was that if you are going to make a management change, it is worth having a look inside your own organisation first to see if the right person is sitting there already. Looking around the dressing room there seemed to be two obvious candidates. There was the striker Owen Coyle, and he was initially my first choice: he was easy-going but driven, and was as keen to help others as anyone else at the club. He wanted to get into management and, not unimportantly, I liked him and thought I would enjoy working with him. It was a huge temptation to plump for him right away.

The other candidate was Billy Davies, who was already coaching the youths as well as being a vital member of the first-team squad. Billy's work ethic was incredible, bordering on unhealthy. Billy was a strong character – like me, he was small in stature, about the same height, the same age, and also from a rough working-class area in Glasgow. We were both fitness fanatics too. We had played against each other many times as kids, when he was at Rangers and I was at Celtic, then later together with the Scotland youth team. He had been a very good player, and still was. He was, however, far more driven than me, and our personalities were very different; feisty doesn't come close to covering it for Billy.

Like many football managers, Billy could be unforgiving: cross him once and you could be dead to him. Even if I didn't like it, this was a common trait in the game, and I accepted it as part of that insatiable desire to win at all costs. I liked Billy's lighthearted fun side, but knew well enough that there was a darker harder shadow lurking, one that could be considered resentful or vengeful. If I gave him the job, I felt these characteristics might be softened by the fact that John Boyle and I were lacking in these traits. I thought he would have a strong enough character to deal with the ups and downs of management and maybe, just maybe, without trying to mould him, we might just smooth off a few of the rougher edges. I knew, though, that I wouldn't be able to change him too much, such was his strength of character. Neither would I be able to make him do as I pleased, but that was fine with me.

The deciding factor was that I thought it was crucial to keep Owen in the team: he was an excellent striker I knew well already, particularly from his days with Bolton Wanderers. Had I made Owen the player–manager then it might have negatively affected his on-field performances. Maybe it wouldn't have, but it was a chance I wasn't willing to take.*

Billy made it clear to me, even before I had decided to consider him, that he would dearly love the manager's job. He wasn't being pushy, just showing an unbridled enthusiasm. I was interested to see his reaction, when I finally told him he was going to be the next manager of Motherwell.

He looked intensely, straight into my eyes: 'Thanks, Pat, I am incredibly grateful and deeply honoured. And understand one thing: you don't know how hard I will work to make this a success. No one in the world will put more effort into a job than I will into this one. You have my word on that.'

I didn't doubt him.

Jim Griffin, who had also been coaching at the club, was another I thought very highly of. Happily, Billy chose 'Griff' as his number two and added the fiercely honourable former Motherwell stalwart Miodrag Krivokapić to help on the training ground. I hoped that I could now be totally hands-off with this part of the club.

At the end of that first month the time was drawing near for me to deliver my initial findings to John. I ended up giving them to him early, verbally and forcefully in the car park of McDiarmid Park, home of St Johnstone, after a 5–0 utter capitulation. The last few games had not gone well: three

---

* Both candidates went on to manage in the Premier League, so I think my instincts were right on this occasion. The dressing room soon boasted another who would eventually go on to manage in the Premier League, and then even higher: one Roberto Martínez. He would have been a dream manager. We got on famously and his Spanish ideas were years ahead of his time.

defeats in a row against Hearts, Dundee and Celtic before this pounding in Perth. It meant a run of two points from 18 and a blunt report delivered in the warm evening air, with me frustrated and still overheating from the game I had just sweated through for 90 minutes on the pitch. With his wife Fiona standing beside him, I said, 'Regarding the team, I'll give it to you straight. If the squad stays as it is, and there is no increase in the playing budget, there's about a 50–50 chance of relegation, and that's probably being very optimistic. Good management might make all the difference in this scenario. But don't worry about young Billy, even after today's fiasco. He'll be good enough to get the best out of them.'

John still looked a bit shocked after the defeat less than an hour earlier, but he also looked serious. He then asked the million-dollar – indeed, considerably more costly than that – question: 'So, what do we have to do to save the situation?'

It was time to level with John, regarding how much it would cost to run this club successfully, and I expected that it would take his breath away. I hadn't finalised the financial side of the report quite yet, but I had the headlines: 'There are two other possible scenarios. If you spend an extra £1 million every year on top of the current £1.1 million wage bill, it will guarantee comfortable safety, and maybe even some good cup runs. Considering what you've already promised in the press about being the third force in Scotland, I would recommend that. If you want to spend that sort of money, and if you think you can improve the business and increase income streams from your end, then this can work. With any luck the increased relative success should eventually boost the fan base and the revenue – as will some of the plans you've suggested regarding ticket pricing and work with the local community.' I stopped for a moment, just to let the gravity and the possible costs sink in. I also probably needed a breath myself having just torn about ineffectively on the field that day, trying and failing to salvage something from the carnage.

As fans and some journalists milled about just out of earshot, he said nothing important, other than, 'Are you feeling OK? You seemed to be working very hard out there.'

I nodded, recovered a bit and with a deep breath thought I might as well carry on and give him the full story in one hit: 'The third and final, gold-standard option costs up to £2 million per year. The upside is we could be as high as third, which is what you have been suggesting in the press conferences, which I really do reckon you shouldn't say again until it actually happens! This is still a long way behind the wage bills that teams such as Hearts and Aberdeen have, but I believe we can get there in a short time with that sort of investment. I use the word "investment" in this context because, with that backing, I can build up the youth-development department at the same time, and maybe in as little as five years we could start making some money back for the club from there, certainly more than is coming in just now. The youth development isn't bad, but is a bit ramshackle – even so, it is one of the best things about the place.'

John was deep in thought, listening intently – maybe a little in shock and probably waiting for some sort of silver lining – so I thought it was worth pitching in with my own personal opinion at this point: 'That's a lot of money for you to spend, John, and my advice would be that you don't do it unless you are confident you will have the funds and are willing to keep ploughing that sort of money in over the medium to long term.'

To my amazement, with Fiona beside him nodding along, he said after only a few moments consideration: 'Let's go with the gold standard option.'

'What?! Are you sure? I can see you've already spent a few million just buying the club before I got here. You have also promised huge sums upgrading the facilities. Just a cursory look at the basic infrastructure such as the pitch, the stadium itself and the training facilities suggests you have a lot more to spend there too, and you aren't going to get any of that back. I'd guess you're probably in for £3 or £4 million already, and you have only owned it for a matter of months!' I didn't add the last three words I was thinking at the time: '*Are you mad?*'

John was adamant, but even that early I thought he and his investment needed some protection. The money would have to be spent wisely, if possible, and if I got my way I would do everything to ensure it was – as much as you can in a business where there are absolutely no certainties.

12/
CRUSHED

We probably looked like a very young, naïve and inexperienced group, from owner all the way to manager – after all, Billy and I were still only in our mid-thirties, and we had just had a stinker of a start. In the background, though, there was also the wise counsel of wily old campaigner Willie McLean. He was at the club in an advisory capacity, watching upcoming opposition and checking out possible new players. Soon another elder statesman, Davie McParland, was acquired to head the repurposing of youth development. Again, he was Billy's call. Davie had been the Celtic manager many years before, among other jobs, and was hugely respected in the game and by me personally.

There was a lot of hiring – and, yes, a very little firing – at the time, but mostly it was shuffling people into roles better suited to their abilities. This was usually as a result of me talking to them, listening to them and understanding where they thought their expertise was being underused. JB and I weren't keen on callously dumping people who had worked for the club, but, sadly, it is impossible to change this much in a company without putting a few noses out of joint, and there were one or two who were understandably miffed and left. During all this it was important to get some players in quickly that would strengthen the group – relegation in that first season was a real possibility, and none of the plans made any sense unless we stayed in the top division. Billy sent me off to watch Derek Adams of Ross County, and I agreed he would be a good addition. What's more, his personality and integrity would be a great supplement to the group. He was another one who went on to become a very good manager. It seemed that just about everyone at the club was better cut out as team manager material than me. I have been wrong about many things, but it turned out that I was spot on with that thought.

From the outside it was suggested openly in the press that I was Billy Davies's puppeteer, and that it was me who was really managing the team. They obviously knew the square root of nothing about the strength of Billy's character! There is no chance that he would have allowed that, but it rolled along as gospel in parts of the Scottish press for a while.

There was, however, one piece of advice outside my remit, and only one, that I offered unsolicited to Billy Davies about signing a player. Sitting in his office, I suggested he really ought to take me up on just this one. It had come to my attention that Ged Brannan, with whom I played at Tranmere, was ready to leave Manchester City. He would be a considerable upgrade on what we had at the club. He could play in either full-back position, at centre-back and in central midfield, so it was like getting four players for the price of one. This was not a punt, this was as close as you get to a nailed-on certainty. Ged was easily good enough for Celtic or Rangers, never mind Motherwell. His attitude was perfect and he would be a base from which to build the rest of the future team.

Billy accepted it would be my only piece of advice in this area, and very soon we got Ged in.

That day in his office, having given him the tip, I said that in future I would very much stand aside and would only ever give an opinion on a player if I was asked. I stayed true to my word on that, however sorely I was tempted otherwise. My thinking was simple: what's the point of me hiring a manager then trying to do the job myself? That would be downright stupidity as well as arrogance. In the end, Billy rarely asked for input, and that suited me just fine.

After I had finished with my Ged Brannan sales pitch, Billy had an interesting proposal in return, one he asked as a favour: 'There is an apprentice at the club who I don't think is going to make it in the game at our level. We shouldn't lose his personality around the place, though. I worked with him when he was with the kids' teams, and he has a mixture of comfortable confidence, lighthearted fun, constant hard work, and he never complains about his lot. He is always positive, helpful, funny and friendly, and he really lifts the atmosphere around the whole club. All the top pros like him, as does every kid, cleaner and cook; he is one of those unusual special people who everyone wants to be around. Could you find a job for him here?'

I knew immediately who he was talking about. It could only be one – local lad Andy Thomson, and I didn't miss a beat: 'What a brilliant idea. I reckon I have just the job for him, helping with the kit among a few other things in the football department and in the dressing room. That would keep him involved with everybody day to day.'

Billy had been thinking along exactly the same lines. There aren't many people that would be given a job mostly down to their fabulous personality and universal popularity, but Andy was one of the special few who – because of that personality and, yes, maybe even those boyish blond-haired striking good looks to set it off – everybody loved.

There was a day when a couple of the bigger characters and more experienced players in the team were having a blazing row in the dressing room at training. Andy, just an apprentice, walked in to do some cleaning, as the kids were expected to do, and instead defused the entire situation by winding both up. I was amazed by his control of the moment and how he turned the tension off in an instant, replacing it with laughter. I was a senior player, the chief executive and I was right there in that dressing room, but I couldn't have dealt with the situation half as well or as intelligently as young Andy did. He even gave me a little wink as he walked out, sweeping brush in hand.

Billy Davies had another ace up his sleeve that I was unaware of: nepotism as a positive force. John Spencer, previously of Chelsea and now of Everton and Scotland, was also his brother-in-law. He wasn't getting a game at Everton so Billy said he could get Spenny up on loan. Now that was a real jump in quality: he was just what we needed to propel us away from the relegation danger zone. Clearly there was no way we could afford to actually buy him – his wages, never mind his transfer fee, would have blown my budget to smithereens. Like most people I am not generally a huge fan of nepotism, but this was the proverbial gift horse I couldn't ignore, for the short-term benefit it could bring.

Spenny arrived in a blaze of glory and scored the winner in his first outing, a 1–0 victory against the mighty Rangers at Fir Park under the floodlights. It was an incredible night: already in early October the 12,000 fans seemed to have bought into the excitement that John Boyle had tried to instill in the club, even if my instinct was to try to rein in expectations, at least in the short term. Spenny was an incredible bundle of energy on and off the field. Nobody was safe from his banter in the dressing room, even and sometimes especially, the chief executive. His attitude was a blessing and a saviour for me, because the lads now understood that at training, during a game and in the dressing room I was fair game and there would be no repercussions. In that sphere I was one of them, if a slight outsider – but then I had been that throughout my career. It only changed when they came into my office wanting to discuss something, and, for most of the players, that seemed to work perfectly well. I wanted to be the trusted older player as well as the 'nice boss', someone you could talk to and ask advice from when I was in the office. But in that office, and away from the actual football, there was other work to be getting on with.

As the season progressed, conditions were improved at the club – for instance, we decided that all the staff would now eat together; the players would NOT be separated from everyone else like a bunch of prima donnas. This was to underline that we were all in this together; a central tenet of John's outlook.

John, for his part, wanted ticket prices reviewed and, if possible, reduced. In fact, John, Billy and I agreed that everything at the club would be reviewed for possible improvements as soon as possible. It was an exciting, intense time, but there was plenty of youthful energy around from the three of us to push it along.

There were one or two occasions when it was unclear if a problem should fall under my jurisdiction or the manager's. In these instances Billy and I were usually happy to delegate between ourselves. The way it generally worked was that if it was a weird uncategorisable one, it would end up on my desk. A case in point: one lad was sent up to my office from the manager with a very delicate and a very west of Scotland problem. I had a particular liking for this lad, who was one we had high hopes for!

'Pat, I've got a new girlfriend,' he said. 'We've been going out for a month.'

'Yes, I know. You were with her in the bar after the last game. She seems very nice. Is there a problem?' I knew there must be, otherwise he wouldn't be in my office.

'I need some advice. You see, I really like her, but the thing is, she is Catholic, and my dad will never accept her.'

That particularly rancid old chestnut again! I was quickly discovering that being the chief executive threw up many unexpected and interesting quandaries. I thought for a moment. 'Well, you've only been going out together for a month, so why don't you spend a little more time getting to know her before crossing that particular bridge? Why cause a fight with your dad if the relationship might not last? You'll have caused problems that you don't have to face. In six months or a year, then it might be worth seriously reconsidering. You could even introduce her to your dad just now. I mean, she hasn't got "Catholic" stamped on her forehead, so he'll be none the wiser.'

He wasn't convinced. 'I think he'll find out.'

'How?'

He dolefully replied, 'Well, her uncle is the archbishop.'

When he then told me her rather Catholic-sounding name, my help was now limited to, 'Good luck with that one, mate.' At least he wasn't a bigot and, as the generations go by, hopefully fewer people in that community hold onto these outdated divisive attitudes.

There were a multitude of other jobs that wouldn't be obvious from the outside but were vitally important in the organisation. For example, I discovered as soon as I got into the club that there were no routine heart checks being done for cardiomyopathy, something I had helped champion in my time with the PFA in England. The physio and the club doctor were tasked by me to get that programme set up as soon as possible. Sudden death syndrome due to undiagnosed heart problems had killed a number of players and other sportsmen who outwardly seemed supremely fit and healthy. There are no warning signs, so the checks were set in place to go ahead as soon as the medics could sort it out with the local hospitals. The cost implications were waived by me immediately – this was more important than money.

There was another problem with the laundry and strip maintenance. The women working in the tiny poky laundry rooms under the main stands were clearly overworked, and the conditions were poor, bordering on a health hazard. Everywhere I looked there were good people working hard but deserving better conditions and often better pay.*

The trouble was that there were large and small problems everywhere I turned. Sorting out confusion with the match-day programme sellers felt like a full-time job in itself for a while. Other problems on the Fir Park pitch amazed me, and could have led to serious punishments from the league.

I was practising some free-kicks alone at the stadium one afternoon, mostly to clear my head and have a break from the growing stress of the

---

* This is not a criticism of the previous regime, who had run a very tight ship in financially testing circumstances. I liked the former owners a great deal, and the Chapman family were still happy to have some involvement in the club, even if they no longer owned it. JB was always gracious and accommodating, so they were invited and expected to be in the boardroom post-match, in pride of place where they had always been. They were helpful without being overbearing. To some, it must have looked like this brash new money had swept the old guard away with no due respect or regard. But that couldn't have been further from the truth.

office work. I couldn't figure out why it was easier to score at that 'away' end than it was at the 'home' end. Something felt wrong, and it wasn't just the psychology of the gnarled old pro preferring one backdrop to another. Eventually I paced out the distance from the goal line to the 18-yard line, only to discover it was the 16-yard line! Utterly staggered and worried what the league would think if they found out, I got the lines re-marked that afternoon. Had that 16-yard line been there for ten years or just ten games? I had no idea. Nightmare averted, I started wondering if there were any more big and obvious errors that were hiding in plain sight.

A while later I was rewatching a goal that we scored from a free-kick from that precise area outside the box and, once again, I thought, 'Something feels wrong about that goal.' Surely it wasn't the old 16-yard-line problem again? I paced it out quietly on my own one afternoon, but the full 18 yards were correctly marked out. I tried a few free-kicks myself and, yes, it did seem easier to put the ball into the top right-hand corner. 'Surely not?' I thought. I got the trusty tape measure out and, yes, the crossbar on the right-hand side was about six inches higher than it was at the left-hand side!

Many pitches in Scotland are built on slopes, and Motherwell is one of them, so I thought that might be the problem. After further investigation I discovered it was down to rubble compacted into the hole where the goalposts were placed. Not a good enough excuse, I grant you, but gauging that the opposition were as likely to benefit as us, I got it fixed and decided against informing the authorities.

Other odd things kept cropping up. Not long before John Boyle had arrived, Motherwell had just imported what looked like a job lot of players from the Continent. I thought it was a highly questionable thing to do just before a new owner stepped in, but I was assured they had all been assiduously scouted and checked out. I decided to investigate. I wanted to see how that money was spent, how much each player had cost and, crucially, how much of the money had gone to agents and which ones.

When I tried to find out the exact details of the deals I was told that there had been a small fire and all the documents relating to the transactions had conveniently gone up in smoke. I never got to find out the details, but I decided there and then that I would be on top of these deals in future. Every penny would need to be accounted for if we were going to run a trustworthy club that we could be proud of.

Giving up on getting the details of those transfers, I turned my attention to the new players themselves. Some were not bad, but others weren't even close to the standard we needed. One specific player caught my eye in the first training session. It wasn't just that he was not nearly good enough for this level, but he also didn't move or particularly look like a professional footballer in terms of his co-ordination. This was something I had never come across before at this level. I had to find out more.

He had been bought not from a top league team, but a fourth division team in Germany, where he had spent a single season after being in the sixth tier! It started to make sense after our chat. He was a lovely lad – smart, friendly and very open – even if he looked like a front-row rugby forward. He was open enough to tell me, 'I vos actually zurprised Muzzervell bought me, because I vos more of a basketball player than a vootballer!' Oh dear, I would like to have got a hold of the details of that transfer, but apparently those had gone up in smoke with the others.

Three months in I realised unsurprisingly, that the work-rate was going to be too much for me. The commute to Motherwell from our new family home in the eastern Borders was a minimum of three hours round trip, usually more like four with the traffic, and I was doing it every day. I was planning to delegate as much as possible to the people I trusted, but the work-rate wasn't decreasing even though I had done some of the heavy lifting by getting the new management team in place, and we'd strengthened the playing squad a bit. Work just increased to fit any spare time, and I found that I was exhausted and wasn't seeing the family at all – the opposite of what I had envisaged when we moved back home to Scotland. I told myself that this dual job could only be for the short term. I had, at most, a year or two left as a player, but working flat out like this, I probably wouldn't last to the end of the season!

I tried to find more hours in the day, but it was hard. A typical day, if there was such a thing would be:

6.30am: Get up.

7.00am: Leave the Borders, usually before the children get up, to drive to Motherwell.

9.00am: Arrive at Fir Park. An hour in the office dealing with the early dilemmas of the day, then planning what happens after training.

10.00am: Get changed. Rush to training. Train with the team until midday.

12.30pm: Quick shower. Meet with the manager to see if he needs anything (being totally dedicated, he always does). Lunch at the club with the staff (to pick up anything from them that I need to know). Add those points to the 'to-do' list.

1.30pm–7pm: Club business (i.e., sort out travel problems, contracts, training-ground difficulties, policing issues, stewarding, press queries, SFA and SPL matters, etc., etc., etc.)

7pm–9pm: Drive home. Try to fit in some food. Think about the challenges of the day and what needs doing tomorrow. Plus work calls on the hands-free phone.

If I got home at 9pm that would be considered a good day; often it was much later if there was a lingering problem at the club. The help I'd promised Annabel in the home was already looking like a distant dream – my entire life was being swallowed up by the job. I never wanted to be a football manager mostly because I didn't want to give my entire life to football. But, somehow, that was happening in this role after only a few months. Nevertheless, I told myself again that the difficulty was playing and doing the other job at the same time, so it was a finite problem.

When JB realised I was being pushed to the physical limits and beyond, he looked at the situation logically: 'You have to find some more hours from somewhere. What about the travelling? Have you considered getting or hiring a helicopter to fly you to and from the Borders? That would save you nearly three hours a day. You could maybe even learn to fly one yourself.'

In terms of pure logic, it was unarguable. However, the cost, not to mention how it would look – as well as the small problem of the danger, and Annabel not being too impressed with me buzzing about the skies every day, hail, rain or snow – meant that neither I nor the idea were flying. I did smile at the thought of the players seeing me landing a helicopter at training already in my kit – that appealed to my sense of the surreal.

Doing all the work would have been impossible at that point without the help of a few important people. JB moved his friend Alasdair Barron in as club secretary, and his help was invaluable. He was one of those people who pretend to be businesslike and heartless in his job, but was far from that as soon as you made the effort to get to know him. He came from a totally non-footballing background, and I know that he found football folk a very odd bunch to start with. As the years progressed, however, there were times when I thought he had almost gone native – the game can do that to you. Without Alasdair's knowledge and diligence on the administrative side of the work I would have sunk without trace.

The other huge character was the 'football' secretary, Betty Pryde. She had been doing the same job at Celtic – that is, she was PA to the manager as well as doing a lot more than just that – but coming to Motherwell was like coming home for her. Billy Davies, working on advice from his agent Jock Brown, had asked me to employ her. A stalwart Motherwell fan, she was fiercely loyal to the manager without ever being less than totally helpful to me and anyone she felt was trying to do the right thing for her club. Every club needs a Betty, the mother hen, someone so dedicated they have to be forced to go home at night. Betty became a mother figure to everyone and was brilliantly efficient in her duties to boot.

The other great help around for me at that time was Dr Bill Harvey, my father-in-law. As far as I was concerned, he was one of the finest people ever to have made an appearance on this planet, and not just because he let me marry one of his daughters. He was a former GP from the 'old school', the type who was available and caring for his patients 24 hours a day, seven days a week. Bill had retired, and I was considering asking him if he wanted to do some of the driving, once or twice a week. He got there before me, saw how stretched I was, and offered before I got a chance to ask.

I worked in the back seat on those journeys, and suddenly found an extra three hours in the day without hiring a helicopter. Just as importantly, his wise counsel – only given when asked, and then shared with delicacy – was invaluable. He was as good at reading people as anyone you could meet.

Because of that help I even started to find the odd few hours to remember what our previous life had been all about. Annabel and I managed to get to see Pulp and then Massive Attack (with Liz from the Cocteau Twins singing with the Bristolians) even if it meant Annabel and I meeting up at the venue and not being able to travel together.

Finally, after some months, I managed to organise one day when I could stay at home with the family, with the prospect of trying to relax a little with them. I told everyone at the club, 'Only contact me tomorrow if there is a real emergency – it has been an incredibly tiring and stressful three months.' The phone call didn't take long in coming, early on that harsh cold December morning.

'Pat, it's Billy Davies here.' I could tell by the tone and his formality that this was not a normal call, something was seriously amiss, he sounded as if he was in shock. 'Pat, it's Andy. He's dead.'

'Andy?' I knew a few, but which one?

'Andy Thomson, Pat.'

It didn't compute. I racked my brains. Andy Thomson. Do I know any Andy Thomson's? Apart from, obviously, the young lad who is the life and soul of the dressing room for whom we had agreed to manufacture a job. But obviously it can't be him.

Billy seemed to understand my internal monologue. 'Yes, it's young Andy.'

It is impossible to describe the awfulness of the moment. Billy's next words made it even worse, if that was at all possible. 'It happened in his bedroom last night. They think it was a heart weakness. Someone has suggested sudden death syndrome. But it is only a guess.'

Something told me that is exactly what it would be. At my behest the club had been in the middle of finally getting the players tested, but, clearly, they hadn't got to Andy yet, who was still on the youth playing staff. Maybe the tests would have shown up an arrhythmia; maybe they wouldn't have. We will never know the answer to that; we had lost him the day after his nineteenth birthday.

As a club we did everything we possibly could for Andy's family, but as he was their only, beautiful sparkling son, I could not comprehend the level of pain his mum and dad were going through. Billy Davies, J B and I went to the Thomsons' home to offer every support we could. I struggled to comprehend the strength and bravery his mum was able to show, at least outwardly, at that time. I am not sure why, but it somehow seemed just that bit more impossible to take on board when the individual was such a huge and beloved character, clearly among the most popular if not *the* most popular person at the entire club.

Being strong myself and getting help for anyone who needed it at the club became critical. I made it known we were available whenever needed, and if anyone needed counselling help to cope, we would organise it. I called the league and told them – I didn't ask – that Motherwell FC would not be fulfilling their fixture against Dundee the next day. They fully understood, and Dundee were equally accommodating, but I wouldn't have cared if they weren't. We couldn't have considered playing a game of football at that point. From his apprentice teammates to the first team, all the way to the ownership, past and present, there was desolation, and that is not an exaggeration. I can recall some dark days in football, but this was easily as bad as any other time I can remember in the game. The fans were in shock too, and there was nothing we could do to make this any better. I still miss Andy to this day, as does every single person who ever met him.

13/
NO DANGER

Andy's funeral was a traumatic affair, but somehow the club managed to pull itself together afterwards, aided enormously by everyone helping each other. Footballers themselves are an incredibly resilient breed, they have no choice.

Chairman John Boyle was still being generous. There was a night out for the players and their wives before Christmas, as well as a players-only night out, all paid for out of JB's pocket. We were still quietly supporting those who were suffering, but by the New Year a positive feeling had returned among the first team. A run of wins against Dundee, Dundee United and then Hearts, twice, in the league and cup showed that things were going in a positive direction on the field. In my diary and in my 'Red and Blacks'* I noted the same phrases week after week: 'The boys were brilliant.' 'The team were superb.' 'The effort is incredible.'

---

* 'Red and Blacks' were books with lined paper that JB suggested I take notes in every day. They were important back then as a check on what people had said and when to ensure people couldn't change their stories, particularly in contract negotiations. Just as fortunately they have been invaluable in researching this book during what was a chaotic time, with days, weeks and months of mayhem blurring into each other.

I also noted that JB had gone from not really wanting to know about football, to making a few suggestions about the team: 'Shouldn't we play Ged a bit further forward this week?' Or, 'Maybe you should tell the manager that he is being too defensive away from home.'

I really didn't know if he'd been to any, or many professional games before he'd bought Motherwell, so from no knowledge of the game to wanting some influence on the tactics in less than six months was quite a thing!

'John, you don't hire a specialist in any walk of life and then start telling him how to do his job. You let him get on with it. That's what we do with the manager,' was my constant refrain. I understood that successful businessmen who have 'invested' in football sometimes feel they should have some input, but then every single person in the stadium thinks they can do better than the manager. Admittedly, John had more skin in this game than most. He was paying for all this, so why shouldn't he have a little shot with his 'toy' now and again? That way lies madness and real danger, as plenty of clubs have discovered – as have plenty of managers. Well, that meddling wasn't going to happen here with me around – not from JB, and not from me either! It showed, however, that JB had a true interest and passion for the business already. This was no sideshow or short-term, faddish hobby on his part – he was getting much more engaged with what happened on the pitch, which was a good thing in so many ways.

Every game and every week in the press was a rollercoaster ride. A couple of defeats and it felt like the end of the world, or the end of the John Boyle experiment at least. Two wins and it was a brave new world where anything was possible. What we needed around then was a relatively quiet time for a month or two, time to concentrate solely on the football. As they say in Scotland, 'Aye, right!'

First, I had to deal with a dilemma that was arising regarding John Spencer. The loan period from Everton was running out and he was due to move back down to Merseyside. This was always the plan. I had no problem with him going back; he had given us the lift we needed at a very difficult time, both on and off the field. The fans, however, decided it might be a good idea for us to buy him. The media were suggesting that if Motherwell were to take the 'next step' they would have to secure Spenny on a full-time contract. Understandably, the manager Billy Davies was keen for us to keep a quality player, and Spenny was exerting some pressure by espousing his love of the club too. JB was hearing the mood music and said to me, 'Why don't we push the boat out this one time and get him? It would send a real message to the fans.'

I appeared to be on my own on this one. This was an important moment, and I had to make my position emphatically clear at a meeting with JB in the club's boardroom, where I stood my ground: 'Are you completely out of your mind? What about the messages it sends to everyone else? Spenny is great, but financially he is way out of our league. His wages are three times more than anyone else and ten times more than some of the others. Do you understand the mayhem that will cause in the dressing room when they find that out? Which they will! How am I supposed to have any sensible negotiations with players and their agents when they think that is the sort of market we work in?'

During the diatribe JB was trying to get a word in edgeways, but I wasn't for stopping: it was a crucial to me that he understood the whole picture. When I was just a little more animated, JB compensated by being much calmer: 'But think about it, Pat, it's a one-off.'

'No, listen, John. You've given me a budget for wages, and I can't get him without destroying it completely – and that's before you consider the transfer fee, the signing-on fees and all the other sundries that we'll be expected to pay for. It is absolutely not on.'

JB tried again with a pacifying air and an arm on my shoulder. 'He's a great lad, Pat. He has such energy, he is such a big positive character. The fans love him, so do the press. He is, I believe, a very good player.'

'Look, John, I like Spenny a lot and, yes, I agree he is still a top player and a top bloke too – but this is exactly the sort of reckless behaviour that I am trying to save you and this club from. The sad truth is that he is out of our league, literally and metaphorically. I can't allow this to happen, even though I would love to have him here. There is no point in having me in this job if you don't listen to my advice on this.'

I was there to help make the team as good as possible, but it had to be with at least some financial sense. It was a prime moment to give JB some solid advice in this alien world he had parachuted himself into. Not overspending was front and centre of my thinking; this business eats up fortunes because it plays tricks with the ego and plays on your heart strings like no other.

Unfortunately, John had an answer that just about stumped me: 'What if I buy him for you and it has nothing to do with the budget I'm giving you?'

As ever, generous to a fault, but was it welcome? It didn't help that at this precise moment the manager Billy Davies joined us in the boardroom and my position suddenly became significantly trickier. I tried to carry on, but with a little less vim and vigour, if I am honest, now that the manager was listening intently and staring at me incredulously.

'First of all, I don't see how that works, legally. But are you saying I can get John Spencer, a top-class Scottish international striker, on board with no extra cost to my budget at Motherwell?'

At this point Billy was now beaming and delighted, knowing that he was getting a fine player, who happened to be his brother-in-law, for the sum total of diddly squat! Billy rightly had to consider the short-term needs for his team, but I was more concerned about the longer-term ramifications. Neither outlook was right nor wrong; it was just two different perspectives from people with different strategic needs.

For once, it was me who was blustering now: 'Clearly, it is impossible to turn down if we're getting him for free, but I am still not comfortable with it. It still leaves the problem of the green-eyed monster lurking in the dressing room. I am guessing you will just add a huge extra lump sum to your initial investment to pay for this deal?'

I had weakened to the point of capitulation, realising it was an argument I wasn't likely to win against both of them. If the fans knew I was scuppering this 'investment', they wouldn't have been delighted at that moment either – in fact, they would have been furious with me. Even so, I wasn't happy about the direction and grumbled on: 'Personally, I think you are mad, but it's your money, I guess. Just so you know, I won't be doing that contract if it isn't in my budget. I have to keeps my costs separate, but I'll be happy to look over it briefly before it is ratified. I will also have to get down to Everton to see if I can get him for a reasonable transfer fee. There is also the problem of taking two days off all my other work, getting the train down to Liverpool and back with all that palaver.'

John thought for a moment more: 'Why don't you fly?'

'There aren't any flights from Glasgow to Liverpool.'

'Just a hire a private plane, then.'

That was classic JB, his international business brain operating in a league and at a club that didn't and couldn't function at that level. I generally didn't think about hiring planes – or helicopters – but the next morning myself, Billy Davies and Willie McLean were flying south in a tiny four-seater. The cost wasn't nearly as onerous as I thought it would be – then again, it wasn't a private jet. It was like a taxi on wings with propellers not Rolls-Royce engines, and, for some reason beyond my comprehension, no heating either. It was bloody freezing at 20,000 feet.

It was an odd meeting. The last time I had talked to these people at Everton I was merely a player leaving the club – I didn't expect to be chief negotiator flying in to buy one of their players just six years later. I eventually talked them down from around £500,000 to £350,000, which was precisely £350K more than I felt we could or should be spending.

I was true to my word. For the first time since I had arrived, I took no part in sorting out this contract when it was agreed with Spencer's agent back in Scotland, after another bitter flight home. I did have a quick glance over the figures, however, just before it was signed, then immediately collared JB. Apparently at the end of the more detailed contract negotiations Spenny and his people had asked for a car. At Motherwell, for the manager or CEO, that would mean the loan of a second-hand Mercedes C class, worth £15,000–20,000. JB had waived through this request blithely as Spenny's team walked out the door of his office. I could see another possible problem here – on top of the huge weekly wage (which, as I correctly predicted, soon got out and infuriated the rest of the team) and said, 'John, Spenny didn't say what type of car he wanted. He could turn up with anything! I don't want to be cynical, but you have left yourself wide open there.'

As I had promised to look over the agreement at the end to check for errors, I quickly had that part of the contract reworded to say that, 'If the player leaves the club before the end of his stated contract, then the car would return to the ownership of the club as soon as the player departs.'

A couple of days later Spenny swung into the car park driving a brand-new black Jaguar XJS with white leather seats that came in at a cool £68,000. We could have had three young players contracted for a year with that figure alone.

The core of the new team had now been put in place by Billy. Andy Goram was a world-class goalkeeper at his peak with Rangers, and he hadn't lost much if any of his ability by the time he arrived at Fir Park, even if he did come with some personal baggage. Every day in training he would make at least one impossible save. He was a legend in Scotland, but his scruffy appearance and slightly chunky shape made him look anything but the perfect specimen for a world-class keeper. He was only ever known as 'the Goalie', and you don't get a moniker like that from an entire country unless you are extra special.

In front of him we had Shaun Teale, who had been at Aston Villa in the Premier League in England as well as with me at Tranmere, with Ged Brannan and Finnish international Simo Valakari in central midfield, then Spenny and Owen Coyle or Lee McCulloch in attack. Stephen McMillan at left-back already looked English Premier League standard to me, so I was confident we had made a huge leap forward in a very short time.

I can't say I was relaxed, because you never are in football, and there was still a multitude of vexations every day, but at least I could leave organising the football itself to Billy Davies and his team.

It seemed peculiar from the outside that I was his boss, except when I had my kit on, then suddenly he was my boss and could drop me whenever he liked. He did drop me most of the time, using me as a substitute 13 times that season, giving me a meagre 11 starts. That didn't exactly sound like the actions of a guy who was being worked from behind by me.

I could sack him, of course, at any time if I wanted a game, but I had chosen him and thoroughly admired his work ethic, even if, as time went by, he became evermore demanding with his requirements. This isn't always a negative trait in a football manager; I suspect Sir Alex Ferguson was very demanding with his bosses throughout his career. I had to trust Billy's judgement in team matters, so the outcome was that I was the only player in the entire club who didn't have the right to go and knock on his door when he wasn't in the team. I never mentioned being sidelined once, just accepted my position, even though deep down I thought I could have added more on field if I'd been given more opportunities.

I was, however, getting to that age when, even if I played just averagely for 45 minutes, I always asked myself the same question: 'Am I too old now?' I generally believed that average performances were more to do with me not getting enough game time and thus match fitness was sometimes an issue, but, yes, obviously the other work was wearing me down as well and my play wasn't regularly at the high standards I set myself, without being particularly bad.

From out of the blue – the royal blue, as it turned out – we had an unexpected series of front- and back-page newspaper splashes involving Andy Goram. A picture surfaced of Andy, from many years before when he was at Rangers, at a supporters' event in Northern Ireland. He was standing alongside some locals, and beside him was a sizeable UVF* banner. Odd that it should only appear now, long after he had left Rangers and also just in time for the build-up to our upcoming game against – who else? – Celtic, whose fans wouldn't hugely appreciate the Loyalist overtones. It was the biggest

---

* The unionist paramilitary organisation, the Ulster Volunteer Force.

story in Scotland at the time, and we found ourselves in the middle of it. It became clear very soon that this was not going to be a one-day wonder.

'The Goalie' claimed no knowledge of what the banner beside him had on it, or memory of the photo – one of thousands that had been taken of him in the intervening seven years. 'Wee man, have you looked behind you in every photo taken of you over the years?' was his semi-reasonable sounding comment to me.

That cut no ice whatsoever with those demanding he be sacked immediately. It was delicate, complicated and it couldn't be ducked by me.

But I had no intention of sacking him or even disciplining him. Maybe Rangers, the club he was at back then and representing in the photo, might say something, though I doubted it. In any case, it was just as likely that a Celtic player or former player would be pictured in next week's paper in front of an IRA flag, surreptitiously positioned behind him without his knowledge! It could even have been me! I had recently been speaking at the Tommy Burns Supper, a rather cool Celtic supporters' club event in Edinburgh University, and although unlikely from the fabulous group of fans I was with that night, it only takes one smart arse, or indeed someone with chicanery on their mind, to put something up in the background as I smile for the cameras.

At this point it felt like the press were having a concerted and specific go at our club and all of us running it, as there had been a series of negative articles that felt designed to undermine the work we were trying to do. I quickly dumped those thoughts – it is just how the print media works; it wasn't personal, it was just our turn, and they would have done the same thing to anyone else. But the truth is that it feels damned personal when you're dealing with it in the moment. Understandably, the Goalie went to ground, while some members of the press and the odd paparazzo camped outside the club. A few even made it all the way to the Borders and my home, turning up outside the front door! On each occasion I did the same thing, I invited them in for a cup of tea instead of letting them stand outside stupidly in the cold. What was the point of that? I had nothing to hide from or be ashamed of, and they were just doing their job.

However open or sensibly we behaved, though, it wasn't going to stop the shit storm in the papers, on the TV, on the radio and from a decent number of irate Celtic fans. The phone-ins were full of it, apparently (I wasn't listening to them), but thankfully social media didn't exist back then, which was a small blessing! Talking of blessings, maybe the fact that JB and I were of Catholic origin helped just a little; we couldn't be described as bigots favouring our own antecedents. Then again, we were seen as 'turncoats' by some on the green side for not sacking our protestant keeper – sacrilege! So, even our backgrounds weren't a huge bonus, really.

When we eventually tracked the Goalie down, JB, Billy Davies and I tried to explain the situation to him. It was a tense meeting, but I tried to be supportive and sensible: 'It feels terrible to be in the middle of this just now, Andy, we get it. But it will blow over eventually, it always does. We'll stand by you and take as much of the pressure as we can on your behalf. We'll face the press, so you don't have to, if that is what you want. You just need to ride it out.'

Andy's reply changed the atmosphere again, and not for the better: 'That's all very well, but I've just been told there's been a paramilitary threat made by the IRA to take me out during the Celtic game at the weekend, and I don't mean for a pint of Guinness. You can share some of the pressure, but you won't be standing stationary in the goal, ten yards in front of the Celtic fans, knowing any one of them could have you in the crosshairs of his high-powered rifle.'

He had a point. 'Well, I'll be on the pitch,' I said, 'and Billy will be a sitting target in the dugout too.'

'Yeah, but you weren't pictured in front of the flag with the red hand on it,' the Goalie shot back.

Again, a very salient point. Andy had annoyed Celtic fans in the past, and many felt they had good reason to be even angrier with him now. Had John Boyle and I disciplined Andy it would have been seen as a Catholic conspiracy by the other side, as John and I were obviously considered 'Tims', though neither of us had been religious in that way for decades.

Andy refused to play in the upcoming game, even though the three of us tried hard to convince him otherwise. The threat was 'probably' not from the Provisionals but rather some nobody causing trouble – but that 'probably' hung heavily in the air. Also, if he didn't play in this one, then how was he ever going to play in another game against Celtic? We played them at least four times a season and we were always in dire need of our best keeper on his best form on these occasions.

But the Goalie was adamant, so I accepted his position and came up with the wording for the next press conference: 'The four of us – Andy, John Boyle, myself and Billy Davies – have met and, after much discussion, have decided in the end that Andy will indeed miss the next game due to the current furore in the media over a historic picture that has surfaced.'

The idea was to relieve some of the pressure that was building principally on Andy alone, as he was extremely distressed by it all, not to say a little frightened. It was a truthful statement, if not the entire story – Andy, of course, was the only one who thought he shouldn't play against Celtic. The press spin was given with a willingness to be compassionate for a guy not dealing well with the pressure of an entire country on his case – as well as another one over the water, and the odd death threat too.

JB and I stood shoulder to shoulder at the press conference. As it finished, with Andy obviously absent as it would have become a circus with him there – and he wasn't particularly enamoured with the Scottish media at that moment anyway – I watched most of the journos go into their 'huddle'. It was as if they had to agree what their party line would be, and I understood their desire to do that. If most went in one direction, and another went for a softer line, then the outsider might get dragged over the coals by his editor for not going for the jugular while the others did. Having never been invited into any of those huddles back then, I am only surmising this is what was happening, but it felt from the outside like they were getting their combined stories and angles straight.

The next day's news ran with the story that it was specifically Billy Davies who would not let Andy Goram play! Exactly the opposite of how

Billy felt, and he was understandably unimpressed that my idea of how to play it with the press had resulted in him now being thrown under the bus. He had an exceptional way of showing his displeasure. He never ranted and raved at me; if really upset, as he was this time, he would sit silently behind his desk in his office and wait for me to speak. He got the apology he deserved, and I added, 'Billy, I'll fix this. There is no way you should be taking the hit here.'

'Good,' was his only reply, and I was determined to keep my word.

My problem was that now the story was blazing away and I knew that any fuel would just keep it going. It was so big, however, and Billy had been so wronged, that another 'presser' was needed at the club. Again, I personally and patiently explained to the assembled throng, 'It wasn't Billy but a collegiate decision after JB, Billy, Andy and I had spoken together. It definitely wasn't the case that Billy had not allowed Andy to play, so it was unfair and indeed untrue for you to have run the story in that way. Billy does not deserve this.'

At the end of the conference I asked if I could speak to them as a group entirely off the record, not in a sly way but just to fully inform them of what had been said and why. They were intelligent people and I wanted them to understand the full story – that there were no untruths, just not the entire story – and there were good and compassionate reasons for me doing that.

I underlined the decision was indeed taken after a discussion between all four of us: 'The thing is, it wasn't Billy who decided the Goalie wouldn't play, but solely Andy himself. This wasn't divulged because Andy is in a very dark place and I was just trying to help the guy a bit. Surely that is only being kind considering the huge pressure he is under and the death threats he has received?' I trusted the journalists would appreciate the humanity of the situation.

Quite a number led the next day with the line, 'Nevin admits to being a liar!' No I didn't! I just didn't give all the facts, and for good reason. I had rarely if ever talked 'off the record' before that, but I certainly haven't done so since. When the story is big enough, there is no such thing as 'off the record'. I know this now. My getting the stick did take a little of the pressure off the Goalie, so there was some upside to it.

This probably led to some people having a jaundiced opinion of me, and it was almost funny to witness how diametrically opposite I was being portrayed by parts of the Scottish media compared to the English media.

The Goalie didn't play, and we lost 7–1 after going down to ten men early when John Spencer was sent off. Following the game, the story slowly fell away in the weeks and months that followed, and Andy came back – but the whole episode left a big impression on me. Did I take it personally? Not at all, I just happened to be in the way again when a major story broke. There is the odd journo in Scotland who I still see at games, who isn't able to speak to me or look me in the eye, and I thought I was the one who suffered the injustice! I continued then and now to be open and friendly with everyone, nonetheless – the other road of bitterness, rancour and lifelong grudges is not a healthy one.

The manager, though, found it harder to be so forgiving, as I suppose many people would, and I didn't blame him. He was quickly portrayed as being paranoid, and it stuck whether it was true or not. I explained to him before every Friday press conference that it was just a game with the media. They, particularly the red tops, have to eke out a story while the manager tries to get his own narrative across, just as a politician would. Initially Billy would talk for an hour, giving his time freely and openly, but there would sometimes be one line, either taken out of context or without the caveats added, that would be the story the next day. He would understandably complain to me bitterly at the unfairness of it: 'They know that it's not what I meant; they heard all the rest of it. Why should I ever trust them when they are always twisting the truth or not telling the whole story? Why have they got it in for me?'

I'd played for nearly two decades and been PFA chairman. I understood the deal. 'It is not personal, Billy, even though it feels like it; it's just the gig. If you take it personally and show you are wounded, they'll see that as a weakness and pick at that sore for even more stories. It's the nature of the beast. You must rise above it.'

He struggled to accept it. And when feeling wronged or not backed he couldn't hide his anger; it was already becoming more ingrained on his face. 'But they write things that I never said.' Billy was fastidious at keeping notes on the statements that were not only wilfully misinterpreted but, now and again, from his point of view, blatantly made up.

Driving home after one of these conversations, I had an idea. I often sat in on those weekly press conferences but only took part in the most extreme circumstances. I never got involved with discussions on playing matters – that was Billy's area – so I sat at the side, not on the podium with the manager. At the next press conference I walked in and pointedly put down a tape recorder in front of the manager and clicked it on, then sat away from the podium at the side, well out of the way. I did this for every subsequent 'presser', and it seemed to have at least some effect on the quotes being attributed to Billy. The important secret to own up to here is that over the coming seasons I never once put an actual tape in that recorder – neither the press nor Billy ever knew that.

The biggest story I didn't want to read about was relegation. That was avoided with four games to go in an away win against my old club Kilmarnock. We finished in mid-table with 13 points to spare, and the lack of jeopardy at the end was a huge relief. I could finally breathe easily for the first time in months. It was without doubt the most relieved I have ever been in my entire time involved in football. The feelings in elite sport are usually about the happiness of winning, and savouring the glory or the sadness in defeat then coping with failure. I hadn't realised up until that point just how moving an emotion relief could be.

The rest of the job wasn't getting any easier, but it was interesting, and it was educational. Until the last few weeks of the season I hadn't had time to consider what I felt about this 'new' job because it had been so full on from day one. Maybe always making sure I appeared calm and in control added to the stress, but I thought it was important to give out those vibes, especially as I was so young for the role. Any obvious crack or angry outburst would have been construed as a weakness or an inability to cope.

Even though the work wasn't much fun, I didn't consider leaving at this point, mostly because this was only the beginning of what we were building. We had done little more than lay the foundations, but it had been a backbreaking slog. The real work JB wanted to do, and the results of our toil, would only become visible in the next season and beyond – if we got things right. But it really felt like it was worth hanging on in there to see the results.

What I did realise was that I hadn't found a moment to think about myself, and precious few to think about my family, even if I did make sure I got home every night – which was always one small victory I enjoyed. But the life balance of working hard to provide for your family and being there for them when you should be was skewed way too far to one side; the wrong side, as far as I was concerned. I am not the only person who's promised to change their work–life balance and not managed it, but at that point I was failing miserably in my attempts.

Failing to be a good and present husband and father while doing something you enjoy is one thing; failing to be with your family while doing a job you don't even enjoy much seems mad – from the outside, at least – but we get dragged into it, by circumstances, by others and by ourselves.

The 1998–99 season had been, considering the delights of simply being a player in the previous campaign with Kilmarnock, a shock to the system. It had been exhausting and stressful from the day I arrived at Fir Park. Some players feel that being a footballer can be a stressful occupation; well, try being a CEO on top of that. I know which job is the more stressful of the two, and it isn't kicking a ball around! There were good days, but the problem with being 'chief executive' at a small- to medium-sized company is that when things go well, others enjoy the plaudits while you sit in the background enjoying their success.

My role was to be where the buck stopped when things went wrong – that is when you take responsibility, as indeed you should. Every problem from the personal to the business side, and every difficulty – whether it came from the cleaners or the manager – landed on my desk. That is why

I kept on playing, because training and playing was the fun part of it all, while the rest was often tortuous. Still, surely it would get easier in the second season now that I knew the job and had done some of the heavy lifting already.

Surely it would.

14/
YOU NEVER CAN TELL

One of the things that almost always leads to confrontation at football clubs is when the two opposing cultures are forced to work together. The football department hates being told what to do by the business side, the people who usually own and pay for everything at the club. Wealthy businessmen who have been successful in their own sphere often find it infuriating to be told to 'butt out' when they try to get involved in the football department. Like most people, including nearly all fans, the owners think they know as much and sometimes more than the people who have been working inside the game, on the field, for a lifetime.

Keeping a buffer between the manager and the chairman John Boyle became a constant bane of my life from the start of the second season. In the early days I would explain to the owner that just before and after games, the dressing room was not his realm. As a player I knew how it felt like an intrusion – unless the owner was specifically giving us something, such as a bonus or the promise of a few days in the sun.

If the owner waltzed in and tried to speak on match days, the manager would also feel his position being undermined, whatever was said and however eloquent or well-intentioned it was. Even with the best will in the world, and with the best intentions, it is almost invariably a bad move at some level for the owner or chairman to hang out too often in that sacrosanct space. I remember explaining this to the chairman, and him replying, 'I can go wherever I like; I own the club, after all. And anyway, I am just trying to help.' Which indeed he invariably was, but sadly it doesn't work, especially in the long term.

After matches I would go up to the directors' boardroom at Fir Park, ostensibly for a debrief but often just for a chat with JB and the others milling around in there. Only a few months into the first season John took me to one side of the room and made a tentative suggestion: 'I was thinking . . . I might tell the manager which players I think should be playing a bit more. You know . . . just in passing, in a relaxed way, during a chat. Maybe both of us should do it? We could explain some of our tactical thoughts to him while we are at it. The other people in the boardroom all seem to have ideas that might be worth sharing too. What do you think?'

Some of the others in the room seemed to know what the conversation was about – they had been talking – so I explained in a voice that carried a little further across the room than was absolutely necessary, 'You can if you like, but he and most managers are more likely to do precisely the opposite to what you want, just to make the point that you are interfering in their work, and they aren't going to accept it.'

As a novice in the sport it was perhaps a bit presumptuous on JB's part to want to give advice. It was, however, unfailingly done with an honest desire to help. Giving a manager all the information and as many ideas as possible from as many sources, and then letting him ultimately decide the direction, sounds reasonable in theory. In practice, it rarely if ever works with football folk.

Another difficulty was a little more delicate. JB didn't exactly fit in perfectly with the rugged football types. Behind his back there were those who made the point that he was more than a little effete for the football world. Most, however, were nowhere near that subtle or polite. I had got some of that stuff aimed at me during my career and it was water off a duck's back; I couldn't care less what bigoted and ignorant people said.

I tried to blank the innuendo aimed at John – who was married with four kids, by the way – and even shield him from it. But I could see that what they would describe as his campness was the funniest thing for them in the world of football. The biggest radio show in the country, *Off the Ball* on BBC Scotland, was using a Frankie Howerd voice to send him up mercilessly every week. It was undoubtedly done with some affection but, as with all good comedy, it was biting as well as very funny because of the sliver of reality it portrayed. On one occasion JB and I were invited onto the programme itself by the presenters – super smart Stuart Cosgrove, an old acquaintance from the music papers days in London, alongside big Motherwell fan, the sharp-witted writer and comedian, Tam Cowan. Obviously JB hadn't been a regular listener because he seemed quite shocked at them playing yet another 'titter ye not' skit when the show started that afternoon.

Sometimes it is hard when you are in the public eye to get a grip on how you are perceived by everyone else. I honestly thought it was a good idea to keep John away from the weekly club press conferences in those early days, as a single word or gesture out of place in the football fraternity would have some of the players and the journos sniggering at the back like naughty schoolboys. Some of JB's phrases like, 'One day you're a peacock, the next you are a feather duster,' were repeated endlessly for comic effect. To be fair, you wouldn't hear Sam Allardyce or Sean Dyche using that sort of analogy, so it was peculiar in that culture at that time.

So, keeping JB from speaking at the pressers, more than once I felt like John Cleese in Monty Python's *Life of Brian*, suggesting to Michael Palin's Pontius Pilate, 'You're not thinking about giving the speech a miss this year, sir?' before being ignored as he headed out to 'Welease Woger!' It was harsh on John. I felt very protective of him in this world, even though I had warned him of the pitfalls from the start.

JB and his wife took Billy, myself and our wives and kids to Gleneagles for a social weekend, which wasn't cheap. It was an artless kindness, which I thought was a fine effort to bring the three of us and our families together.

During the trip to Gleneagles our son Simon – whose autism was still a constant challenge, confusion and, to be brutally honest, unremitting strain for us at this point – had a small epiphany that had a huge effect on his later life. The people working at the stunning hotel wanted to take eight-year-old Simon and the other kids to learn to drive in their mini-Land Rovers. We were unsure, to say the least, and indeed frightened, but were talked round, so we nervously let him go while alerting the staff about his autism. On his return we were informed that he was the best driver of all the kids there, a total natural. It was an early sign that Simon might one day be capable of some independence; Annabel and I even thought at that moment, 'This might just be a skill he could utilise in later life.'

At the end of that first season John outdid himself in the generosity stakes. He suggested we should go to a non-Motherwell match together, so I could talk him through some of the subtleties of the game. Up until then I had been playing, or had been on the bench every week, so the chance to talk him through things hadn't happened thus far. It was a good idea, but there was a minor problem: 'John, it's the end of the season, there are no matches to go to.'

'But isn't there a game in a couple of days over in Spain?' he ventured.

I laughed internally at his naïvety: 'Ah yes, that would be the Champions League final between Manchester United and Bayern Munich at the Nou Camp in Barcelona. To be honest, John, you might just find that tickets are a little bit hard to come by at this late stage.'

He reached into his pocket and produced four tickets for the third row from the front, right on the halfway line. Taken slightly aback, I thought I should underline the other possible problems: 'Well, you might find it hard to get a hotel room, the city will be rammed.'

He was unshaken: 'I have an "interest" in the hotel adjacent to the stadium.'

His naïvety was quickly turning into my naïvety. 'Actually, the real problem, John, is that there is no way you will get a flight at this late stage.'

'We'll take the Lear.'

There is officially no comeback from someone throwing out the 'Lear jet' line. 'Fair enough, let's go.'

The trip turned out to be an enlightening glimpse for me into football as viewed through the eyes of those not steeped in the game. The two of us flew down to Manchester to pick up a couple of JB's acquaintances en route, who professed to be United fans. The first statement when they got on board made me question the depth of their knowledge: 'That Roy Keane is hopeless.' It went steadily downhill from there, as their trenchant and alcohol-induced opinions were given with great conviction but absolutely no thought for any small input I might have in the discussion as a current player who had not only watched 'the hopeless Keane' but had actually played against him. Flying over a beach en route to Barcelona, one of the new passengers looking out of the window and spotting a beautiful coastline, suggested, 'That looks like a great beach. Why don't we buy it?'

Lear jets are small. On the plus side you don't have to go through the usual airport hassles with everyone else to get on – you get your own plush departure areas – but, for the most part, you can't fully stand up straight once inside the plane.

On board the four of us coped well with that minor irritation. We were the only passengers lounging in the large, sumptuous leather chairs, but we were frequently joined by the co-pilot, who was serving fabulous food and plenty of drinks – well lots of nicely iced champagne anyway; the beers were not needed. Flying around the planet by Lear jet is not the best way of keeping your feet on the ground, metaphorically or literally. Fortunately, I was acutely aware that I was a flying visitor in the rarefied atmosphere of this strange world.

We were sat in just about the best seats in the stadium, right on the centre-line, yards from the turf. I didn't dare ask how much the tickets had cost. The tension grew from the first minute as one of the most memorable games in Champions League history developed right in front of us among a passionate and absorbed crowd. JB watched intently as the Germans took the lead from a Mario Basler free-kick awarded by the world-renowned referee, Pierluigi Collina, his famous bald head being roundly abused by all the United fans beside us. United came back at Bayern but couldn't score despite the best efforts of David Beckham, Ryan Giggs, Teddy Sheringham and a host of other stars in red.

With ten minutes to go Manchester United were still a goal down and I was explaining to JB, as best I could, how Stefan Effenberg and Lothar Matthäus were stifling Sir Alex Ferguson's men with their intelligent positioning when our two 'United supporters' in tow suddenly stood up and announced, 'We have seen enough, this is rubbish. They are never going to win this. Let's go now and get to the bar first.'

I picked my jaw up off the floor as they and JB stood up to leave. I grabbed John and couldn't stop myself, the old earnest east end of Glasgow righteousness kicking in as well as a little embarrassment in the wider company. 'John,' I hissed. 'You can leave now if you like, but here are a few reasons why you shouldn't. First, it is offensive to every Manchester United, or indeed any, football fan who would give their right hands to be sitting here now. You have hot- and cold-running champagne in a private jet waiting for you; you'll get your drink in good time. This is history you're watching here. It doesn't matter who wins, you stay to the end to take in the atmosphere and watch the aftermath, including the trophy lift that is the culmination of European football for the entire season. There is also the not insignificant point that Alex Ferguson's Manchester United have been known to score the odd late goal! Finally, if you walk out now, I will not come back to work for you at Motherwell next season because in my eyes you will be the biggest football philistine that has ever owned a professional club!!'

I'm not sure if JB knew what had hit him. He'd seen me exasperated before, but never like this! To his credit, John sat back down as the other two made their way out. As the clock hit 90 minutes it was still 1–0 to Bayern and JB made to get up again just as Peter Schmeichel was edging upfield, in case United won a late corner-kick. 'Absolutely not, stay there!' I hissed again. 'The guy over there holding the board is suggesting there are three extra minutes of injury time, in case you hadn't noticed!'

Two minutes and twenty seconds later Teddy Sheringham and Ole Gunnar Solksjaer had both scored and United were champions. In those incredible moments I believe JB finally understood the true unparalleled drama and elation that football can provide. I reckon he fell fully in love with the game then and there. At the time I felt delighted that he'd seen the light at last, and that I'd been a part of that.

But some years later I thought, 'Maybe I should have let him leave early that day. It might have saved him a great deal of money and just as much heartache chasing those football dreams that would be impossible to catch . . .'

15/
MOVIN' ON UP

We had survived the first season, with more than our fair share of trials and tribulations. Now it was time to finally settle things down to truly begin to see the Motherwell project through at a more considered pace – which would hopefully be less stressful for everyone involved. We had a strong squad, the manager was committed, and the structure of the club was already looking a great deal better from my perspective. This was the season to start looking up instead of down, as far as the league was concerned.

The budget for the football side of the business was exactly where it was supposed to be – except for the additional John Spencer costs – and I could see a clear path ahead.

From my own point of view I still felt fit enough to play a part in the side if the manager needed me – but, at almost 36, I knew this would almost certainly be my last season as a player. That decision would have to wait. I had been playing professionally for 18 unexpected and accidental years already; this extra season was nothing more than a bonus, though I would give it my best shot.

It hadn't got beyond August before I realised that the idea of this being a quieter time was very unlikely – even though I had delegated work to specialists in their own departments, and the initial major investments had been made. On field things started well: a diving header from the chief executive, set up by Lee McCulloch, got a point at Easter Road against Hibs – it felt good to still be of some use on the pitch!

That match was preceded by an Under-21s game the manager asked me to play in earlier that week. It was at Cleland, our training ground, and a young Newcastle United team had travelled up from over the border. I was sitting in the sparse drab dressing room with a crowd of our callow kids when the door crashed open. In stomped the imposing figure of none other than Stuart Pearce, by now a legendary figure in the game, clearly playing for the same reason as me, to take care of the youngsters and to keep his own fitness ticking over.

Psycho had boldly strutted in there purely to spook our young lads. He had his customary dark soulless eyes on, doing their usual impression of a 'hangry' shark just before lunchtime. Without bothering to look around he had the gall to walk directly into the middle of our dressing room, fully kitted out in his strip, thigh muscles bulging below the unnecessarily tight turned-up shorts. He was clearly going to be playing. The odd gasp came from the weedier kids before the infamous 'Psycho' opened 'our' large metal box that contained an assortment of studs. He gave it a hefty hoof with that famous left foot so that a load of those studs splashed out. He looked down and picked up four of the largest metal ones he could find, then turned to strut out again. The desired effect of striking fear into the cowering kids was duly accomplished. Or so he thought.

As he was shutting the door, he heard a lone Glaswegian voice pipe up from among these kids. 'What a complete dickhead. Who the fuck was that fat old arsehole?' Psycho was obviously fuming, but the door was closing and he couldn't exactly turn round and walk back in again. Cue all the kids falling about laughing at him . . . not the reaction he was expecting. The lone voice that had piped up was, of course, mine.

As the youngsters lined up to go out onto the field to start the game, there was Psycho already standing there in his centre-back position eyeing them up, trying to figure out who was the offending arrogant little Jock, the one who would clearly be getting the full treatment during the game. He finally spotted me walking into centre midfield with a huge grin on my face. He met it with his own huge smile, realising what had happened. In his thick London accent he called over, 'Oi, Nevin, you little shit, where you playin' today?'

'Centre mid.'

'Well, make sure you come up front and play against me at some point. You'll get the usual facking reception.'

A few short years earlier this would have been considered close to a death warrant, now it was two veteran players enjoying a laugh. I think it might have been the first time we had actually spoken to each other on a football field. I knew all along we would get on eventually, and we did. Afterwards we had a chat about our favourite punky gigs – him telling me again that The Stranglers were still great – and nearly 20 years of extreme competition between us was brought to a pleasant smiling close. The question was: could I do that with the rest of my football career?

The sunny summertime at the start of a season always holds out such hope and expectation. In 1999 this lasted less than a month for me, and it was the beginning of a series of lurching highs and lows that I struggled to make sense of. One morning I was joining in a training session with the lads when two of the senior players made it clear they were not happy with my presence. Shaun Teale and Tony Thomas had both been my teammates at Tranmere, but neither was happy with something that was happening off the field – the usual contract niggles. In the warm-up they started commenting that they thought there was a spy in the camp, pointedly looking at me. Up until that precise moment I was able to keep the executive role and the playing role totally separate, but even though they were very clearly in the wrong in what they were saying – and to his eternal credit Tealey apologised personally just a few days later, without me asking him to – I knew something had changed.

Five minutes later I thought it best to pull up with a 'calf strain'. I stopped, went back to my car and then straight back to the club. I had to decide whether to retire on the spot, or to stick it out, as promised, until the end of the season. If I wasn't trusted in that environment, then I couldn't consider staying in it. I had just about decided to hang up my boots when a few of the lads, led by Ged Brannan and John Spencer, came to say they thought both Shaun and Tony were out of order. I decided to stay on after some serious consideration, but, without making it known, I decided that if it happened again, no matter who said it, then I would stop playing and stop being part of the team immediately. It would never have crossed my mind to discipline the two protagonists or get rid of them; I knew I was allowed in that dressing room only on sufferance. From that moment on, however, I knew that this would have to be my last season as a professional footballer at Motherwell.

It wasn't a bad start to the season, even if there were too many draws early on. But we weren't far from success on the field. Off the field was a different story. The first hint that anything was amiss came from a journalist, one I trusted. He called me and said, rather gravely, 'I've heard on very good authority that Motherwell are skint. I'm not looking for a story or even a quote, it's just a word to the wise, Pat. Be careful.'

I was more surprised than careful when I answered, 'That's news to me. The club is running at a loss, but that's all been agreed with JB. My budget hasn't gone over any of the previously agreed limits.' I explained this to the journalist, but he seemed very confident that he had information about the way the wind was blowing from inside JB's main company. I wasn't overly concerned; if JB had a problem I expected him to tell me about it.

Less than a week later a couple of the players came into my office complaining that their signing-on fees hadn't been paid. Now, that did give me a wobble: cash-flow problems are almost always the first sign of financial difficulties at a football club, or indeed any company. I listened to the players, calmed them down and promised to get to the bottom of it right away. The recent warning from the friendly journo flashed to the front of my mind. Surely the owner wasn't pulling the plug on his well-publicised plans to make Motherwell the 'third force in Scottish football' after just one season?

I was promised a meeting with JB soon, but each time we organised a day and a time it was cancelled, or delayed a few days more for financial reports, or something had come up at the last minute, or someone who needed to be at the meeting hadn't been available. It was getting more concerning by the day, but there was nothing I could do until we had a chance for a serious discussion, face to face.

I was fairly concerned then when, eventually, three whole weeks later, JB called me in for a 'crisis' meeting in his sleek new modern offices in the centre of Glasgow. The room was styled in the thrusting young business mode, with lots of chrome and glass, very unlike the stuffier old-money dark wooden décor of the Motherwell boardroom, where I originally thought the meeting was going to take place. This was where his companies were run from. More importantly, it was where the money was released from and where decisions about the other companies were taken, at arm's length. The people who ran those other companies for JB – specifically, the venture capital arm, Hamilton Portfolio (HP) – were situated here, and I suspected they were not hugely impressed with the constant drain on their resources by Motherwell football club. Stewart Robertson,* among others, would have been there and although almost certainly fighting for team HP, I always found him friendly and fair. Even so, this was going to be a tough 'away from home' fixture!

It was tense, and JB was clearly conflicted, but in front of me and, more importantly, his business colleagues he had no choice but to be blunt and to the point with his opening statement: 'The finances are disastrous at Motherwell; we have to offload one of the higher earners right away. The club is in £4.4 million of debt and it can't go on like this.'

I wasn't delighted with this turn of events: 'Yes, I did warn you this was a costly business, but the £4.4 million debt can't be down to the players' wages alone. Our wage bill for the year isn't even half that, and that's before you take into account we have some considerable income too.'

---

* He went on to become managing director of Rangers FC many years later, so he went native eventually and joined the football world.

I decided not to mention that 20 per cent of the entire budget was being spent, against my express wishes, on John Spencer. Surprise, surprise, that cost was added onto the figure quoted at this point, and every ensuing discussion on the matter.

My job, the club, the ideas, the future planning, the financing and just about anything else you could mention had been completely upended within the space of a month, without my knowledge or input. I walked out of that meeting feeling dispirited bordering on devastated.

In the time I had spent at Fir Park I had realised that the club had previously been run frugally on a shoestring but, like a classic old country house, the real running costs were not in the beautiful artworks on show or accrued in buying the property in the first place (which had cost John a few million quid of that debt up front), but on the mundane running costs and repairs that had been put off, patched up or ignored for decades.

The stadium needed huge amounts of expensive work everywhere, including repairs to the roofs of the stands. John had started off in a blaze of glory, expensively refurbishing the interior posh bits of the main stand. Those were unnecessary costs in my eyes, as success on the pitch should have been the first priority. Even the pitch itself was a disaster, and after various remedial works the contractors eventually came clean with me: 'The stadium is built in the wrong place for the water table. Every drain beneath the pitch has collapsed over the years; the drains are big enough to walk through. Fixing them will cost millions. It might be cheaper to bulldoze the place, sell it off and start again somewhere else.' Motherwell fans would have been appalled.

One set of agronomists explained that laying a new Premier League-style pitch might just work: 'They're far more costly, obviously, but it might be worth a shot.' There were no guarantees and, personally, I had a concern with those pitches anyway – they are too hard! I worry that, in years to come, the injuries players get from playing on those pitches every day – they are used at the training grounds too – could become another scandal in the game. I was told that the reason such pitches look better is because they wear better in specific areas: 'You never get that brown worn patch in the middle of the field from one goal to the other with these new pitches,' the soil specialist said proudly.

'OK, how about you lay a "runway strip" of the new pitch style from one goal to the other, leaving the rest of the field to its more forgiving, softer and better-to-play-on style?' I replied. He said that would be impossible and too costly, but he clearly didn't want to think about it as his profit would be diminished. I wasn't only trying to save money; I was also trying to save my players and their future health.

Even the plastic pitch recently installed behind the stand at Fir Park was a disaster. It was 3G, but its softness underfoot vanished within weeks – cue tons of costly rubber crumb being added to soften it. That didn't help much as it quickly became rock solid again, making it useless for the first team to train on. I was then informed that it too had been built on the wrong foundations and would cost the equivalent of a year's playing budget to fix it.*

There had been no set training facilities at Motherwell before we arrived – they had to find ad hoc surfaces around the area often in public parks, just like Kilmarnock had, which was not exactly the best way to run a club or entice decent players to it. This was clearly not uncommon at the 'elite' level in Scottish football outside the top handful of bigger, wealthier clubs. A regular, decent quality, purpose-made training surface is a minimum requirement to improve players and develop younger ones. We had sourced this 'to let' and it was another considerable extra cost we now had that some other clubs hadn't taken on board.

---

* When talking about old-school pitches versus modern I try not to sound like an old fart just saying, 'It were tougher in my day, lad.' Trying to play skilful, fast, dribbling or passing football was obviously harder with bobbly surfaces. I always wondered how the best of the modern players would cope in those conditions. Then Spurs played Man City at Wembley a few years back the night after an American football game had destroyed the pitch. How would they cope? The answer was, 'Not very well.' Their quick-passing style was close to impossible. I was secretly a little happy that, for once, David Silva, Kevin De Bruyne, et al. struggled when confronted with our conditions from the 'old days'.

I had already started ensuring that youth-development funding was given priority, and their budget was ring-fenced, but the youngsters coming through would take a little more time. Billy, who had worked in the youth department and had a great talent for spotting a developing player, assured me, 'There are four or five who are not too far off the first team; they'll get there, but you can't rush them. It might take a couple of years, but you can rely on them getting there eventually and being valuable assets in time.'

It was a positive note on which to end the chat but Billy and I both knew that there was clearly a financial problem looming, one that had no obvious easy answer, other than downsizing very soon. Planning is hard enough, but when the financial goalposts are moved it makes life very difficult, bordering on impossible. Four days after the meeting in Glasgow I got a call at home to inform me that there were bailiffs at the club, demanding payments for some outstanding debts. A few days after that the company that had been providing our training ground demanded months' worth of payments that apparently had not been made.*

I called the guy in charge of releasing our agreed funding from John's holding company, and he had an interesting angle: 'We need to save money. Do you really need a training ground? Can't you just train on the home pitch at Fir Park every day? That would save money, wouldn't it?'

I tried to stay calm: 'We could, I suppose. But the pitch would be destroyed in a fortnight, and it would be unplayable for large parts of the rest of the season. So we would have to forfeit matches, which doesn't sound like a great idea, financially, from where I am standing.'

---

* Well, they sometimes provided our training ground. There were always excuses as to why we couldn't train – it was often 'unplayable', or we would 'damage the turf'. They did always want the money to be paid on time, however. There was a period of three months when it was 'unusable' 49 times! One day they said it was flooded again, but it was a lovely sunny day. I drove up there. The pitch was in perfect shape, and Rangers were training on it! It had been frequently 'unplayable' when we were about to play Rangers!

Cash flow was clearly a pressing problem for JB's umbrella company, but I managed to explain to him and the other financiers that there was value in the playing staff at the football club, and that panic player sales never realised their full value in this industry. I also tried to underline it was imperative that they give us a definitive framework to work under. Football contracts last years – you can't just rip them up at will – and, on top of that, youth development doesn't happen overnight. So changes to budgets shouldn't be happening on an ad hoc or weekly basis; we needed to be able to plan sensibly, with a robust financial plan.

Even so, I decided then to double down on youth development, led at the time by Davie McParland, as it might be our future salvation. From day one I had felt it important to keep control of youth development and the running of the first team totally separate from each other. Yes, the managers wanted as much control as possible, particularly back then, but I didn't feel that was necessarily in the best interests of the club. Managers come and go – it is the nature of the industry, whether they are sacked or get a better offer from elsewhere and want to move onwards and upwards. That's fine, losing the manager can be dealt with. But the youth department must roll on unimpeded, no matter who oversees the first team. This was already becoming a bone of contention between Billy and me, but I wouldn't budge.

I also considered looking outside for different ideas, and one came from my old friend Ivano Bonetti. He had incredible contacts, and when we met up he told me some of the star names he could source for the club. Many were Italian and of a far higher standard than we could normally consider, but the plan was to bring them to Scotland, use Motherwell as a shop window, then sell them on at a profit. It seemed quite far-fetched, especially as he was talking about some serious world-renowned names. On top of that he said he would be happy to come and play a season at Fir Park himself to help things along.

In extreme times it would have been an equally extreme solution, but I felt our existing plan at Motherwell could still be fruitful and it was also a lot less fanciful and risky. Having said that, the idea of having Claudio Caniggia playing in Motherwell's claret and amber was rather seductive.

Motherwell didn't need any more traumas, but then, at half-time in a home fixture against Hearts, while 1–0 up, the referee abandoned the game when the surface became waterlogged. We had just spent £60,000 on the pitch, but it still couldn't even host a game in the rain. Cue the usual opprobrium from the press also raining down on the club. I was back next morning trying to stick my fingers in the wall of the financial dike. But the infrastructure of the place was a mess and leaking everywhere. Everything needed money spent on it, just when the money tap was being turned off. The rain clouds were gathering in every sense.

I knew the rumours were beginning to fly and that the press could smell something was up. The time I spent dealing with the press grew exponentially, and it wasn't spent just talking about the finances. I'd tended to disregard the media during my own career when they talked about me, but now that I oversaw large parts of the club and the people working there, the media were impossible to ignore.

Dealing with the press shouldn't have been such a big deal – it's just that it took up far too much of my time when I could have been doing other more useful things. I couldn't change the situation and, most importantly, I rarely complained. The media were there to do their job – it was publicity, after all – and in the goldfish bowl of Scottish football, ranting was pointless, it was just part of the deal. I liked most of the sports journos at the time, and still get on with them to this day, but I had to underline to any incoming players how different the media landscape was in Scotland, and how careful they had to be.

A perfect example was Don Goodman, the former Wolves and West Brom striker, whom we had signed. He was, and indeed is, likeable, intelligent, funny, gregarious and loquacious. In many respects he was the perfect man for a press conference because he could hold and charm a crowd – but I still gave him the advice I provided for every new player, especially those coming up from England: 'The press corps are extreme up here,' I would start. 'In Scotland we have all the red tops and all the radio and TV stations you have down south, but we also have another layer. There are the local big beasts like the *Daily Record*, and the local radio channels, who are all fighting tooth and nail for ratings. When it happens to you, it will not be personal, everyone gets "done" at some point. Just be careful. Any phrase out of place, or that can be spun to sound like something else, they can and will use. Just remember *when*, and not *if*, it happens, it is not you, it is just the way the media work up here.'

Don looked surprised. 'I am not stupid or naïve,' he said. 'I'm friendly and open. I've worked with the press in tough situations before. I can handle it. Anyway, I like talking to the press; I like giving them something. In fact, I might work in the media myself one day. I'll be fine, Pat. It can't be that bad, can it?'

I had worked in London and Liverpool, where the press is known to be hard on footballers if they step out of line. But they were kittens in comparison to the Scots.

Within the month Don was in my office and furious: 'I'll never speak to any of those jokers ever again. They just make up garbage that you didn't say; they are a disgrace. How do they expect players to trust them when they stitch you up? Is it because I'm English?'

It was noticeable Don didn't say, 'Is it because I'm black?' He thought being English was a bigger problem in Scotland! I thought it was neither: it was just his turn, and they would do the same to anyone. The 'rules' of the game were different in Scotland and England.*

Soon after the abandonment aberration against Hearts, we managed to get a game played at Fir Park. Aberdeen travelled down for what became one of the most unforgettable games anyone there would ever see. I started.

---

* I had first encountered this apparently vicious side of the Scottish press pack while playing for the national team years earlier. I'd had an extremely positive press down south – far too positive if truth be told. When I turned up for a Scotland game, one of the journalists had written, 'I lie awake in bed at night in fear that Pat Nevin will be picked to start for Scotland.' I couldn't believe it and confronted him: 'Why the hatefulness?' He was as shocked and as confused as me: 'It's not personal, Pat. That is just how we do it up here in Scotland. We're just selling papers.'

Our team looked very strong, but with less than 40 minutes gone we were 4–1 down at home with our fans understandably furious. Spenny made it 4–2 before half-time. Could we still get a draw? Within 25 minutes of the restart we were 6–3 down in a game that was getting weirder by the minute. We were playing brilliantly going forwards – both teams had many more chances than the nine already scored – so we threw the kitchen sink at them for the last 20 minutes. Actually, the kitchen sink had been hurled already, so they got the dishwasher, the microwave and the fridge. Spenny got his hat-trick – 6–4; Shaun Teale scored a penalty – 6–5! There were still 15 minutes to play, but try as we might, and we came mighty close, we couldn't get that equaliser. The final score was Motherwell 5 Aberdeen 6.

As I trudged off I remember being exhausted, furious, embarrassed and also confused. It was incredibly exciting; we had been a superb unit up front, but more like the BBC comedy unit at the back. Going into the boardroom after my shower, I had no idea how to explain what on earth had just happened, but at least they all seemed to have enjoyed the spectacle. Motherwell fans still talk about that game affectionately now, but the most amazing thing was the fact that 11 goals were scored and, in between the sticks were Jim Leighton and Andy Goram, the two best Scottish goalkeepers of their generation! You can add your own line here about Scottish keepers – Jimmy Greaves in the old days would have had a field day. Some of the pressmen were not slow to mention the amateurishness of that game, and I couldn't argue with them.

The next press furore came when one of our Dutch players had done the classic overseas newspaper interview that ended up in our red tops. Apparently, he wanted 'to punch the manager in the throat' – clearly a Dutch phrase; as ever he claimed it was 'lost in translation'. It was a little more hassle but by this point that sort of story was no more than a trifling matter for me – even if it enraged the manager, who wanted me to sack the midfielder.

The problem was that every other week there was a dramatic angry newspaper headline that had to be managed. Crisis management always fell squarely on my shoulders as CEO, and it was wearing. Especially as it usually had absolutely nothing to do with me, but I would still be the one standing in the firing line.

There was the odd quieter day, which I relished – and on one of those, while at home minding my own business, JB floated his own business idea that maybe Motherwell should join forces and merge with local rivals Airdrie. I have no idea why he suggested this, or how serious he was, but the newspapers picked it up and ran with it. OK, it's on a smaller scale, but it got the same vicious reaction from both sets of fans that the Liverpool owners would get if they said their club fancied merging with their 'little' neighbours Everton. The brief quiet spell was over. That media meltdown lasted for weeks, and although I was sanguine, it came very close to pushing JB and his wife into walking away from the club altogether, mostly because their children were caught in the crossfire and were being picked on at school. John was an emotional man, and this piqued his emotional state more than anything.

The underlying problem was that each time I got John to settle on a reasonable budget and agree on the finances, something like this would happen. This time, unusually, it was entirely his own fault: he should have run that idea by me first. I would have killed it on the spot. But after abuse like this from the press, and many of the fans, JB would then back off the promised financing going forward. Doubtless there were those cash-flow problems in his other businesses as well; many, as far as I could see, weren't flourishing the same way his original holiday companies had.*

Every time something positive would happen, like a win, you could rely on a crisis days later. Three points on the Saturday, and the next day Shaun Teale was hammering the owner in the Sunday newspapers. I hated disciplining players on these occasions – remember, I am a union

---

* He suggested I invest £20,000 in two of his businesses. I got around £5,000 of that back in the end. They were the worst investments I made in my entire life, with one of the businesses, JB's main venture capital outfit Northern Edge, eventually being liquidated. I should have stuck to rare vinyl – that's much more secure. I can't complain, however, as others almost certainly lost far more than me.

man at heart – but sometimes there was no other option. At such times that poacher-cum-gamekeeper dilemma was among the most morally difficult things I had to deal with. In the end I simply tried to be fair. I would not be excessively punitive – in fact, quite the reverse – but then JB generally wasn't the spiteful type either, so there weren't too many big disagreements when those very rare workplace fines or punishments were handed down.

I came to expect the worst from the media on any story, but it didn't always happen. At McDiarmid Park against St Johnstone I raised a few eyebrows, not least the referee's. I got the ball in the opposition's box, twisted round the defender but, as I was going past him, I tripped over my own foot. Obviously, I was beginning to show the signs of ageing – I would never have been so elephantine when I was younger. As I picked myself up I spotted the referee running towards the penalty spot, clearly intent on giving me an unwarranted penalty. I caught his eye and shouted, 'No, no, it wasn't a penalty, I just tripped over.' The look of shock on his face was mirrored by the defender beside me, whose emotions went from anger to astonishment in a millisecond. The referee glanced at me again as he slowed down and mouthed, 'What?' as he brought down his arm that had just been straightening to theatrically point to the spot. Did he hear me right? 'No pen, ref. I just fell over!' He elegantly changed the direction of his run from a direct line into a beautiful arc and waved play on.

I wasn't being a martyr or a goody two-shoes, it was just the natural, right thing to do. It would have been grossly unfair; the defender wasn't even that close to me. The match was drawn and afterwards I knew there would be a press reaction. Was I saintly or was I letting the manager down? Those extra two points gained, had we converted the penalty, would have been very helpful.

The journos asked what had happened. I explained it all in a matter-of-fact way, and they said, 'Fair enough,' and left it at that. They didn't make a big deal out of it either way, but it underlined that you really couldn't judge which way the newspapers were going to run with a particular story or incident. I expected some devious stirring in the tabloids trying to drive a wedge between the manager and me, but nothing happened. Even Billy didn't bring it up, which was maybe even more surprising.

Was I becoming too distrustful or cynical, seeing problems in everything that the press would or wouldn't write? Or was I just being sensibly cautious? I'm still not sure, but it showed the pressure that we all felt back then, even me.

After one decent run we got all the way up to third place in the league, and there were some brief happy days to be savoured, but I always feared something was about to go wrong.

I didn't have to wait long. Billy picked two Under-21 players in the squad for the game against Dundee United, which we subsequently won. The problem was that one of those youngsters was a goalkeeper, and the rules stipulated there needed to be two 'outfield' Under-21 players on the teamsheet. It was little more than a technical breach, but breaking this football rule could cost us all three points if the league took a dim view of it – certainly afterwards Dundee United were pushing for precisely that outcome.

I had been one of the advocates of the 'Under-21 rule' in the first place – to help promote young Scottish players – so I wasn't in a great position to argue. I kicked myself for not noticing it before the match, or even during it, but it was an honest mistake, and Billy accepted responsibility. I felt this could be one of the biggest scandals we would face at the club; we looked like rank amateurs and I waited for the press storm – but it never arrived. The club secretary Alasdair Barron and I 'played a blinder', as my diary recounts, when we went to the SPL hearing, and got off with nothing more than a warning and a £1,500 fine. It didn't reach the media to any noticeable extent.

I wasn't above using the media myself if I thought the situation called for it. We had a player sent off unfairly and I decided to make an appeal against the decision, to save a suspension. Unfortunately, there were only a couple of TV cameras at the game, and they didn't give clear enough evidence of his innocence. There was, however, another camera, our own wide-angled club camera we used to oversee tactics. I checked out this footage and it clearly showed that our man hadn't made contact with his opponent. It was the miscarriage of justice I suspected, but the rules didn't allow us to use that footage, as it wasn't officially sanctioned.

I thought this grossly unfair and decided to use my old VHS splicing skills from back in my Chelsea days. With a little help from an unnamed source in a TV studio (your secret identity is safe with me!) I put our camera angle in between the other two and showed it to the relevant committee. Fortunately, they bought it, and we got our player back for the next game. Was that immoral? I argued to myself that it was a miscarriage of justice: bigger games with more cameras would have had an advantage, and that particular law was an ass. Well, the argument suited me anyway.

All of these situations bled into each other; dealing with one at a time would have been fine, but I was spinning a huge number of these plates together at the same time, as well as being a full-time player. My head was spinning after a cup game away to Arbroath that was unlike any other I had played in in my life. Gayfield Park is only a heftily launched centre-back's clearance from the North Sea on the east coast of Scotland, and on this Saturday afternoon the wind had come straight down from Siberia without troubling to stop off for a rest on the way. We knew there was a slight problem when our goalkeeper Andy Goram thumped a goalkick as hard as he could just before half-time, and the ball went over the crossbar . . . his own crossbar! The referee looked over at me and shouted through the gale, 'This is pointless, isn't it?'

'Absolutely; it's a joke.'

He nodded and abandoned the match because of wind – the only time I have ever known that to happen during a match in all my years in football. It was funny, but the smile was soon wiped off my face. If I thought we were then going to have an easy weekend in the Sunday newspapers after the match was abandoned, I was mistaken. We were in the mire again. A bunch of 'Motherwell casuals' had allegedly tootled along to the local pub and, eschewing the proffered famous local 'Smokies', had instead busied themselves fighting and making Nazi salutes to any interested passers-by.

Another week of amateur sleuthing followed for me, speaking to various fans on the quiet to help track down the culprits. Eventually, I was able to point the police in the right direction: anyone from the far right wasn't going to get an easy ride from me or the chairman. Another small group turned up in the Motherwell family home section, not an area renowned for its offensive behaviour. The match was against Celtic and their travelling fans reported seeing far-right regalia and Nazi salutes aimed at them. Enraged by these bigoted and racist 'Motherwell fans', they wanted an apology. I could smell a particularly offensive rodent. More detective work led to me discovering that this small band of supporters were recently Rangers fans but had been banned from Ibrox for their extremist actions. They were never allowed in again but, as ever, it took time, effort and a lot of work with the press guys to get the true message across.

I understood that the newspapers were constantly on the lookout for the more salacious personal stuff, and our new signing Saša Ćurčić provided them with some very juicy tidbits. He had what I considered a hilarious disdain for the Scottish press. He couldn't care less about what they thought or what they printed: 'They are just stupid, provincial arseholes who have no importance beyond this minuscule country stuck out in the corner of the continent that nobody else gives a shit about. They can write what they like. I don't care. I have nothing to say to them.'

They did write what they liked and, to this day, I don't know if Saša did or didn't take drugs; tell Brian Little to 'go and fuck your mother'; if Saša's marriage was a sham just to get a work permit; or, indeed, if he did have a poo on his former manager's bed. But I suspect he didn't do any of the above. What I do know is that he truly didn't give a shit, wherever it was positioned! Oh, yes, and he did turn out to be a very talented but maybe unsurprisingly very unreliable player that Billy had brought to the club for a short time.

It was an unusual delight not having to make any efforts whatsoever to protect a player from his perceived misdemeanours. Press guys would call up and say, 'We are going to write all this stuff. How are you going to make excuses for him?'

For once I could say, 'I'm not. Write what you like and take it up with him, but I strongly doubt that he'll talk to you, other than telling you to fuck off.'

After what felt like a period of persistent negative headlines in the press, I understood why the owner was getting fed up with it. I was finding it gruelling myself at this point; but who really wants to spend millions of pounds only to be confronted by a host of problems every week, be pilloried in the newspapers, and see no clear way of getting out, while continuing to spend a fortune? I tried my best to shelter JB from the worst, or at least show him that all the other clubs were also getting it in the neck now and again. That it wasn't personal; it was just the business.

I always had the backstop that I had originally told JB that I thought buying a football club was a mad thing to do; it would cost him a shed-load of money and that fame is not all it is cracked up to be. I think by then he had begun to fully understand the reality, and that it might have been sound advice.

Just when I felt as if I might be overwhelmed by the constant ever-changing insanity of the season, a few rays of light began to shine through. First were the Motherwell fans themselves: 2,500 people turned up for an open day, five times as many as we might have reasonably expected. Clearly there was a 'buy in' from some fans after the efforts we had made, and the money John had spent.

However, we were then inundated with complaints from fans who didn't care for the more radical concepts we'd introduced, such as cheaper tickets for kids (the 'kids for a quid' initiative), free entry for women for certain matches, some other games having specially reduced prices for everyone, and running free supporters' buses from nearby towns. The objection was: 'Why should we buy season tickets when, once you factor in all these discounts during the campaign, our season tickets paid for up front might work out more expensive than just turning up and paying at the gate every week?'

They had a point. Cash flow at any football club is a major concern, and money coming in at the start of the campaign from those fans' season tickets was vital. So this was a real dilemma. But the discounts were all part of a long-term strategy aimed to build up the core support from a young age, to tempt those who were not regulars and reward families. There were many in the community who were well onboard at the open day. Families milled around the pitch and stadium, checking out the stalls and meeting some of the players and staff personally. It underlined to me that the positive customers for any business are usually quietly satisfied, but that those less enamoured, even if a minority, are more vocal. I couldn't be angry about the season-ticket complainants, however: they might not have all shown up for the open day, but they were the true dedicated fans, the backbone of the support, and they didn't deserve to be aggravated by us.

Yet for all the efforts at positivity from the new ownership – the unarguable increase in the quality of players on the field; the improved league position; and better facilities on match day such as more food outlets, a better match-day programme and improved toilets – it still wasn't translating into increased crowd numbers, unless there were 'special' discounts. I had studied marketing to degree level, and everything we had put in place suggested there should be an upturn in match-day footfall, but it wasn't happening yet.

I had always warned JB that football was an unusual business, that it didn't always follow the normal rules, and that this 'experiment' of his may take a generation or two to bear fruit. Even so, we expected at least some increase in the numbers coming through the turnstiles – but, for a period, they actually began to dip to lower than they were before we arrived, which was confusing and deeply dispiriting.

A few fans I talked to suggested: 'The new regime just isn't popular with some of the old fan base.' And there were some dark mutterings of certain fans not trusting 'those Catholics'. I dismissed that idea out of hand, but maybe there was a deeper mistrust, or just disbelief, that this would work out in the long term. The donkey character in George Orwell's

Animal Farm repeatedly used the phrase, 'Donkeys live a long time.' Meaning, 'I have seen this all before and it doesn't end well.' So maybe it wasn't bigotry but wisdom from those doubters.

Just when I needed it for my sanity there was another boost: a run of games that were nothing short of awesome. I had laid on the winner for our now much sought-after youngster Lee McCulloch up at Inverness just before the 11-goal thriller with Aberdeen. We then grabbed 16 points from 18, including two wins against the mighty Celtic. The 1–0 at Celtic Park, clinched with a superb Kevin Twaddle goal, saw us play 60 minutes with ten men after Shaun Teale was sent off, but we still held out for all three points. The 3–2 home win against Celtic, with Don Goodman, Ged Brannan and Derek Townsley all scoring, was also a pulsating match, which seemed to suggest that one season in, we could already stand toe to toe with the best in Scotland. Even though it was only November, we were realistic challengers for third place, and managing to do that so quickly was clearly pretty impressive.

The problem was that the spiralling costs that would keep us there were clearly not going to be borne by JB. I had to deal with that dilemma one way or another, and soon. Cuts in playing staff would be essential, but with good sellable value available in one or two players, I felt there was no need to panic – it was perfectly doable even if holding onto a top-three spot would become very unlikely once I'd sold those players. I did feel sorry for Billy Davies more than anyone else at this point; he had shown he could build a good team and do it quickly. Alongside me, he would now have to manage a budgetary decrease which would reduce the quality of the players available to him. It felt unfair on such a keen young manager, but sadly that was the new economic reality. I didn't hide any of the bad news from him, and he got it right between the eyes straight after I did.

The ownership changed its mind three times regarding the team budget during that successful month alone. It was a classic case of a new owner getting carried away and then his financiers getting inside his head and underlining the fiscal foolishness that football tempts you into. I didn't disagree with them; I never had. As the old adage went: 'The best way to make a small fortune when owning a football club is to start with a large one.' All the time I tried to be the calmest person in the room, however difficult it became.

What was needed was certainty, clarity and an ability to plan. In a variety of reports and speeches to the board I pleaded my case for a sensible, controlled way forward – and in the heat of the moment they would agree, only for minds and budgets to be changed a week later.

In any football club you have a rough idea of what the income will be from gate money, TV, advertising and match-day corporate sales. There are other sundry ways of upping that a bit, but the two other major income streams at Motherwell – the owner's largesse, and the possibility of selling assets, specifically players – were the big imponderables. In all honesty I would have preferred a considerably smaller budget all along, but one that was secure, where we could have worked on building the club slowly instead of trying to race to the top, or at least onto the podium. There were other difficulties and, by now, even if I still had the 'swan-like' appearance on the surface, I was paddling furiously beneath. The next trauma was when the relationship between Billy Davies and his assistant manager Jim Griffin broke down. Billy stopped trusting Griff, but Griff seemed bemused and insisted that he had no idea why this had happened.

Griff left and was total a gentleman about the whole affair; my admiration for him since has never waned. He had been a club stalwart, had been part of the triumphant 1991 Motherwell cup-winning side, and I liked him. Even though he was upset and understandably felt he was treated unfairly by the manager, he still came into the dressing room and gave a rousing positive speech to the entire squad before walking out the door, head held high. I was upset to see him go, but when it is a choice between the manager and an assistant coach, there is only ever one winner, even if I did try very hard to talk Billy round – but he stuck doggedly to his demand for me to remove his number two, who had been there a year.

Managers want their own people around them, and they almost always get them – but that one stung. Griff's only negative words to me about Billy were his last before leaving the club, 'I think he might be getting a bit paranoid, Pat. Watch out for that.'

The *Daily Record* then called me to let me know that they were going to run a story that JB was on the cusp of selling the club to some guy in Uddingston. Thanks for the heads-up, John! Actually, I had more intel than any of them could have known. I had played briefly at Clyde with this guy Tommy Coakley, who was the suggested buyer, so I suspected I could work well with him if he did buy the club and I decided to stay on. Which, to be fair, was becoming an exceptionally big 'if' by this point.

I could have done without any more stress, but now the manager's already brittle relationship with JB was becoming increasingly fractured – something that was totally understandable, even predictable. From the manager's position, the financial rug was being pulled from under him, and he was acutely aware that poor results would inevitably eventually lead to his own sacking and a negative effect on how he was regarded in the game. He was ambitious, a dedicated hard worker who wanted to get right to the top.

The chairman, from his perspective, felt the manager was ungrateful, considering the opportunity we had given him, not to mention the sizeable amount of money already spent, none of which JB would ever recoup. The tension between the two would spill over when the owner sometimes came down from the directors' box and stood by the touchline at the end of games; it got far worse when one night JB walked right out onto the pitch post-match, drawing the attention to himself in front of all the cameras, in an attempt to show solidarity with the team.

As we know, for football folk, this area is sacrosanct, and the tension grew daily from then on. The owner then decided to insert a new fitness guru friend of his into the dressing room, infuriating the manager. Billy already had his own team in there and could live without the meddling intrusion, thank you very much. 'Why employ more people when we are trying to save money, and are they just spies in the camp?' was Billy's reasonable-sounding position. Even if the guru did have a few decent ideas himself, the growing tension was affecting the atmosphere around the squad.

As ever, I was the man in the middle, trying my best to get what now felt like two warring factions to work together. One by one the board members were losing trust and belief in the manager – a few hadn't wanted him to start with. Their usual line was, 'He's paranoid.' I would remind them that most managers get sacked, so maybe a healthy paranoia is a useful trait to have. It is difficult to say when suspicion about others' attitudes slides into unreasonable and obsessive behaviour. Billy once asked if I could get his office screened, in case it had been bugged. JB thought it was an unhealthy attitude but, on the other hand, I know for a fact that industrial espionage has happened before in football.

In the middle of it all I had what was probably my own personal favourite moment at the club up until then – in fact, one of the favourites of my career. We were facing Hearts in a crunch game on a Tuesday night under the Fir Park floodlights. They were then the true third force in Scotland, but after our good recent run of results a win would put us back third in the league, above them but behind Celtic and Rangers, obviously. Sky showed the game live, and it was another cracker. We didn't have anything close to their budget, but with everyone fit I thought Billy Davies had already built a team to match theirs. This was the night we would find out.

Lee McCulloch scored midway through the first half for us, which was great news all round. Hearts themselves had made a respectable bid for him a few days before and there was tentative interest from Spurs, among others. The main stand was teeming with scouts surreptitiously checking out our young striker, while others were also keeping tabs on left-back Stephen McMillan. I knew we would need to cash in on Lee eventually, but it was important to maximise his value. Even more important to my mind, though not conveyed to the owner, I wanted Lee to be given the opportunity to develop his career on his own terms. He should have a major input into deciding when to go, and what club to go to.

A truly magical moment for Kilmarnock, beating Rangers in the last minute at Ibrox on a day that was momentous in many positive and negative ways. (I'm buried in there somewhere.)

Winning the Ayrshire Cup with Kilmarnock and,
more importantly, celebrating with a great bunch of friends.

Signing for Motherwell with owner John Boyle right at the start
of the most tumultuous period in my career and life.

Having just left Kilmarnock for Motherwell I soon found myself directly
up against my great friend Dylan Kerr at left-back when I was on the right
wing for the Steelmen. No quarter was asked or given, but the second
the game finished we were back to being best mates.

The new management team unveiled at Motherwell: (left to right)
Brian McClair, Jim Griffin, Me and Billy Davies.

It still felt odd to be the person with most control over an entire top-level football
club in Scotland. To be honest, it didn't sit comfortably most of the time.

There were ups and downs, but this was probably the high-water mark for me at Motherwell – scoring the winning goal against Hearts with six seconds left to go to reach third in the league behind the Old Firm. At that precise moment, the sheer joy of the game I loved was back, if only briefly.

Looking less than enamoured at a press conference with John Boyle. It is fair to say that I was struggling to find much fun in the job once I stopped playing.

One of the biggest moments in Scottish Football? We, the 'Other Ten', decide to resign from the Scottish Premier League. Honestly, I am not trying to hide by standing at the back on the right.

Parading Motherwell's new management group of (left to right) Chris McCart, Terry Butcher, Eric Black and me. It is clear to see I have a renewed enthusiasm with the brilliant new team I had tempted to the club.

James McFadden celebrates scoring after coming through the Motherwell Youth System, which I was proud to help build further. I was pleased with the legacy I left behind, at least in that department.

The moment, caught on camera, when all hope of saving Motherwell
from administration was lost. The sadness and despair is not for me but
for the people inside those doors behind me. I look and certainly felt
older there than I do today, more than 20 years on.

After Motherwell there was another career, and one with more fun, travel and
adventures than I'd had at Fir Park. I struck lucky with BBC Radio 5 Live,
Setanta Ireland, Chelsea TV, BBC Scotland and, above, with Channel 5.

The game blazed on. Gary McSwegan equalised for Hearts early in the second half and, from then on, the tension grew. Billy Davies sent me on midway through the second half to see if I could help us win it. Ninety minutes came and went with four more to be added at the end. Scarcely a single fan had left the enthralling affair, with the atmosphere continuing to build as injury time leaked away. After some heavy pressure from us the ball broke to me and, with six whole seconds left, I scored a decent goal curled in from an acute angle on the left-hand side to win it.

There are a variety of reasons why it is one of the favourite moments from my entire career: the tension of the situation, the six seconds left, and it being against our closest rivals at that point. That goal and those three points took us back into third place. There was also the reaction of the fans, who were ecstatic, alongside the joy of my teammates.

As the game ended amid huge celebrations, Lee McCulloch (Jig), still a young man, but a lovely lad right down to his size ten boots, came up to hug me on the pitch. As the cameras were on us both, the two scorers together, he called into my ear over the fan's roars, 'Please don't sell me to them, Pat.' I knew he fancied a move down south, so I explained, 'Jig, you'll go to the club that suits you best. It will be your decision and yours alone. But why don't you just enjoy this moment while it lasts and forget about everything else for a little while.' It was an odd discussion and an even stranger moment to have it, with the celebrations exploding all around us. We didn't even cover our mouths with our hands to hide the words (as the modern players do), but I would stay true to those words with Lee.

Ged Brannan, Lee, Spenny, Derek Adams, Derek Townsley and Don Goodman, among others – people who I liked a great deal – had smothered me in the celebrations after my winner. Nearly all tall lads, they pinned me to the ground, so much so that I almost couldn't breathe. I think it was excitement! In that moment, it was all about still being accepted, being part of the team and the simple joy of the football once again.

The unpredictable and extreme changes were difficult to process, however. In just over a year at the club we had briefly reached where we wanted to be – and, of course, the owner John Boyle was particularly delighted that night and very emotional too. When I asked him later what he thought of my winning goal he said, 'I have no idea. I was too stressed. I was in the boardroom pacing up and down with a stiff drink to help calm me down.' In those moments I saw an echo of his ecstatic excitement back at the Champions League final in Barcelona. This time he walked away from his seat early, but now it was because he cared too much about the game. There may have been all sorts of problems on the horizon, but for a very short while, maybe all the way until the next morning, it was joyous again.

16/
DON'T LET PROBLEMS GET YOU DOWN

In classic JB style, just as I was trying to save money anywhere I could at the club, the chairman and the manager finally agreed on something. It would be a good idea to take the lads abroad for some warm-weather training. It might cost a bit, but it also might boost morale for the run-in, as we tried to hold on grimly to that third-place position, which was the ultimate goal.

JB dipped into his own pocket and personally paid for the trip, but by now the undercurrent of negativity was growing around the club due to the rumours about the financial problems. With a few days planned together in Lanzarote, I had already sensed the anxious atmosphere in the first-team squad, but, as I had some quality time to talk to the lads in an open and honest way, I thought I'd use the trip as a way to flush out any underlying issues. At dinner on the first night at the hotel, I took a moment to say a few words to everyone there: 'If any of you have any pressing problems, just come to my room tonight and we'll have a chat. There is no point in allowing things to fester, so come along and let me know, and if I can help I will. Be open and say what you feel, it will go no further than me.'

Fifteen people queued outside the room with an assortment of complaints, and it didn't start well. These are my edited notes from the meetings:

The first player said, 'The tactics are shit, the manager is crap and he is also a wee prick.' Not a great start.

No. 2: 'The assistant manager is a paranoid wanker; the club is a disgrace, and I'll only come to the dinner tomorrow night as long as I don't have to sit beside that fat poofy bastard Boyle.' These first two players wanted out of the club, to be fair, with their contracts paid up. They were getting no joy. The language was totally offensive, but I couldn't complain, as I had told them that they could be open and frank. At least I knew the strength of their feelings.

No. 3: 'I'm seriously unhappy about the club going public, saying they can't afford to keep me on. They bought me, agreed the contract, and this stuff in the papers is making my life very difficult. Oh, and so you know, Pat, I know it's not you who is leaking these stories.' Unbelievably, the club's position on the player had been written in the programme notes before one of the games by JB's financial adviser, so it would have been difficult to argue that I was the culprit.

Nos. 5, 6 and 7 had exactly the same complaint about being portrayed as overpaid by the money men; each was angrier and more offended than the one before.

No. 8: 'I want a new contract and a wage increase.' Fairly routine stuff, but unlikely to happen in the current financial climate.

No. 9: 'I am not signing the new contract you have offered me. It's not enough. Others are on more than me, and I don't care about the club's finances; I care about mine and my family's finances.' The dilemma I had warned JB about when he set out spending big at the start.

No. 10: 'The club secretary won't release payments I'm due for my relocation to Scotland. My lawyers will be in touch, or I might just go in and break his nose when we get back.'

No. 11: 'My bonuses have been worked out wrong. Can you sort it? Preferably tonight!' We were in Lanzarote; it was now late in the evening. I explained it might be difficult tonight, but I would contact the secretary in the morning.

No. 12: 'The manager thinks I am plotting behind his back – I'm not – and now he won't play me. Is he paranoid?'

No. 13: 'The training facilities aren't good enough.' Agreed.

No. 14: 'The food isn't good enough in the club canteen and the weather in Scotland is crap.' A first-world problem followed by one which I suggested he take up with his God.

No. 15 then walked into my room, with an impressively long list of complaints, but this time it was the manager!

I think three players on the trip managed to quietly understand that they were being paid decent wages for doing their jobs, and had some semblance of perspective about their problems. After that, I just about gave up – they were a seriously disgruntled group. But then I remembered that this was frequently the case when I was just a player. I always felt there were plenty of players who weren't happy unless they were unhappy, complaining about something or other, whatever the circumstances. Some just like a good old moan-up and a chance to blame anything that is going wrong on somebody else.

In reality, everything on this occasion was rooted in the same question: is the money running out, and what effect will it have going forwards? It was mostly fear that was driving those grievances – other than the one about the weather.

The chairman was flying in the next day to join us, and I explained to him beforehand that if he did have the 'open session' he was considering with the players, 'It might be long, difficult, embarrassing and it might be bordering on impossible to fix any of the issues. In fact, it might just leave you fuming, in that you have just paid a few grand to give each of them a free *holiday*!' As it was, he was too unwell to take part, and he really was – a fortunate state of affairs for all concerned in the circumstances.

The run-in to the end of the season was not an easy one, but it was helped by our best players being back and on form, especially Ged Brannan and Lee McCulloch. The week before the final game the arithmetic was simple: if we beat Rangers and Hearts lost, then we would finish in third spot, with the promise of European football next season. It should have been exciting; it should have been a celebration of reaching the highest level possible for a non-Old Firm club, and doing it within a couple of years. Sadly, it was anything but that.

There had been a further discussion with JB and his people. I was informed of the outcome by a phone call from Los Angeles. It was simple, and it was becoming tiresomely repetitive: 'Sell! Sell! Sell! We want you to get a bunch of players out and we want them out quickly. John Spencer being the highest earner is obviously first on the list. Ged Brannan [the captain], as well as Lee McCulloch and Stephen McMillan [the jewels that had been brought through from the youth system], all must go. As well as Andy Goram [the Goalie]. They all have to be off the wage bill over the summer.'

If this wasn't hard enough to swallow, Billy and I were told that Finnish international Simo Valakari would not be given the new longer contract that he had been promised. The idea of going back on a promise was particularly painful; it was totally alien to how I thought a business should be run by decent people. Honest, honourable hard-working men like Simo didn't deserve that.

'If you could possibly also offload another eight players on top of that,' they added, 'it would be much appreciated.'

This was bordering on traumatic, considering the efforts that had been made to get to where we were.

There was also another player who might have to be released, one who wouldn't be a particular problem – me! This time it was the manager, not me or the chairman, who had to decide. In some ways Billy had to be brave when he asked me into his office. In there I binned the chief executive's hat and was, for the moment, just a player sitting in front of the manager – albeit one I had appointed – wondering if he was going to be offered a new contract. Billy was impressively straightforward: 'Pat, this is a tough one for me, but considering the financial situation and the quality of the young players coming through, I'm going to have to make some painful decisions. And this is one of them. I'm not going to offer you a new deal for next season. I could give you the entire spiel if you want it, but I am sure you would prefer it simple and straight. You know the score.'

Sitting there in front of Billy, it was still in my power to sack him on the spot, if I liked. I knew it and Billy knew it too. I am sure he also knew me well enough by then that I would not to be so self-obsessed to pull rank on him. I felt I had another year of playing left in my legs; I had kept myself very fit. However, I said to Billy, 'You are the manager and that is your decision to make. I will respect it and will not even try to talk you out of it. I chose you as the gaffer, and I will do the right thing and accept your judgement.'

It may well have been the easiest dumping of a player Billy ever had. Maybe I could have put a bit more meat on the bone, or just saved him the agony by announcing my own retirement, but I thought it was good for Billy to be able to show the power and control he had in the situation, not only to others but also to himself. I could also have mentioned that I had decided months ago myself that I wasn't going to play another season for Motherwell. There just wasn't enough fun left in it, and when you added in the politics, the travelling (still three or four hours every day) and the constant hassle of the chief executive role, there was no way I could face that for another season, even if the legs were still fine and I was up to it physically. This really ought to have been more than a brief wistful moment for me. The official ending of my 19-year professional career should have been a time to pause, think, consider my own feelings and worry about how I would cope mentally with such a huge life change. Maybe I should have been looking back on everything that had happened from the day I joined Clyde, moved to Chelsea, then Everton, Tranmere,

Killie and Scotland – along with all the adventures on the way. But I couldn't do that on this day – there was too much work to be done. It was time to be practical.

The reality was, seconds later I was out of Billy's office and back in mine in the adjacent building, trying to help sort out the problems of other players who were leaving the club, as well as organising the paperwork for those who were getting offered new contracts by the manager. Those wistful considerations would have to wait. This ability to compartmentalise I had learned from being a footballer came into its own, as I took meeting after meeting and did my best to get through the day.

So my playing days were over. But a far bigger problem was that for the last two years I had seen precious little of Annabel, Simon and Lucy, other than late at night when I got home, always exhausted and always on the phone dealing with the latest nightmare engulfing Motherwell. Finally, retiring felt like a blessed relief, and there was not even a second's worth of regret or doubt as I drove home that night to tell Annabel, 'I'm done with playing football, it's over.' She wasn't disappointed; she knew it was time, as much as I did.

There was another bonus for the club and my budget calculations. Having Mr P. Nevin off the list did help the balance sheet a little, if not my own personal bank account. I was a long way from being one of the top-earning players, but you must look for the positives in every situation, and at that point every little would help to get the books closer to balancing.

My final professional game, a week later, was a surprisingly good one to bow out on: the crucial tie against Rangers for third place, at Fir Park. We unexpectedly won 2–0, with what would clearly be the last hurrah for that group of players and, indeed, the entire plan that John Boyle had initially set in place for the club. It had taken two seasons and we were within a hair's breadth of the fabled position that the owner had touted from the start. There was a little satisfaction to be gained in the thought that we could have improved further, had the finance continued at the current level or even just a bit less. As a sportsman I was hugely competitive, always believing we could win whatever the odds. As a CEO I also had to be realistic: chasing third place would now be a thing of the past.

Unfortunately for us Hearts also won their final game, and so the chance of European football evaporated on that sunny day in the middle of May. I knew that was probably for the best, because I was aware that the team would soon be torn apart. If we were going to be substantially weakened, we didn't deserve to be our country's representatives alongside Celtic and Rangers.

I now had a decision to make, and it looked like a fairly straightforward one for me. It was time to tidy things up and allow John to take Motherwell in a new direction. I didn't have a great deal of interest in joining him on that journey. My black and red diary reads, 'The boys were fantastic against Rangers, the best display so far. Great day, though soured for me by JB asset stripping the club and I'm 95 per cent sure I am leaving. Finished 4th, miles ahead of those below us; an excellent year on the pitch.'

My playing career had all been one long, interesting and mostly enjoyable accident. I had managed to get through it with no massive ill feeling towards just about anyone. I'd had adventures; it had opened doors and introduced me to interesting new people and places. In that moment I was back to being that 19-year-old kid who had taken a couple of years off his degree, who was now finally getting the (admittedly slightly delayed) chance to start again. Would I miss the playing? Yes, I loved the actual football itself, and the training, and, of course, the fabulous feeling great fitness gives you. Would I miss the adulation, the autographs, the notoriety, the whole ego trip? Not a chance in the world. None of that had ever meant anything to me anyway, so there wasn't the slightest sadness in those departments.

My dad was at Fir Park that day against Rangers, and I knew he would miss coming to see me play, and maybe that was the biggest twang on the old heart strings. But the time was right, and I was convinced I would not look back; there would be other adventures ahead. My personal diary was so understated it is almost laughable. The entire entry read, ''Well 2–0 Rangers. Last ever game. Oh well.'

17 /
HIGHER THAN THE STARS

The job offer from Motherwell in the summer of 2000 was intriguing, if a bit short on actual detail. JB suggested that, as I was no longer a player, I could now be chairman and a board member. Director of Football was a given. I would be youth development co-ordinator; I would have total control of buying and selling players. I would oversee the overall direction of the club, which as far as I could see at that point meant running it down to a much lower level. I would also be the club's representative on all the SPL and SFA committees. I could happily live without those committees, but somebody had to do it. I would be press liaison officer, website overseer, and a 5 per cent shareholding in the club would also be mine if I wanted it. The financial package was not much different to the wages of a below-average player at the club, though there was the obligatory loan car thrown in.

JB also told me at this point that the manager wanted me to be based in the main offices away from the players; he wanted me to step back from day-to-day work with the football department. I was quite disappointed by that; I had only ever tried to help Billy – or, more precisely, be there if he asked for help. The board, to a man, had reiterated that they thought Billy was paranoid and wanted him out. But I reminded them we had just finished a whisker off third in the league, so a few strains in the day-to-day relationships might just be worth it.

I understood why Billy wanted to control as much as he could, but it was painful to think I would be marginalised to some degree if I stayed on. I thought he should have known me well enough by then to trust me. I had given him the job, and I was sticking by him when, unknown to Billy, the others weren't. But so be it. It was his call and, as ever, I would respect it. On the positive side, being further away from the players would likely deplete the already overloaded in-tray. That was something to consider. Although, of course, on the other hand, none of this would matter if I was going to leave. What to do?

I was called in to Glasgow to see JB and his financial adviser, Andrew Lapping, for a meeting about the next season. It was probably time to let them know that I was happy and indeed keen to leave now. Their opening gambit, before I could let them know, was, however, yet another surprise: 'Just to let you know, Pat, we have changed our minds, and you don't have to sell all those players right away. It is your judgement when to sell, particularly McCulloch and McMillan.'

I picked my jaw back up off the floor: '*What?!* You've changed your minds again!!!??' I gasped. 'How on earth do you people ever develop a strategy in your other industry? Football is a weird business, but even for football these changes at this pace are ridiculous – and, I'll be honest with you, I've struggled to cope with them lately. You've got to understand that it would be impossible for me or anyone to plan a route ahead if you keep making these bizarre handbrake turns.'

I had begun to realise by then that this was just the way they worked, and that each of them dealt with the ups and downs in their own way. JB might be ashen-faced one week then rosy-cheeked at the next good result; Andrew Lapping could look utterly panicked but then be super-laidback seconds later; while Stewart Robertson always appeared pleasant, relaxed and convivial, though he could have been thinking or feeling anything, for all I knew. I got on very well with each one of them on a personal level. If they had a good week in the markets, or one of the companies they had bought with their venture capital arm had been sold at a large profit, then that would change everything in a positive way – but only briefly. The opposite was the same, if the markets or investments slumped. I had nothing to do with those businesses, other than knowing that they sent the club on the same sickening lurches. As the meeting went on I found myself reasoning, 'Maybe I could just consider this as an interesting adventure? Yes, be dedicated to it, don't waste the man's money, but go along for the ride; it won't be as hard now I'm no longer a player. In fact, maybe I could even get back to doing some of the things I liked, instead of giving my entire existence to this mayhem. I could do the TV and radio work without worrying about getting back into training the next morning. I might even get to see more gigs again. Above all else, I may at last be able to have some semblance of the family life I had missed for the last few years. Should I have a go at this and see if I can find a balance?'

I absolutely didn't want to be tied to it, if it continued to dominate everything, so I made a suggestion to John and his team: 'This might sound odd, but how about putting no timeframe on my contract? We just shake hands. If I want to leave at any moment, because I don't like the direction, then I can just walk away and there is no comeback from you. If you want me to leave, just say so, and I will leave that afternoon – no comeback, no compensation, no complaints. Just trust on both sides that we work together for as long or as short a time as either of us wants it. Also, I don't want the 5 per cent ownership, that's yours, as is the chairmanship. How does that sound?'

They thought for a little while – I guessed trying to see the angle, but there wasn't one, and JB quickly understood. I bet there are very few executives demanding to work on the basis that they can be fired at any moment without compensation. I was being honest. It was important not to take advantage of JB's kindness and wealth, but I also wanted him to understand I was happy to walk out if I didn't like the way the club was being run. There were plenty of other people hanging around him, doing a perfectly good job trying to rip him off. I wasn't going to do that.

For once – after talking to Annabel and explaining we could stop at any time – I was the one making the handbrake turn; I decided to stay on at Fir Park. Admittedly, Annabel was less keen, and it was a very tight call in the end because, like many working-age people, we were shoving our real lives with quality time together further away into the future. But, like almost everyone else, there was still a financial imperative to work to keep the family solvent. On the other hand, clearly you shouldn't keep putting your life off forever. Well, you can, and many of us do, but you should always question whether it is right, needed or you are just following the expected societal norms.

I reminded myself, when I got a spare moment or two, that I never wanted a career inside this industry. The fact I could stop at the drop of a hat was a comfort. But the hardest thing to explain away to myself was doing a job which hadn't really been a lot of fun so far. OK, it was interesting, even fascinating at times – I had told everyone exactly that when I was asked. But I had also put in two years of hard graft, so it might be worth sticking around for a while to see if it had all been worth it. I knew that it wasn't something I was going to do for the next 15 years. Then again, I'd thought that about playing football when I signed for Chelsea at the start of my first accidental career, and that lasted nearly two decades.

There was also the fact that I had grown to feel a great warmth towards Motherwell, specifically the supporters, who were generally a considerate bunch. You can't generalise about an entire fan base, there are so many different factions and opinions, but mostly they understood the realities of supporting a team that was rarely going to get the chance of a cup final or experience a European adventure. It's easier to be a fan of the bigger clubs who regularly have those glory days, sometimes once or twice a year, than it is to stay loyal to your small hometown club. It was the same reason why I had grown to love and respect Tranmere Rovers fans just a few years previously.

Days later I got an unexpected phone call to add a little confusion. It was my old mate Ivano Bonetti from those Tranmere days. His plan from last year had come to fruition, but not with me at Motherwell. He had arrived as the new player–manager at Dundee. 'Pat,' he said, 'do you fancy coming up here to Dundee and working with me? You could even play on for another year, both of us in the team together. How much fun would that be?'

There was a moment when it sounded like an offer I couldn't refuse. When my old Italian pal told me the star names and the standard of the players he was going to get, as well as some of the undiscovered gems he would entice, I was amazed. We had aimed high at Motherwell, but Ivano's plans were stratospheric. When I listened to his business plan, which had evolved and grown since our chat 12 months earlier, it sounded both bold and risky, but with a fair wind it could also work. On top of this I still fondly recalled those times training at Tranmere when we had such an incredible understanding. He was right: this could be that chance to have the joy of playing together. I could even squeeze in another year of kicking a ball and getting paid for it!

Exciting as it was, the offer had come just a few days too late. I had made a promise to Motherwell. I had shaken JB's hand on it, so it was time to knuckle down and get on with the job, though I would keep a close eye on Dens Park, Dundee. Had the offer come a week earlier, I would probably have taken it.

I also had a few ideas and plans to put in place myself at Motherwell, even if they didn't involve the likes of Italian international Fabrizio Ravanelli and Claudio Caniggia, Diego Maradona's wing-man for Argentina. To his word, Ivano eventually tempted all of them and more stars to the City of Discovery, but in the end his rollercoaster was maybe even more extreme than mine at Motherwell.

We hadn't gone abroad as a family that summer as Simon's autism had played havoc with the previous year's attempts to chase the sun. Any flight delay meant a change to his routine or plan, which would still lead to him becoming incredibly agitated. Meltdowns in public places were torture for the family. Poor little Lucy always helped as much as she could, but it wasn't easy on her, as well as Annabel and me, and, maybe most importantly, eight-year-old Simon himself. The previous summer when the plane finally arrived late at Newcastle airport, further nightmare news was relayed to us to stress Simon even more. We were going to have to walk across the apron to get to the plane, instead of walking down an enclosed gangway. This, we thought, was designed to make Simon crack.

Somewhat surprisingly, he wasn't too bad and held my hand calmly as we headed towards the plane. As I went to walk up the steps onto the plane I bent down to pick up a bag and, before I knew it, Simon was off, legging it at top speed and heading straight for . . . the runway. After falling over the bag, I managed to catch him just before he reached the edge of the airstrip itself. The crew were unimpressed and, with limited knowledge of autism back them, we weren't getting much sympathy from anyone as Simon threw another massive tantrum all the way to our seats, clearly upsetting the nervier of the passengers.

I remember thinking at the time that, in some ways, Simon was probably the sensible one. Flying in an aluminium tube, 30,000 feet in the air, travelling at 500 miles an hour . . . don't you think it is scary when you consider that through a different, more logical lens, one through which many autistic people quite literally and correctly see the world? Most if not all things are viewed by people with autism in a quite different way to us neurotypicals – but understanding Simon's point of view without being given the relevant information by anyone back then (from specialists to Simon himself) was a particular torture for us.

Ultimately, it turned out that crashing wasn't Simon's main concern, after all. Eventually we discovered it was just the noise – specifically the volume and the tone of the engines – that he couldn't cope with. He'd always had a problem with machines that made certain noises – we always had to vacuum at specific times and, on journeys, if we had to stop at a service station to go to the loo, Simon and I would have to edge in centimetre by centimetre, in case one of the hand dryers was switched on and he was rattled. As you might imagine, it all made life a trifle complicated for us.

When, years later, Simon eventually became more capable with his speech and communication, he one day calmy said, 'Ear defenders would help me get onto planes.' He hadn't been able to tell us that was the problem; we had assumed it was the more reasonable fear of falling out of the sky at 500mph.

One of the many difficulties we found with Simon's autism was actually deducing what the problem was in the first place. We lost a few summer holidays, including that year's, because of this little piece of ignorance. If only there had been people to talk to and share information with back then. I knew one thing for certain from Simon's early life: that a big part of the rest of my life would be filled with sharing anything we had learned with those facing the same problems after us.

18/
TIME TO PRETEND

It is always imperative to remember that owners of football clubs are, in the end, just custodians of an institution for a short time. In a deeper, more meaningful way – in the long term – the club always belongs to the fans and the community, so you shouldn't take risks that might destroy it. I instinctively knew this, as a real football fan, and it was foremost in my thoughts as I planned for the season to come.

This, 2000–01, had to be the season when most of the changes would be made, but the trick was to manage the financial recalibration without gutting the team and its self-belief, which would lead to the real possibility of relegation. That could put the club into danger of terminal decline, and us mere custodians had no right to do that. So, I would not only accept selling the higher earners, I would be facilitating it, but I would try to ensure it was done only when the time and the price was right. Any hint of a fire sale and your bargaining power goes up in smoke, and the damage left is worse.

However painful it might be in the short term, I could see now that even more time and more resources had to be diverted to our youth-development programme. A good job had been done in the recent past producing the current valuable crop of McCulloch, McMillan and the next kid coming through, a very tidy left-back called Steven Hammell.

Billy Davies had previously been part of the youth set-up as the Under-21 coach; his man Davie McParland would be asked to upgrade the structure further. Over as short a time as sensible, we could then replace some expensive first-team players with those being developed from within. This was not a new idea in Scottish football, but the important part was to try to make sure it was the best system available. I saw this as my most important area of planning for the entire club going forwards.

Even though I was to be apart from the players, I still loved keeping fit, and Billy knew it. I wasn't completely ostracised, and our relationship didn't suffer from the distancing as much as I thought it might – it was only about 50 yards from my office to his in the next building. He asked me to play in a few Under-21 games early that season in order to give my thoughts on some of the next group of youngsters. One early game stood out.

I played a full 90 minutes at Fir Park, between the striker and the midfield, as a 'very' overage player, with Billy observing closely on the sidelines. Afterwards, he asked my opinion on the lads playing around me, none of whom I had been particularly aware of before, while he brazenly ignored the fact that I scored two goals! A few things stood out to me: 'I got a ball played to me from deep by one of the kids, the red-haired one. I twisted, made a few yards and turned, and suddenly he was 20 yards ahead of me in the perfect position for a through ball. I have no idea how he got there so fast. It was a brilliant movement, and he did the same thing time and again. That was special. He could have a future.'

Stephen Pearson would end up playing for Motherwell, Celtic and Scotland. Billy nodded in agreement with my judgement. Then asked,

'Anyone else impress you?'

I thought again: 'One of the lads in midfield was tough, no nonsense and very mature; he rarely made a bad decision when passing and was impressively tidy.' Keith Lasley went on to play nearly 500 games for the club, later becoming skipper and then assistant manager. 'Both of them have got a chance, even if the red-haired lad catches the eye a bit more.'

'Anyone else caught your eye?' Billy asked with a knowing smile.

Had I missed something? Playing in a team for an entire game should give you a decent idea of the quality around you. I thought again, and considered them one by one before hesitantly suggesting, 'Well . . . the left-back seemed to have something about him. He was good on the ball, but his positional awareness was awful. He just played off the cuff, but he couldn't defend to save his life.'

Billy nodded, 'You got there in the end. He's the jewel in the crown and will be the best player we have at the club, and maybe the best this club has produced for generations.'

It underlined why Billy, and indeed the best people working in youth development, are so far ahead – and why I delegated all this type of work away from myself. I couldn't see it, well not on that first viewing anyway, but James McFadden did, of course, become the jewel not just for Motherwell but for his country too – but as a top-class creative forward. Billy probably knew before me that our saviours were already in our midst, but they needed time, they needed polishing and they needed the right pathway.

There were other positives when you looked at it closely with an optimistic eye. Season-ticket sales were up 30 per cent in a year, though decreased prices were probably as important a factor as last season's excellent league position. The original idea was to build the fan base from the bottom up but, although I always argued that this would take a generation, if it happened at all, it was still a very heartening start to the campaign, even if we didn't take in much more money.

On the other hand, dealing with the worst football agents was the most disheartening job I did in football – but it had to be done. My relationships with the agents became more complicated and time consuming as I started planning the eventual sale of players. I also had to work with them to help source some cheaper replacements.

I did have my initial method still in place when managing agents. My first question was, 'Do you legally represent this player?' If the answer was yes, I would underline it: 'So, you work for them?' If it was yes again the third statement was always the same: 'Excellent. If you work for them, then they will be paying your fees, so don't ask for money from us, because you are not employed by us.' Unsurprisingly, this didn't go down very well with some agents, who fancied two payments for the same transfer. Amazingly, it was not uncommon in the industry, even though it could lead to conflicts of interest as well as temptations to carve up deals and payments. I tried to work with the reasonably honest agents – but even so, it was rarely easy. That was the nature of the industry, though, and I understood it.

We needed a new centre-back, and Billy targeted Greg Strong, an honest, robust and fittingly named player then at Bolton Wanderers. They were playing hard ball with us, as was their right. Eventually I was given permission to talk to Greg, and was pushed directly towards his agent, David Speedie! Speedo and I had been teammates at Chelsea, and though we had a fine on-field understanding, he was the most difficult teammate I'd dealt with in my entire career. The thought of me doing a 'deal' with him now seemed to scupper the possibility of us getting Greg. Much to my surprise the business was eventually done, with a surprisingly limited amount of rancour. Speedo must have mellowed as he aged.

Every deal had its own idiosyncrasies, there was no standardised way of doing things. Young Stephen Pearson just got his dad to do his. Scott Leitch, who was a great pro, looked like he might be difficult to lure away from Swindon Town for an acceptable price. Cue finding out that his agent was John Colquhoun, somebody who I could trust. The deal was done in hours, while others might have dragged the negotiations out for months.

There were some dreadful 'agents', who were an embarrassment to their profession. One had a player who we wanted to sign from the Continent. The agent sat in my office with the player. I laid out my offer, and he replied with his demands, which were predictably around double what was on the table. As the haggling continued, he would turn to his player and speak in French, to safeguard their confidentiality without having to walk out of the room. My French isn't fluent, but I had enough to be *au fait* with just about every word they said. It wasn't a great idea, to suppose that no Brit can understand anything other than English.

He compounded his arrogance by asking his player to leave the room, then brazenly explaining, 'My lad would sign for peanuts, but we could make sure that the deal was cut so that we could both clean up on the excess. We could go 50–50, without anyone else knowing, including the club. What do you think?'

I made it clear I wasn't that type of person, but got the player signed, gave him a fair wage for his talents and sadly also had to allow the player to overpay his corrupt agent, who didn't deserve a penny. It was an inexcusable attempt to stitch the lad up by someone purporting to work for him and his best interests – but I did the best I could for the player in the circumstances.

The first question the lad asked me just a few weeks later in his broken English was, 'Is there any advice you would give me about Scotland or Scottish football?'

I looked him meaningfully straight in the eye and, with as much kindness as I could, said, 'The best piece advice I could possibly give you is "GET A NEW AGENT!"'

Happily he got the message and soon after got a new agent too.

Agents sometimes tried to insert themselves into deals that were already almost done – deals they'd had absolutely nothing to do with. It was not uncommon for an agent to call and say he was representing a player, or indeed another club, claiming it was he who was making the deal happen (back then it was always 'he'). It only took one phone call to the club or the player to find out if this was a scam, but it was not a rare occurrence. I've seen less brazen bare cheek on an episode of *Love Island* but I guess sometimes it must have paid dividends for those unscrupulous agents, when distressed selling clubs had to move quickly.

The agents trying to scam the system were rarely open about it; they chose their words carefully. It must have become known in the darker parts of the community that I wasn't taking a slice of the pie personally because, after a while, I stopped getting those types of shady offers. Doubtless there was plenty of it going on in the game back then, otherwise why would they try?

I had already realised that this could be a very grubby business, with the politics in the game being just as iniquitous as the outright sleaze. If I dealt with only people I knew to be upright and trustworthy, that meant there were quite a lot of people, many of them powerful and well connected, who were out of my orbit. Maybe I was sticking my head in the sand regarding the realities of the business sometimes. If I am completely honest there were moments when I had to manipulate situations myself, politically – but I always hoped it was for the right reasons.

Was not telling the press the whole story about Andy Goram acceptable? Was 'playing a blinder' to get us a limited fine when we made an error on a teamsheet decent behaviour? What about leaving a tape recorder in press conferences, even if there was no tape in it? There was also the tampering with the video tape to hoodwink the SFA disciplinary committee. I had to be careful not to slide into that mucky world. I reckoned most who did never really realised that, after first dipping a toe in, they were suddenly in so far they couldn't get out again.

Next item from the in-tray was tying up our midfielder Derek Adams on a new contract. The fans didn't always love him, because he wasn't showy, but he was a superb influence on the group and as selfless a team player as I had ever known, which often goes under the fans' radars. He was the best natural finisher at the club, but for some reason the goals didn't flow quite as easily as they had done for him before he joined us. I met up with his agent, an old friend and former international colleague, Eric Black.

Eric had been coaching but had become disillusioned with it, which I totally understood after what had happened when he assisted John Barnes during his ill-fated time as Celtic manager the previous year. Everyone in the know thought Eric was a top-quality coach, and I felt it was a shame that he was 'just' an agent, and I told him so. He might have thought I was buttering him up as part of the deal to get Derek Adams to sign, but I wasn't. Not surprisingly, he was an honorable agent who behaved impeccably throughout and went to the trouble of talking me through some of the other players he had or could provide. His knowledge and reach were startling. The deal was done to re-sign Derek and, for once, doing business with an agent was actually pleasurable, due to the honesty and decency of the man. Eric Black was someone I could work with again.

There were good and bad agents, but there were even some question marks over national associations, though that admittedly fell far short of corruption. We had spotted a young Irish attacker named Stuart Elliott playing for Glentoran. At the last minute, during the negotiations, the Glens suggested an extra £20K payment if Stuart became a Northern Irish international. John Boyle said to me, in front of their negotiator, 'That sounds reasonable; if he is a full international then he is a more valuable player.'

I took JB aside: 'I will make you a solemn promise, John. If you agree to that condition he will be playing in green and white at Windsor Park within the year. You're just throwing £20,000 away. Don't fall for it – or at least make the deal for ten international appearances not just one. That would make him a seasoned international with real extra value.'

I was outvoted and the day after he signed for Motherwell, with the ink scarcely dry on the contract, Stuart was called into the Northern Ireland squad. He was good enough and did go on to play nearly 40 times for his country, but it was some coincidence it happened right there and then, at what some might think an indecent speed.

Despite the pre-season meeting, JB was still putting some pressure on me to sell players, and the best I could say was, 'All in good time. We have some valuable assets, but you should always sell when the market suits you.' Though why I was saying this to someone who had infinitely more knowledge of the real financial markets than me is questionable. I guess I was just trying to speak in his native tongue.

There were still some increasingly incredible ideas being floated at board meetings and in the boardroom after matches – but, to be fair, those sometimes surfaced after a few drinks. There was a suggestion around then that the entire club could be sold to an agency called Premier Management, in London. This kite was flown far enough for me to fly down south after it, only to discover they were just interested in our sellable assets, McCulloch and McMillan. It was a wasted journey and a waste of my time. Had I not organised it to coincide with some TV work I was doing for Channel 5, I would have been more than miffed.

Working for Channel 5 as the studio guest for their UEFA Cup games was becoming more regular, and those trips to London were a fabulous relief from the pressure at Motherwell. Every two or three weeks I would pop down, and the stress of the day-to-day trials would just melt away for a day or two. Nobody down there cared or knew about what was going on back up north. Covering the likes of Roma v Arsenal, Newcastle v Troyes or Inter Milan v Ipswich was more like therapy than a job.

Back home there seemed to be the possibility of 'an understanding' between Motherwell and Aston Villa, which also led to high-level meetings between the two clubs. After one such meeting I ensured that everyone fully understood that ownership of two different clubs could be 'problematic' within the current rules. So, if anything was to be done it had to be done carefully, sensitively and legally. When it became clear that Motherwell were not going to be bailed out by the much wealthier Villains, JB and his team went cold on the idea very quickly. The chance of getting some of their most talented youngsters on loan, which was my special interest, was also gone. That was a shame, as it could have been beneficial for all parties.

Other attempts were made to increase income. I spent a lot of time talking to the police, trying to get them to allow us to play on Friday nights, to capture a few local Celtic and Rangers supporters, just as Tranmere had done with Everton and Liverpool fans – but they refused to budge because of issues with their staff rotas.

There were rumblings that Celtic and Rangers were trying to get out of Scotland and join the English system, where the real money was. These possible moves south often appeared in the media just before a round of TV contract negotiations began, putting pressure on the 'little' clubs to acquiesce to the Old Firm's demands. It wasn't subtle – well, not to my eyes anyway.

During an early SPL meeting about a renegotiated TV deal I asked, 'Do you really think any middling Premier League team would want you two behemoths clumping around on their patch, when you would be sure to take their positions eventually? Turkeys generally don't vote for Christmas.'

There was no reply. I suspect they felt they had better intel than me.

At Fir Park one afternoon at a board meeting I mused, 'The only legal way for the Old Firm to get into the English league would be to buy an available northern English club and build them up. If you bought, say, Workington Town, theoretically, over time, you could make them Workington Celtic or Rangers.' It was just a thought, an experiment I'd consider a bit 'out there', not unlike franchising – and I wouldn't have condoned it. Months later I discovered that, without my knowledge, Motherwell had apparently entered into an understanding with Workington and had even been talking to Carlisle United.

Apart from the usual ways of trying to increase revenue, such as sponsorship and improved executive packages, there was also merchandising, and some of the ideas were bizarrely creative. Like: 'Have you ever noticed the Harry Potter Gryffindor scarfs are the same colours as Motherwell scarfs? Surely we should get some capital out of that in the club shop?' I will own up to that one at the start of Potter mania, but would underline that the Steelmen wore claret and amber long before J.K. Rowling had written about Harry and his chums.

I will not, however, accept any involvement in the idea of a players' calendar designed not unlike the Women's Institute's infamous publication. The idea was that the better-looking players would be pictured naked, except for a football or some other Motherwell regalia strategically positioned to hide their . . . modesty. We had plenty of very good-looking lads and, even though I dismissed the idea out of hand, any female Motherwell fans who were asked about seeing pictures of Ged Brannan, Lee McCulloch, Michael Doesburg, Spenny and Benito Kemble undressed seemed much less negative about the idea. I promise I wasn't against the concept because they wouldn't be using me, but more the idea that the owner JB would get dog's abuse for it, and that it didn't sit well with our progressive outlook anyway. That idea was floated and scuttled very quickly.

There was a feeling of desperation in the air, but it was imperative that I didn't buy into this panic mode; decisions made in haste now would have the club repenting at leisure. Things were not helped by having a difficult start to the season on the pitch. There was a run of single goal defeats in games that could have gone either way, including tight 1–0 losses to both Celtic and Rangers.

Our experienced star strikers, who were the most expensive players on the books, saw their goals dry up, with John Spencer only scoring three that season and Don Goodman just one, albeit against Rangers. Neither seemed to be doing anything different or putting in any less effort, but, obviously, without a creative player like yours truly they weren't getting the supply. (That wasn't even close to the truth about me, but I did think I could have helped a little had I still been available. But, of course, that ship had sailed, and I had accepted its departure.)*

We had a whole bunch of injuries, illnesses and suspensions when an important home game came along. The squad available to the manager looked threadbare and very youthful. A senior figure in the club then came to me with his cunning plan to save us. On the day before the game, he suggested, 'Pat, it is going to be well below freezing. If we get the groundsman to soak the pitch with fire hoses tonight, by morning it will be solid and rutted and the game will be cancelled. We'll have half the team back when it's rescheduled! Let's do it, it's worth the risk.'

When I eventually stopped looking like a startled vicar, I countered, 'Well, let's see if there are any possible downsides if I agreed to do this. Our pitch is a disaster area anyway, with the destroyed drains. The hose on

---

* Billy, to his credit, did come back to me a couple of months into the season and asked if I would consider returning to the squad to give him another creative option. But, tempting though it was, I decided against it, probably wisely.

all night might just kill the surface for the rest of the season. And what if it leaks out that we have cheated like this? First, I would sack you, then I would sack the groundsman for allowing you access and, finally, I would sack myself. The club would be a laughing stock, and we'd get docked about ten points. That's before we've considered letting the fans down and the costs of the cancellation to them. It also happens to be immoral. So, on balance, I probably won't sanction that particular action.'

It was clearly a proposition born of desperation, and, yes, he had the club's interests at heart. In his eyes, 'when' we lost tomorrow's game it would be my fault, because I wasn't brave enough or didn't care enough to take a chance. Maybe this was no great show of my honesty from me, just another example of my tiresome earnestness and the fact that I thought it was simply a dim-witted idea. As it was, we won the game 2–0 against St Mirren and picked up three vital points.

Fortunately, our young striker Lee McCulloch started banging in the goals as well as improving his all-round game at an alarming rate. He had become inseparable from Ged Brannan and was being positively influenced by the professionalism of our captain who, along with new signing Stuart Elliott, had become one of our most regular scorers. Derek Adams was chipping in with a few goals too, as well as delivering some steady performances. You could not hope to have better characters than those four in your team, and I hoped to keep them at the club for a while yet.

The corner was finally being turned, and things were even more positive by the start of the new year. We had to reach a position of security in the league and then, and only then, could I consider the departures of McCulloch and McMillan. I thought that the longer we kept them, the more likely there would be a bidding war, as more clubs were taking notice of them every week. That would be the perfect financial scenario not only for the club, but for the players themselves, giving them good options and better bargaining positions.

This patient approach was becoming a harder sell to the owner and his people, however. Then, out of a clear blue sky, a stark message was delivered to me on the phone: 'Hamilton Portfolio [JB's umbrella company] could go under if we don't get half a million pounds of the money Motherwell owe ["*owe*"!] us immediately. You need to sell now, right now; the value doesn't matter, and we don't care who you sell to.'

I refused to flog any player on the cheap, and wouldn't panic. A week later they informed me their panic was over, and I wasn't to worry about the £500K right now. Thank goodness I wasn't rattled by the original message and hadn't flogged McMillan or McCulloch – or both of them – for a pittance. I'd got used to the financial lurches and was confident my way would be the most cost-effective in the end; short-termism is catastrophic in this business.

All the other usual media mayhem was still carrying on around us. Shaun Teale was going, but the sting in the tail was another vicious article in the *Sun* newspaper slaughtering the club – well, John Boyle and Billy Davies, mostly – for not giving him the contract extension he wanted and felt he had been promised. J B was annoyed, but this time he was much easier to talk down from his hurt and anger. He was finally learning that this stuff just comes with the territory and goes just as quickly. It was a fairly mundane hatchet job, and most people could see it for what it was. JB, for once, took some pleasure going on the front foot and reacting presciently in the press, going as far as threatening Tealey that he would never play for the team again. I remember thinking, 'Well played, that man.'

One win in those first ten league games had initially left us in a treacherous league position and, of course, the media understandably felt the manager's coat was on a 'shoogly peg', as we would say in Scotland. One by one the board members were becoming more vocal about sacking Davies, because of results but also what some of them felt were his increasingly tiresome personality clashes. Billy and I were fine: I accepted he was just trying his very best under what were increasingly difficult circumstances, and I stood by him. We needed a strong character to get us through these tough times – and doubtless even more challenging times to come when we had to sell players. If that meant a bunker mentality from him, then so be it in the short term.

Communications, however, began to break down between Billy and Davie McParland, the head of the youth department. Within weeks I was hearing passionate complaints from both sides every day. Then Billy's relationship with the club secretary, Alasdair Barron, became strained. Worse still, the chairman himself began to further lose patience with the manager, the mutual trust and respect for each other dwindling daily. The atmosphere was rapidly becoming toxic within the club. At the management level, it felt like I was the only one trying to get everyone to work together. These tensions were all growing from the stresses of downsizing and the looming cutbacks. The run of bad results was matched by the run of negative stories in the press. 'Davies on the verge of the sack,' ran in the papers most weeks, which must have been very stressful for him. Seeing as I was the only person who could sack him, maybe talking and listening to me instead of the papers was the best call for Billy – but, even so, I knew it wasn't easy for him.

One of the most difficult moments slammed into us from nowhere in the January of that season, in a game against St Johnstone up at McDiarmid Park. I was standing in the tunnel post-match when one of Perth's finest pulled our young full-back Stevie Hammell before he got to the dressing room. He was being accused of racially abusing their winger Momo Sylla.

One of the greatest difficulties of doing the job was I couldn't plan or prepare for these problems that arose seemingly out of nowhere. There was also the delicacy that I had spent a lifetime making stands against racism in football, and in life, but here I was having to advocate for someone directly accused of abusive racist language. This was a very serious charge, even though Sylla himself had heard nothing untoward – the complaint had come from fans. I knew Stevie's personality well, and to say that sort of thing would be 'out of character' wouldn't even come close to covering it. But the two policemen weren't to know this.

Stevie was aghast, devastated and clearly shocked even at the mere insinuation, but he was also angry and indignant. He thought he was going to be thrown into the back of a police van and transported to a cell with his strip and boots still on – and the boys in blue were not doing or saying anything to stop him feeling that way. At this point the media fallout was the last thing on my mind; I had to help the young lad get to a safe place. Sometime later I discovered, after a little digging, that this was not the first such 'complaint' from that specific area of the ground. Lubo Moravčík of Celtic, another player with impeccable personal credentials, was accused of a similar unsubstantiated outburst.

The press were understandably all over the story. Young Steven was beside himself with worry, and needed lots of help in the moment, then days and weeks afterwards, as his character was being destroyed. Eventually I sourced a video of the game and went through it frame by frame. After analysing it closely, my diary entry leaves no doubt about my own considered legal thinking on the matter: 'This is total crap; he is totally innocent! He was miles away from those fans; they could never have heard what he was saying.'

In the end, the case was dropped, but it was a long, drawn-out and stressful affair for young Steven. In such cases, whether fair or not, comments like 'there is no smoke without fire' and 'mud sticks' are commonly used, whether there is a conviction or not. It is grossly unfair.

The problems kept coming. Andy Goram, 'the Goalie', was also under pressure again. This time he was being chased about his private life, and I was getting regular reports that his drinking was getting out of control. He turned up one morning with the booze still strong enough on his breath to just about intoxicate anyone who got too close, but he was battling to straighten himself and his life out. Somehow, his performances on match days and in training were still of a very high standard. Being followed and reported on everywhere he went wasn't helping his mental health, though.

There was also an argument with the players over the season's new bonus schedule. I knew this problem better than most – it had happened at almost every club I had been with at some point. The press may have begun to grasp the financial pressures on the club, but some of the players either hadn't done so or didn't care. The bonus negotiations were leaked to the press and, yet again, we saw the standard headline: 'Motherwell in Crisis'.

Right after that a delegation of players came to talk to me. I braced myself for the outbursts, even though I was quite hurt by the apparent actions of the group going to the press while discussions were ongoing. They filed into my small office, led by some of the more senior players, including reserve goalkeeper Stevie Woods. Woodsy was always a sensible, intelligent and considerate guy whatever the circumstances. He was also funny, as well as being utterly honest and trustworthy. He was one of the players I could only think of as a friend, so I was happy to see him in the party.

I didn't have enough seats in the office for the six-strong gathering, so as they stood I stood too, all very uncomfortable. I hated being on the 'other side' of the desk, seemingly against the workers, but I felt I could explain the delicate situation to them, if only they would listen and not get angry right away. I was braced and ready for the showdown, with all the figures at my fingertips, though I was far from relishing the discussion. They surprised me, though, with their opening gambit: 'Pat, we're really sorry but the press have stitched us up on the story about the bonuses. We've agreed that we would like you to inform them that all media appearances from now on should go through the club, preferably you. We can't trust them and we don't want to talk to them.'

Not exactly the meeting I was expecting, or indeed had prepared for. I was happy to help, but I also knew that from the outside it would look like I was the one trying to control the players' output with a kind of Stalinist efficiency when, in fact, the opposite was the case, it was them asking me to provide a buffer. These days agents do that job, but not many of our players had day-to-day agents back then, just people who would turn up for the big pay day when the new contract was due, or when the player was being transferred. But I was happy to take a little more pressure to help the lads – there was enough stress on me already, so what difference was a little more going to make?

One of the questions regularly being asked of me, and one that had been asked from day one at the club, was, 'So, what is it you actually do at

Motherwell?' The temptation to get annoyed was only momentary, but it underlined that, from the outside, apparently all that ever happens at a football club is that a bunch of players train and then kick a ball about in front of the fans a couple of times a week. When all is said and done, apart from the games, everything else is secondary – so I understood the question. There was, however, a lot more going on, which would have taken most of the day to explain, and, much to the surprise of the questioners, I didn't have that sort of spare time on my hands to talk them through it all.

The latest missive from on high was that I had to get the players' wage bill down from £2.8 million per annum to £1.6 million. In fact, this drop of over 40 per cent in the wage bill was something I felt I could engineer by the start of the following season and still keep us safely in the top league. It would leave us a far weaker team, but if we could blood the up-and-coming youngsters throughout the current campaign, it was doable. I was acutely aware that whatever I or anyone else said, the manager would then get the blame for the ensuing bad results, even though it would be clear he was losing many, if not most, of his best and most experienced players.

I was still working at 100mph, constantly firefighting and with precious little time to see my family and live a life. On almost every drive back home I asked myself the same question: 'Do I really want to keep on doing this?' I could just about cope when I had a little head space, and all the problems weren't crushing in on me at the same time. This wasn't how it was supposed to be, and not the way I envisioned the job when I had agreed to it at the start of the season. This third season at Motherwell was supposed to be easier now that I wasn't actually playing, but it was proving to be anything but.

Everywhere I turned there were serious issues to be dealt with. I gave statements to the prosecution, the defence and the police regarding a court case involving paedophilia allegations against a former coach at Celtic Boys' Club, but I wasn't called for the trial. Child abuse could happen anywhere, and I realised I had to be proactive to ensure all was well at Motherwell. I called our youth coaches together and told them, 'If anyone has suspicions of improper sexual behaviour, my door is always open; call at any time and speak to me in the strictest confidence.'

A few weeks later I had a visitor with the dreaded line, 'I'm concerned about one of the youth coaches.' He told me the name and it wasn't one I had heard of before. 'What are your suspicions?' I asked. 'Have there been complaints? Have you witnessed questionable behaviour? Has anyone else? Has a kid said something?'

He answered confidently: 'Well, I think he is gay. He kind of acts a bit light in the loafer, a bit poofy sometimes. Y'know what I mean?'

'Surely that's not it,' I thought to myself. 'So, what has that led to?' I asked.

'Well, nothing. But surely we don't want that sort coaching our kids?'

I answered in a kindly manner: 'I can't sack someone for being a bit "light in the loafer". Being or acting gay isn't a crime, but come back if you have any real evidence of misconduct.'

I could have been angry, but I knew there were many who felt the way this guy did, and some still do so today. It is part of the worst side of football culture, and one that I hope we will finally see an end to soon.

Fortunately, the team suddenly found some form and, more importantly, there were a couple of clubs who seemed to be in an even more precarious financial position than us, specifically St Mirren. It's still the case today: it's all about the money. Whatever you say about the great managers and their tactical genius – in the end money is as important in bringing long-term success as anything else in football, however painful that is to digest.

The real money that was going to save us would come from TV and from developing then selling players. Those two areas looked healthy right at that moment, which was a blessed relief. There was a new TV deal on the horizon. Celtic and Rangers were ominously demanding an increase in their percentage of the money, which was already the lion's share, but hopefully that was just the usual sabre-rattling bargaining from the big beasts. Survival in the medium term seemed a little rosier, even Hamilton

Portfolio were a little more hopeful, and I could see what looked like a slightly smoother road somewhere ahead, albeit in the distance.

The selfish truth was, however, that being 'Director of Football', as I was now currently labelled, didn't suit me long term. The constant flow of problems to solve – some worthy, others selfish and capricious – was dragging me down. Spending days on tiresome small complaints knowing I should have been spending my time elsewhere, sometimes anywhere else, wasn't helping matters.

One argument about acquiring hypertonic drinks lasted weeks. In the end I snapped, 'Just go out and buy some bloody Lucozade!' That took two weeks when it should have taken two minutes, but I was often too polite to just say it right away in case they took offence. I got frustrated with the time-wasters. Because of them, I wasn't finding enough time to help and praise the good colleagues, who were still in the majority, and quietly knuckling down and getting on with their jobs.

Doing everything on a shoestring budget was tiresome, when week by week we had to revisit costs. Can we get a cheaper coach company for away games? Can we stay in cheaper hotels? Can we travel to even the most distant away games on the day of the game to save paying any hotel bills at all? And that was just the travel; every other area was slowly being cut back too.

Another negative factor was that I was now divorced from the things I loved about football, and married to the things I disliked. I knew this couldn't go on forever. Others apparently liked wielding power and controlling people's destinies. I couldn't see the attraction. During those long dark drives home that winter, I planned my exit strategy. Before leaving Motherwell I would reset the finances, recoup some of John's money and leave the club in a good place economically and structurally.

The change in direction to a cheaper version was no longer being hidden. There was a press story that said, 'Boyle's experiment is over.' My party line would have been: 'It's a recalibration.' Which it was. My blunter, more honest reaction to the headline would have been: 'No shit, Sherlock!' It was blindingly obvious that the plug was being pulled.

19/
I DON'T RECOGNISE YOU

In the Motherwell boardroom after home games, you would find our own board members, the former owners, the visiting team's executives, as well as a few invited guests. The atmosphere was always forced – a stiff conviviality. If your team had lost, the last thing you really wanted to do was to engage in polite small talk with the opposition's owners who, even if they weren't being smug and self-satisfied, it almost always felt as if they were.

After these defeats John Boyle would do the rounds of the little groups, delivering the expected pleasantries, and then sidle over to me at the first opportunity and say, 'We can't go on making financial losses like this forever, Pat. Are you sure you know what you are doing? Will the young players' values not fall if we continue to lose like today? If we are relegated and we haven't cashed in on their value, the club might be unsavable.'

These were difficult times, when I had to be strong with JB and hope that I was being honest with myself and not just hopeful. 'These players are good enough and they will improve more as time goes by,' I assured him. 'There are a few weaker teams in the league, so we'll be fine. I am convinced we will stay up. When I feel we are safe from the drop, I promise I will start the sales, but not before. It is time to hold steady, not to panic. I am not being cavalier with your money, just sensible.'

Not only had we lost by a single goal to the Old Firm teams – who each had individual players that cost more than our entire squad combined – we also lost by single late goals against Kilmarnock and Dunfermline, each one a crushing blow, as was the 86th minute equaliser by Aberdeen to deny us two points a few weeks later. For a while the season felt jinxed, and it didn't take a statistician to realise that a measly five points from the first 30 was 100 per cent definite relegation form, but I still felt we had a good enough group of players to recover, and that our bad luck wouldn't last.

The owner had become a less frequent visitor to the club in this third season of his ownership, though he rarely missed a match day and those drinks in the boardroom. He might have been busy in his other businesses, but I suspect part of the reason for his absence was that he'd got fed up with turning up for constant grief from players, fans and staff about their problems at the club, now always finance related. I didn't blame him for swerving those discussions.

Fortunately, the quality of the team, and indeed the manager's decisions, bore fruit eventually. What became clear as the season progressed was that I could not let individual games affect the way I planned the next stage. That is easy to say but very hard to do. Every defeat feels like the end of the world, but that day-to-day or week-to-week panic had to be dealt with by the owner, the manager and the players. That would be the fans' and the press's domain, I couldn't get sucked into it: someone had to have a longer, wider overview.

By late February 2001 I believed we were just about safe from relegation, and the time was right to fulfil the promises to the chairman, to slash the wage bill and get some money in. It was time to press the button – I just hoped it wasn't a self-destruct button.

First to go was Ged Brannan. Wigan were the main suitors, with Tranmere Rovers also trying to get their former star back. Unfortunately the Rovers clearly didn't have the funds. I loved that club, but this had to be hard-nosed business. I talked Wigan up from £100,000 to £175,000 – daylight robbery for a player of his quality – but because he was nudging the dreaded 30th birthday, that was the market value. Most importantly for Motherwell, this was one of the top earners off the wage bill. For me, personally, it was the hardest deal to do. Ged was our most important player, often skipper and the perfect pro who never let the team down wherever he played. Ged was as undemanding a player as you could meet. He had a great relationship with all his teammates, was as kind as he was committed, and was also well respected and liked into the bargain. It felt like cutting the soul out of the team – and on top of that I was losing a good friend. I had no option, however: I had to cut the wage bill by over £1 million. That was the deal, and he had to go.

Soon after there was an approach for both McCulloch and McMillan, or Jig and Studs as I knew them, again from Wigan Athletic, who were preparing for a serious and eventually fruitful assault on the foothills of the Premier League. This was the critical moment: if I could maximise the fees for these sales then I felt much of the financial stress would be relieved on the entire club. I found myself preparing mentally for the negotiations the way I would have done for a cup final. I needed to know the values of every other player of similar ability who had gone south, and everything I could about Wigan's financial situation. I got myself into a state of mind that was totally alien to any previous contract negotiations I had been involved in. I had to be as hard as nails this time.

McCulloch and McMillan were two of our best players, but they deserved the chance to go to the next level. So although the team would miss them massively, now was the right time to act or, to be more accurate, cash in, for all parties concerned. Hearts and some other clubs were still sniffing around Jig, but both players told me again, personally, that they preferred Wigan.

Just before I got things moving with the Latics an agent representing Wigan called while I was in my office and said someone at John Boyle's company had already been in touch that morning. '*What?!* Who the hell was that? I'm dealing with this!' I was angry already, but furious after his next line: 'He told us that we can have both for £800,000 on the nose, here and now, less agent's fees, of course.'

For the first and maybe last time in my in my executive career, I banged my fist on the desk in front of me, then shouted down the phone, 'Absolutely not, whoever gave you that bullshit line must have been pissed!' I had to get this back under my control and quickly, 'I am the only one who can ratify this deal, and even £1 million isn't close to being enough for these lads – they are top players and, anyway, I've already got other offers on the table for well above that figure.'

It took a while, but I managed to convince the agent and Wigan that they had been communicating with a 'rogue dealer' within the organisation. In a brief one-sided phone call later, I let the individual who suggested the £800K know what I felt about me now being hamstrung in the negotiations.

These negotiations would all be done by phone. They took two days of calls: the deal was on then off again a number of times from both sides – it was classic brinkmanship – but I couldn't afford to sell them cheap. Then again, I couldn't afford to lose the deal altogether either. Using all the charm I possessed I eventually got them up to £1.35 million, with further appearance bonuses to be added in time, and with no agent's cuts coming off from our side!

Just sitting in my office with the phone glued to my ear, getting coffees delivered on the hour every hour, I had made the club nearly £600,000 extra in just a few days with some hard negotiating. This was undoubtedly a great result considering how I'd been undermined at the start. Lee McCulloch trusted me throughout but Stephen McMillan was understandably getting more stressed as it dragged on. I knew they would get their moves eventually – my hand was nowhere near as strong as I implied – but I couldn't share that knowledge with them at that point!

Well into the second evening, and with my office now darkening after sunset, it appeared we had a deal. So just when everyone felt the negotiations were over and we were all mentally exhausted by the efforts, and desperate to get back to our homes, I pushed the deal a little further at the very last moment. While Wigan doubtless had me on speaker phone, I was alone in that gloomy office in Motherwell when I lobbed in my final demand – make that grenade: 'Let's discuss the sell-on fees now. If you make a huge profit on these guys, we should be due a percentage of that.' I removed the phone from my ear about six inches at this point and reclined way back in my chair, while looking at the ceiling and cringing as well as smiling at my own cheek. I didn't need to hear the full explicit explosive force from the other end of the line, but what I caught was as funny as it was furious. There were a few northern swear words that I had never heard before.

Gordon Taylor, back in my time at the PFA, had always underlined how lucrative these last moments of negotiations could be. After the shock and horror from both sides – mine feigned – I agreed to be reasonable and give something back: 'We'll just take a percentage of the sell-on fee for one of them. But I get to choose which one.'

Left-backs were at a premium just then, and I knew the position having played against a few in my time. McMillan was good enough to be an international and to play for a bigger team in the Premier League – an Andy Robertson of his time.

Lee was a striker, the more obvious choice for a sell-on clause, but to make it up front in England is a tough call. He would always be good in his position, but Stephen could be great in his. I was under pressure to make a quick decision, seeing as it was my idea and they were still grumbling away. 'I'll take the sell-on clause with McMillan.' The grumbling stopped. Wigan seemed perfectly happy with that, and they were right to be. Sadly, I'd made the wrong choice and it served me right for being so pleased with myself during that phone call. Stephen was unlucky with injuries and retired after a successful initial period; Lee, on the other hand, continued to improve and was eventually sold on to Rangers. Had I chosen him, Motherwell would have got close to a six-figure bonus four years later. Some you win, some you lose.

When the deal was finally done it dawned on me that I had managed to have an entire career in football and had never fought particularly hard for my own deals – but when it was someone else's money, or the club's finances,

I found I quite enjoyed the cut and thrust of the negotiations. I suppose it was just the fact that I could never say of myself: 'Do you know how great I am? I am worth a fortune.' Maybe I should have had an agent during my career – but, then again, I was paid enough to get by over the years, so why worry?

It was a revelation that I enjoyed this specific little side of the business – no part of my personality or previous life suggested I would get any pleasure from this haggling at all. On reflection, maybe I thought, 'This is just a game – one that needs some deep understanding of my own and the opposition's positions. If I play the game well, there is a reward, not financially for myself, but for my club.' It was intellectually challenging. Maybe the thing that made it easier to deal with morally was that I knew the buyers could afford the money – certainly we needed it far more than them. There was no guilt.

The fire sale was far from over. The next to leave was John Spencer, whose wage costs were still eye-watering for a club the size of Motherwell. This is in no way a dig at Spenny: that was his value, and John Boyle had agreed to pay those wages and the fee – but it was totally unsustainable. He left for a happy and successful new career in the US as a player and then a coach*.

Even though I strongly advised against buying Spenny in the first place, and was promised those costs would not be lumped in with my

---

* Remember that £68K black Jag Spenny got when he signed? This was a super-car, more like the Batmobile than a bog-standard Merc. With Spenny leaving, it was now ours. But what the hell to do with it? A local garage offered £17 grand, a loss of almost £50K. Apparently only two types of people liked those cars: millionaires who wanted them new; and boy racers who couldn't afford the tyres, eye-watering insurance, bankrupting services, the initial £17K or, indeed, the fuel. The joke was that it could pass anything on the road, except a petrol station. Embarrassingly, I didn't trade it in. I kept it instead of getting a loan of the second-hand C Class Mercedes I was due for the same value. But what an incredible car to drive – if a tad brash in the interior-décor department! I argued to myself that I needed a safe, comfortable car because of the 200 miles covered every day – total nonsense, of course. Being followed by the police, or boy racers – either of whom you could burn up effortlessly if tempted – was not the worst downside. The lasting effect was that I've never enjoyed driving as much since. Everything else in my price range is utterly bland in comparison.

budget, naturally, they were when the losses were discussed. His contract alone accounted for nearly 20 per cent of our entire playing budget, and you had to add in the fee for buying him on top of that. It was the single, biggest and most expensive financial mistake JB made at Motherwell – apart, arguably, from buying the club in the first place!

The sales still hadn't finished there, however. Out of nowhere came a call from Manchester United. They wanted our veteran goalkeeper Andy Goram. There are two things to note here. First, there was no way on earth that I was going to stop Andy getting his chance to go to United – even if it was for free. And, secondly, the Goalie was the last big earner – losing his wage from the budget would give us breathing space to start the rebuild with the new, albeit much smaller, budget. I couldn't, however, allow United to know this.

So, once again, I had to play hard ball for a while and keep my poker face steady.

United had a goalkeeping crisis, with injuries and other problems concerning Fabien Barthez and Mark Bosnich. They still had Champions League football, and Goram was still a world-class shot stopper, even if he was creaking a little bit at the edges. It made sense, but it had to be done in a few days as the European transfer deadline was approaching.

There was a snowstorm of biblical proportions that left me marooned in the Scottish Borders for a couple of days. I decided to be unavailable at home with a 'dodgy phone line' and limited internet, but I got the message across that we still had a day or two to do the deal. I knew Andy would go down to Manchester to get a medical and he would be there ready in their offices waiting to sign the papers.

I eventually made it into Motherwell's Fir Park after a four-hour drive through snowdrifts on deadline day. I had always planned to 'cut it fine' and so, at three o'clock, two hours before the window slammed shut, I casually asked United's negotiator over the phone, 'Let's get down to the real business. How much are you prepared to pay for the Goalie?'

I wasn't surprised by his reply. '*What?!* We thought it was a loan deal. We aren't paying a transfer fee.'

I was talking to one of their executives but understood Alex Ferguson was in the same room, or an adjacent one. He would have been furious, I guess. Two hours from the deadline, they had nowhere else to go, no other keeper they could get, and we all knew it. What they didn't know was that I had told John Boyle that if they hadn't agreed to pay us some money within the hour, then I would let Andy go for free. But I had to try this last-minute ploy to see if we could get anything. I explained to United, 'No one mentioned loans. You can't expect us to give you our only world-class player for free. We may be small, but we aren't stupid. You've got to be reasonable. And if you are, I will be too.'

I knew the Goalie would be fuming down there in Manchester, fearing his dream move was in jeopardy. Of course, I would never have stopped it going through, but brinkmanship is part of the business and I had to try. An hour later a 'loan fee' of £100,000 had been agreed, Motherwell's coffers were looking a little healthier, and Manchester United's accountants probably wouldn't have spotted it missing from the loose change box.*

With some of the top players offloaded and the squad lighter, the results unsurprisingly dipped – as in, dipped off the end of a huge continental shelf-sized cliff. After the player cull we managed the grand total of four goals in the next ten league games, and 11 points from the final 36, even though there were no real hidings. There was another 1–0 defeat at Celtic Park and a 2–1 loss to Rangers with another 89th minute goal being the difference.

The final two games of the season gave a little glimmer of hope about the future, and something for the long-suffering 'Well fans to enjoy, just when they needed it most. The 2–1 win at Dunfermline and an exciting 3–3 home draw against St Mirren, with four of our five goals being scored by Northern Irish striker Stuart Elliott, made everything brighter and

---

* It felt huge, even if £100K would scarcely buy a United player a car. But for me this could cover the wages of two, maybe three young players for a year! I was happy enough to allow myself a fist pump, though I am not sure the Goalie ever forgave me for those few fretful hours. Sadly he is no longer with us.

more hopeful than it had been since the sales. I wasn't convinced; it was clear to me that there would be a lot of work to do to replace those lost, and that the job had to be done at a fraction of the cost. Thank goodness I hadn't sold those players any earlier, otherwise relegation would have been a certainty.

Considering the perilous financial position John had said our club was in, I was pleased I'd got the job done – or part of it, anyway. We didn't have as much debt, but we didn't have much of a team either. There were kids coming through who could fill some of the shirts and, eventually, somewhere down the line, they would become valuable assets themselves.

My plan had worked, and though it was stressful, and there was precious little fun during the fire sale, I also knew that the club was now in a far better place financially. John had spent a lot on Motherwell: allegedly more than £2.5 million buying it, then over £1 million upgrading various stadium facilities such as the corporate areas, the directors' rooms, the toilets and roofing, among other things. Less than three years in, however, my original fears that he would get disillusioned with losing large sums of money had come to pass. I hoped that JB wasn't just using me to asset strip the company before selling it on – but he promised me that wasn't the case.

With the financial position secured, there was relief all round. I even got a few handshakes and slaps on the back from the financiers at Hamilton Portfolio at a meeting in their offices, which was a first. The new direction at Motherwell held no great interest for me going forwards, but I'd wanted to leave the club in a decent, secure position. And it was now almost there. With a new, hopefully vastly improved TV deal in the offing, there would even be just about enough cash to rebuild a team of sorts. This organisation could finally be run like a sensible, if less successful, grown-up football club. I almost relaxed for a moment.

20/
BLINDNESS

You get bullies in every walk of life, and I guess it must be a huge temptation
to throw your weight around if you are bigger, stronger or wealthier than
everyone else. Football is just the same, on the pitch as well as off it.
Throw in a dollop of stress to add to the tension and some form of battle is
inevitable in the end.

The SPL clubs met to discuss the next television deal for the league.
Celtic and Rangers had a new outline proposal for the TV money on
offer – one which ensured most of it went to them, whatever happened,
wherever they finished in the league table. If agreed, this would be a huge
financial blow for the other ten clubs.

SPL CEO Roger Mitchell sat in the middle of the two now warring
factions: the Old Firm versus the rest. Roger had already negotiated a very
good overall package and was ready to go with Sky, but this disagreement
between the big two and 'the ten' over how the money would be divvied
up was holding the deal up and frustrating Roger, even if he always
appeared calm and in control. That open, friendly boyish face, always
framed by dark-rimmed rounded glasses, would be aged by others' lack
of willingness to be team players like him. Roger was a businessman to
the core – but even more than that he was a dedicated lover of the game,

as a fan, something I couldn't say with confidence about all the other executives working in the sport.

Alongside those youthful looks, maybe not being the tallest meant some didn't give Roger the respect he deserved. But I admired him and his general outlook on the game as highly as anyone in the sport at the time, whatever the media said. In the meantime, the press were being used as filters for leaks from the disgruntled big two clubs who were not getting their way – and we knew that.

The Old Firm argued that because they had the lion's share of the fans, they alone were attracting most of the domestic and global interest, and so they should be able to trouser a much bigger percentage share of the TV money – even more than they had received previously. It is a perfectly sound argument from their angle, and from the perspective of many of their fans it was fair. The real value for the broadcaster was in the four Old Firm derbies, followed by any other game that involved either of the Glasgow giants. They correctly underlined that the rest of the league games had microscopic value to the broadcasters in terms of eyes and, more importantly, advertising. So, depending on who you supported, the problem was with the greedy giants of Glasgow, or the grasping little clubs living off their scraps who were demanding too much. But how could 'the ten' agree to such an act of self-harm?

The Old Firm were, of course, still casting envious glances – or, more accurately, staring lasciviously – at the incredibly lucrative English Premier League TV deals. That's who they felt they should be competing with, as well as the top European clubs. The problem for the other ten Scottish clubs was not only that we couldn't come close to being competitive with the Old Firm on these terms but, more importantly, some of us knew that without this money our clubs wouldn't be able to survive as going concerns.

As positions became evermore entrenched, I think the Old Firm were initially surprised at the fight being put up by the others – they didn't seem to grasp how serious it was for us. The TV deals tended to last three or four years and, as the end of this one approached, we needed the certainty of that money coming in from the broadcasters. It was almost impossible to plan anything when you considered that this figure could amount to as much as 40 per cent of our club's overall income – roughly the same as annual gate receipts back then – and to suddenly have no idea if it was going to be paid the next season . . . well, without a decent TV deal in place the entire business model simply didn't add up. For a start, it would be almost impossible to service the contracts the clubs already had, never mind buy any new players. But none of this stopped the Old Firm piling the pressure on us, as clubs and as individuals.

Things went from bad to worse when suddenly the wider market began to change. The deal that Roger had almost got over the line with Sky was becoming less likely to remain on the table as the value of sports rights began plummeting as we bickered. For Motherwell and a few others, it now appeared incredibly bleak, especially as we had just cashed in most of our other chips by selling our best players.

Roger was trying everything to get both sides together, but his bargaining position with the broadcasters was being materially affected by the internecine war that was going on between the Old Firm and the rest. He came up with one other plan: SPLTV, our own channel that could be sold and marketed more directly to the public and would work on subscriptions. Even if there was no certainty that it would make the same kind of money that Sky had offered, I thought it was a decent way to let Sky know that they didn't have a monopoly – whether our channel idea worked or not, at least it was a bargaining chip.

Our own TV channel was, admittedly, a fairly radical idea for its time, and local Scottish production companies like Wark Clements were brought in to help work up the concept. The idea was not as ridiculous as it was portrayed in the press; in fact, in some ways, it was ahead of its time when you consider all the subscription channels that came into being years later. Roger, though, was pilloried in the press for the concept – but neither the chief executive nor his idea was the problem, it was the disagreement between the clubs that he couldn't resolve however hard he tried. The bad feeling continually spilled over into the press, and the stress levels were right back up to maximum again.

Existential problem or not for the 'other ten', the big dogs didn't seem to care a jot: on the face of it we might 'only' be fighting for a decent TV deal, but in reality we were fighting for our futures, the job security of everyone who was working at our clubs, as well as the fans of those institutions and the long histories they treasured.

It was the one topic that immediately sucked out all the usual good feeling that the other SPL meetings habitually had. The impasse was, however, increasingly annoying the prospective broadcasters, who needed to plan their own schedules and budgets. What the Old Firm didn't seem to appreciate was that Scottish football wasn't the broadcasters' first priority, and it soon became clear that with values in the sector plummeting, the deal still on the table could soon be removed if we didn't sort ourselves out as a league. The pressure was mounting daily on all sides.

For Motherwell, gate receipts and TV and radio revenue brought in roughly the same: about £1.2 million per annum each, and in a decent year we could make a further £900,000 or so through other income streams. Without a good TV deal for us it meant, at the very least, many redundancies, losing more players and a serious battle against going into administration. We simply couldn't afford to back down.

Suddenly the stories about the Old Firm moving south into the English Premier League were rampant again. The suggested upshot, if they did leave, was that the league, never mind the TV deal, would be hugely devalued.

I wasn't buying this line. I still had a few contacts down south and it didn't take long to discover the Old Firm moving there was, as ever, nonsense, a complete nonstarter – little more than a bargaining stick to beat the rest of Scottish football with. Celtic and Rangers could maybe join at one of the very lowest tiers, outside the Football League, and make their way up. But, in simple terms, other than buying out lower league clubs, they weren't wanted in the Premier League, whatever they had been told in those clandestine meetings. I also knew that getting it past the PFA would have been bordering on impossible and stupidly expensive! The suggested English love-in had a whiff of desperation about it, and I was smelling something else too.

I was one of the hawks in the 'other ten' who was strongly arguing that it was finally time 'to call the Old Firm's bluff'; it was time to stop cowering in their combined presence. The likes of ourselves, Hibs, Hearts, Aberdeen, Dundee and Dundee United, alongside Kilmarnock and St Johnstone, were each seriously concerned about our financial futures; it was time to make a final stand, so we began to hold our own meetings without the Old Firm. We knew they were working together, so we had to do the same.

Chris Robinson, representing Hearts, was among the first alongside me to speak up and say, 'We are in a stronger position than them, and we can use this situation to our advantage if they aren't going to play fair. We should publicly take the position that we'd be better off without the Old Firm constantly blackmailing us.' It was time for David to give Goliath his long overdue sore face. Our thinking was that if we set up our own league, they could decide whether they wanted to join us. There wouldn't be an 11–1 voting system in our new league. That was the catch that ensured the Old Firm always got their way by voting together to block change.*

Eventually, after some persuasion, everyone on our side except Livingstone FC was in agreement. Livi had a difficulty because there was a Celtic connection in their boardroom – but although they wouldn't be standing front and centre with the rest of us, they also wouldn't vote against us. They would be the 'Swiss' non-aggressors standing at the side, ready to help with negotiations if and when the fighting ended.

I argued that the Old Firm had nowhere to go: they could crow about the English Premier League all they liked, but there was no chance of that happening, whatever they said. They could join the lower Scottish divisions but, with all due respect to the likes of Stenhousemuir and Cowdenbeath, that wasn't going to be a huge sell on the international broadcast markets. If they wanted to they could coquettishly approach some of the bigger

---

* To have any major change implemented in the SPL, the Old Firm had initially demanded there had to be at least an 11-to-1 agreement; 10 votes to 2 would not be enough! The big two then always voted together to veto anything that they felt might negatively affect their own interests.

Scandinavian clubs, and maybe a few Dutch and Belgians could be tempted along for a new Atlantic League – but then that was very unlikely to get a speedy green light from UEFA, a body as resistant to change as the SFA. I was a hawk because I thought that at last, for maybe the first time in history, us 'other' Scottish clubs actually had a stronger hand than the big two, and it was time to play those cards.*

There was a very reasonable argument that said if this battle went 'nuclear' and the Old Firm weren't with us, then any TV deal we would get without Celtic and Rangers on board after the balloon went up would still pay us as much as the leftovers from the carve-up those two wanted to throw us via the Sky dish. There was arguably nothing for us to lose. The uncertainty around the TV deal and the subsequent impact it could have on our club meant that Motherwell's next season would already be more than just a battle against relegation. It would be a fight for survival as a business.

While open warfare was close to breaking out in the league, a cold war had been simmering at Motherwell. I came in one day to find the manager Billy Davies and youth supremo Davie McParland arguing outside their offices. This amounted to a final total meltdown in their relationship, which before then had been merely fractured. The reasons were tiresome from my point of view – mostly just a lack of trust on both sides, office politics that you can find anywhere. In the moment the words being said

---

* I wasn't absolutely delighted with the Old Firm at this point and felt they were not helping the game in the widest sense. That is probably why I wrote this in a *Match of the Day* magazine article at the time, with more than a hint of bitterness: 'Celtic and Rangers did have their own little domestic scrap the other week. Phenomenal atmosphere, if a tad poisonous, but in most respects a terrible game to watch for the connoisseur. A Belgian opened the scoring followed by a Swede before a Dane nabbed a late one in reply. A Dutchman should have been sent off for giving away a penalty, but an Italian defender diverted the referee's attention. Meanwhile a couple of Englishmen and a Welshman argued with a Norwegian about a Georgian diving earlier in the match. Some advert for Scottish football.'

were unimportant, it was the hatred in each man's eyes that was frankly disturbing. I'd had several meetings with them both individually and together to try to thrash it out, but I was getting nowhere. Knowing what was happening at a macro level, these micro-level spats frustrated me beyond belief. But to them, their disagreement was all consuming and the most important thing in the world. After walking out of their offices I would quietly stand in the corridor gently banging my head against the plywood wall separating those rooms.

One of my final efforts to reconcile the pair – after hearing countless diatribes from each, of their mutual mistrust that had now developed into full-blown hatred and loathing – involved getting them both in my office together to hammer it out face to face. I had no chance. As I spoke they both sat there refusing to look at each other or even acknowledge the other's presence. Not a word of consequence was uttered by one to the other during that entire final meeting. The exception being when I asked them, 'How would you describe this relationship?' Both answered in unison, 'Fine!' – with all the honesty and hidden poison of a furious housewife in a 1970s sitcom answering the same question from her husband.

I had learned by then that this sometimes just happens in organisations, as in life. Two parts of the team, or two people, clash; and even if they were as thick as thieves before, there is nothing you can do to fix it once the trust is gone. One would have to go. Even though I got on with both individually and had a high regard for their abilities in their own fields, this internal battle was poisoning the club. Davie was the one to take the hit. It hurt me to do it, though maybe not as much as it hurt and upset him. He was well within his rights to be annoyed in the circumstances.

From a kid I had spent a lifetime trying to make people get on together and I had continued doing that to a fault, sometimes a very big fault. I should have dealt with this sooner, before the poison had seeped out to affect other people.

Billy was also being put under huge pressure while his team was being ripped apart from under him. I have watched many managers over the years in the wider game getting abuse for being hopeless when, from my vantage point of having been inside a club, I know that they are nothing more than victims of circumstance – be it limited budgets, inheriting squads that are nowhere near the value of their costs, or, like Billy, they simply have their best players sold from under their noses.

I felt for Billy, but he didn't seem to be feeling particularly positive towards me. Billy had, of course, managed to see out the 2000–01 season, avoiding relegation by 13 points, even after we sold half his team. From my perspective that was a superb effort in the circumstances, even if that opinion wasn't shared by everyone else. Motherwell's short three-season attempt at punching above their weight was demonstrably over, and they were back almost precisely where they had been before I arrived.

I still had my mantra that this was 'always going to be a short-term gig', but did it deserve one more season of effort after now having done most of the hard work downsizing?

I think John liked the fact that we now agreed that living within our means was the sensible thing to do. I wasn't complaining about the reset, just the manner in which it should be done over a longer period and in a more controlled way.

In the meantime, we needed new players. Billy had been on the search already. Centre back Karl Ready came in from QPR. A new midfielder was acquired, and he couldn't have been a more pleasant individual: Roberto Martínez. He not only became one of the most celebrated figures in world football, but also one of the best people I've met in the game. His career at Motherwell wasn't as successful as any of us would have hoped, but at least he managed to get a wife out of it, meeting a Scots girl, Beth, while he was here.

I was just trying to tie up some of Billy's deals when I got a call from John Boyle at home late one night. He was completely exasperated, and my latest attempt at a quiet family night in with no hassle evaporated once more. John and the manager had clashed yet again – their relationship had been sinking for some time; in fact, it had never got very close in the first place – but this sounded serious. JB was furious, brief and to the point.

The giveaway was always the opening line. He was so desperate to get it out, this time he spluttered it a good octave or two above his usual tone. 'I'm . . . I'm incandescent with rage,' he ranted. 'Get him out right now. I want him sacked in the morning. He's driving me completely mad. I can't cope with his paranoia, I honestly worry the pressure is getting to him!'

I was taken aback by this fury; JB was passionate when he felt let down, but this was a level above anything I had heard before. The relationship between the chairman and his manager at a football club must be solid, but the bond had been completely broken by this point. Was it really worth carrying on with Billy as boss in these circumstances?

The atmosphere wasn't good in too many areas of the club now – but, then again, Billy was working under extreme strain and, most importantly, I knew he was still a very good technical coach. If I pulled the trigger now, it would be for personal reasons over professional ones, and that seemed harsh. But maybe it was still the right thing to do; was it time to replace the ever-growing toxic atmosphere with something more healthy and positive?

The central plank of the idealistic outlook JB had had when he bought the club was that it should be 'all for one and one for all'. Among other things this meant that everyone should sit down and eat together at the club as equals. Billy bought into this ideal originally but, suddenly, for his own reasons, he now wanted the players isolated away from the other workers. It seemed a small thing, but it struck at the heart of JB's ideology – and mine. This was why he was 'incandescent with rage'. I suspected Billy felt he had to build a bunker mentality within the group, as the battle ahead was going to be against the odds and not very pretty, so a tight-knit team unit with a fantastic spirit was vital. From the outside, bunker mentality can look awfully like paranoia.

John made a pertinent point about Billy: 'You know he has fallen out with his original coach, Jim Griffin, then got him sacked. Then Davie McParland, who he brought in, then got him sacked. Now he has fallen out with Alasdair Barron, who I will not sack. Do you think he wants me sacked as well now?' I decided not to mention that Billy had also sacked me, as a player! John felt that all the ill-feeling centred around one man, the manager, and he was no longer worth the hassle. I wavered at this point. I'd had enough of the bad feeling, with infighting surrounding me at both the club and the SPL. I didn't need any more just then.

We had recently signed David 'Ned' Kelly, who I knew to be a striker of real quality, an Irish international and someone very capable of scoring regularly in the SPL. It was a coup and was helped by Billy's contacts – that is, he and Billy were great mates. I knew Kelly to be a big character with strong opinions, but within a week he was standing in my office shouting and balling at me about something he didn't think was right with his contract. As he stood on one side of my desk, veins bulging in his neck as he bellowed, I sat resolutely on my chair, fortunately on the other side of the desk. I calmed him down after a few minutes and, after some reasoned discussion, we came to a perfectly amicable arrangement. But afterwards I thought, 'What on earth was all that screaming and shouting about in the first place? Is he unhinged too?'

I don't think I had raised my voice – or indeed anyone else had raised theirs to me – in all my time at Motherwell. This seemed odd and quite concerning behaviour. Attempting to bully me was a mistake, but on this occasion, as a kindness, I decided to let it slide. After all, Kelly had just moved club, moved his home and his life, so maybe he was suffering from some stress himself. But I would have to watch out for that temper of his – it could be costly on the field. Much more importantly, I underlined to him, calmly, 'If you behave in that threatening way to any other staff member here there will be a severe cost to you. Whether it be a young player or a member of the cleaning staff or a director, we don't do that in this organisation; there will be no bullying culture allowed here. But, hey, we are football folk, and things must be taken on the chin now and then, so we move on.' And so, we did.

I had two other meetings around then that would have consequences later in the season.

We had signed the 14-year-old son of a local businessman called Tommy Coakley. The same Tommy Coakley I'd briefly played with at Clyde. Tommy had apparently done well professionally, vaguely mentioning property at one point, but I didn't really know where his apparent wealth had come from. We got together for a coffee while his son was being courted by the club. The discussion eventually came back round again to his interest in owning Motherwell. Tommy didn't immediately kick the idea into touch and agreed that if it did become available as a going concern, he would certainly listen and consider. He was up front enough to say that it would be run purely as a business – or, at the very least, with limited losses to him in the short term. We agreed to stay in touch, and anyway he was easy to talk to regarding football, as our paths had crossed briefly at Clyde, where I started out.

The other meeting was more personal and very concerning. I got a call from Annabel's uncle, and when I went to see him he relayed a story I found confusing and downright upsetting. He'd had a successful decorating business, but it had been all but destroyed when he claimed an individual and his wife had refused to pay for the extensive works he had carried out for them. I knew and trusted this man's integrity as high as anyone I had ever known, so I listened on: 'You should know what you are working with, Pat. These people just said to me, "We're not paying you for the work. Sue us if you like, we have very deep pockets." It was John Boyle and his wife Fiona.'

To re-use John's favourite phrase, I was now incandescent with rage: 'That's it. I am finished there. I can't work for people who would do that sort of thing.' I hadn't witnessed any behaviour remotely like that with JB myself. It may have been a one-off aberration and it was, indeed, only one side of the story – I am sure John and Fiona would argue it was shoddy workmanship. But I was devastated by the claim. The ever-honourable relative quickly interjected, 'No, don't walk out over this. I'm just warning you. When push comes to shove, remember he will always be a businessman who will do what is right for himself.'

Those words of wisdom I took on board, but it shook me. I thought about it on the drive back from Edinburgh that day, and when I reached home and saw Annabel, it all came gushing out. Her reaction surprised me with its directness. She reiterated more forcefully than ever before: 'It is time to leave Motherwell. It's not right for you, or for us, any more. If you hang about with people like that for too long, you will eventually be tainted by association.' Annabel, who was always supportive, had been pushed right to her limit. She had every right to be annoyed, as well as concerned. In fact, considering she loved her uncle like a father, I was astounded at her restraint.

There were so many strained relationships and now, to some degree, that included mine with John. Annabel and I needed time over the summer to consider the immediate future.

During that summer Channel 5 TV and my friends at Sunset and Vine asked me to cover the Confederations Cup for them as their main pundit. I loved travelling down to London again to do a job that was a constant delight, with people I liked.

Co-commentating and analysing the games was fun, and my employers seemed to like my work. I think my willingness to adapt, work with the technology and with the crew, as well as studying the teams and tactics in depth, piqued their interest. They had probably got used to dealing with one or two less involved 'lazier' players before that.

I had been doing quite a bit for them for a couple of years, but after this tournament they wanted me contracted for the upcoming season. It was impossible not to think, 'How much easier and how much more fun life would be if this was my "real" job – instead of all the heartaches, headaches, exhaustion and stress that the role at Motherwell comes with.' Was it crunch time? Should I leave the club now? All the evidence seemed to be pointing in that direction, even more so than it had before.

But it just wasn't that easy. What kept playing on my mind was that if I walked out on Motherwell right now, I would be leaving just as the money had dried up. That might make it seem like I had only been doing the job because of the flowing dosh. Although I was earning about half of what I had been in the first two seasons – because I was no longer earning a player's salary – it might still have looked, sounded and even felt bad.

However logical it was to leave, bailing out when times were bad just wasn't my style. I much preferred the idea of leaving when the overall financial position was secured, which was something I thought I could still do. Nevertheless, it was obvious that I would have to decide over the summer whether or not carrying on at Motherwell was the right thing to do for me – and for my family.

During the summers back then the SPL had their annual 'strategy' gatherings, held over two days, usually at a hotel somewhere in central Scotland. These were enjoyable affairs where things actually got done, unlike most of the interminable SFA meetings I was also obliged to attend. The chairmen and their CEOs would meet up in a semi-relaxed atmosphere, without agendas, to discuss real problems, concerns and, indeed, new ideas. There was a very positive method and mindset on those occasions, which certainly had benefits – not least the increased empathy between clubs who had previously acted like enemies rather than partners in the business of top-flight football in Scotland. I enjoyed the conference that summer of 2001: it helped invigorate me about ways I could personally help Scottish football going forwards. The people at the SPL and the club owners were generally not a bad lot once you got to know them a bit away from the work environment. I began to waver again about leaving Motherwell. JB and I got on well at the SPL congress, so I decided not to confront him about the allegations from Annabel's uncle, who had urged me not to anyway. In hindsight, I definitely should have, because this was the thing above all else that had angered me during my time at Motherwell. But back then at the conference, it was maybe that the break from the season's madness injected me with some new energy – and, on top of that, I am a sometimes infuriatingly forgiving type of guy.

On the last day of the gathering there was a fun football quiz hosted by SPL secretary Iain Blair. JB and I weren't going to be favourites – JB's knowledge of Scottish football and its history was minimal, even on the SPL, which was only three years old itself. My knowledge of large parts of Scottish football history wasn't great either – give me a nice wee quiz on music, literature and the arts any day – so I wouldn't be playing my joker on this one.

Question one, asked directly to us, was meant to be an easy opener, but it stumped both JB and me: 'Who was the first player to be bought by one SPL club from another SPL club?' John looked at me, and I looked at him. We had no idea, so it was slightly embarrassing to find out that I was the player and John had been the guy who'd bought me.

Annabel and I had talked for some weeks over the summer and, in the end, I decided to stay on at Motherwell to help get the club back in good order and help the good people working there, if I could. But with one major caveat to Annabel: this year, I would absolutely, definitely, 100 per cent leave the club. We agreed that life was too short to do a job I wasn't hugely enjoying, one which wasn't suited to my personality, had held no interest for me before I took it on, and was not allowing any sensible work–life– family balance now. I may have been an accidental footballer, but I loved playing football; being an accidental chief executive, or whatever title I had that particular week, didn't have much pleasure attached.

I also decided to try to find some fun in the coming season – to at least try to enjoy some of the obvious daftness and contradictions the game and the job afforded, instead of being constantly frustrated by them. Who knew, something radical might change at Motherwell and the stress could be relieved? There was certainly no one better placed than me to make that happen. Taking a little bit more short-term joy from the team's victories would be a good place to start, instead of always ceaselessly planning, thinking and worrying about the months ahead. There was also the not inconsiderable fact that these were interesting and incredibly important times in Scottish football, and in the coming season it would be good to try to help get the best outcome going forwards – not only for Motherwell but for the game as a whole.

That said, my big decision had been made: it was a relief to know that whatever was happening at the end of this season, it would be my last.

21 /
THE PROMISED LAND

Billy Davies's job was hanging by the most slender of threads, those threads being my belief in his ability to manage and my desire to give him a fair chance.

After jettisoning most of the best players, we were now living in the hope that the others left over, a few new cheaper signings and our talented youngsters would improve enough during the campaign to keep us safe. The first couple of months were horrible and, unsurprisingly, the results were awful. My search for fun was looking like a forlorn one, but not as forlorn as the manager's search for a win.

The first game was a horrendous 5–2 defeat at Dunfermline that seemed to confirm my worst fears about the strength of the team. There were three home draws that kept the worst of the animosity towards the manager at bay to some degree, but then a 4–2 defeat to Aberdeen before a 3–1 loss at home to Hibernian opened the floodgates. Now there was an open fury cascading down from the stands and onto the manager; an anger that had merely been bubbling along beforehand. Nobody at the club was even trying to be delicate about it now. 'Get him out,' was the demand being echoed all the way from those stands to the heart of the boardroom.

The next league game was against Rangers at home, and it felt like some of our people wanted us to lose just to make the manager's position untenable. We did and it was. At this rate it felt like we could go through an entire season without a win, and the 'Davies Must Go' gang were indignant. On the Monday morning I called the chairman and told him that I had decided it had gone too far with the manager. JB disagreed: 'It's not gone too far, Pat; it's gone way too far!'

Following the 3–0 defeat to Rangers and having bagged only three points from the first 21 available, I finally raised the white flag; many at the time felt I had left it too long. I thought the manager deserved a decent amount of time to succeed, especially as his circumstances had been unfairly and materially altered, but it was all going south too quickly, and it was time to change.

Obviously, I was the one who had to tell Billy he was being sacked, even if I was the last to give up on him. I sat in my office preparing what to say and how to say it, though I was sure by then the decision wouldn't come as a total shock to him. I made sure that everything was in place to make his departure as smooth as possible for him. There would be no briefs or leaks – the press wouldn't be parked outside – and I ensured the club was in a position to 'do the right thing' financially regarding his redundancy. When I trudged down to his office I knew the best thing I could do was to be straight and honest while attempting to be as helpful and as kind as possible. I walked past Betty, his secretary, and she instinctively knew what was happening – I could see the hurt on her face. I walked in and sat directly across from Billy at his desk. I hate the hypocrisy of trying to make something this negative sound positive when it is anything but – but even so, I couldn't bring myself to say the word 'sacked'. He waited silently to hear me out.

'I'm sorry, and I really am, but I'm going to have to let you go, Billy. It's not working and we're in real danger of relegation if this keeps up. I know you are a victim of the club's circumstances, but I guess that means very little to you right now. I'll ensure every contractual promise is fulfilled.' It might have sounded a little less harsh, but it was just as brutal all the same. It was painful for both of us in different ways; Billy much more so. To his eternal credit, he may have been furious and felt as though all the promises made about 'the third way' in football had been pulled from under his feet, but, in the moment, he was businesslike and outwardly took it on the chin with some grace. The only phrase I can clearly recall him saying was in an emotionless monotone, 'I'll give you the details of my lawyer; he'll sort it out.'

There were no personal comments from Billy, either good or bad about the time we had worked together, but, still, it was a horrible thing to have to do. I hated the idea of sacking people because I knew the effect it had on entire families, but the club had to come first and fairness second – there were too many livelihoods at stake if the club failed and we were relegated. The meeting couldn't have lasted more than a couple of minutes, and he started tidying up his desk to leave even before I was out of the seat. I lingered for a moment by the door to see if he wanted to talk further, but he clearly didn't want my company. I got the message, if not loud, then certainly clear. There was nothing further he wanted to say to me. He didn't even look in my direction. I think he was furious with me inside, but he held it in impressively.

In the press conference arranged afterwards to announce his departure, I was unambiguous: 'Billy Davies is an exceptionally good young football coach and he will go on to be successful somewhere, I truly believe that.' This was not a kind or patronising comment to smooth things over, I was absolutely convinced of it. He later got Derby promoted to the English Premier League, and had other managerial appointments, but there often seemed to be bad feeling following him around after that. I hope it wasn't the pain of the circumstances of his first job that caused this, although I suspect it was part of the mix. The paranoia line suggested by the Motherwell board also followed him around. The *Guardian* journalist Louise Taylor cited 'paranoia, self-destructive insecurities and an obsession with conspiracy theories and old grudges' as the reasons behind his downfall in England. Whatever the case, he was a very capable coach who, after Motherwell, routinely got his teams to the play-offs in the English Championship and to the cusp of the Premier League. These are very difficult things to do, and you must possess a certain skill set to do them.*

Football is harsh and can't wait, however, and, even though it was alien to my personality, I had to act quickly. It was time to have a clean slate, and my next port of call was to sort out the youth department, as I hadn't yet replaced Davie McParland. I immediately brought in George Adams from Celtic to fill the void – among the best, if not the best in his field in the country. It was a coup but I didn't stop there. We also managed to tempt Chris McCart from Celtic too, to work hands-on in youth coaching. He was a highly respected coach, but fortunately also a Motherwell man, as well as a great person to have around generally.

These might have been the first jobs to sort, but there was clearly a more important decision to be made. We had to find a new manager. As I trawled the planet searching for the best candidate, someone would have to caretake the position and lead us into the next few games.

I did have some ideas for the new manager already, as anyone in that position should, but to give me a bit of breathing space to check out all the candidates, I asked Billy's two coaches if they fancied doing the job together in the short term, with the thinking relayed to the owner: 'You never know. I chose the previous manager from in house, so it's not a far-fetched idea that, if they work, I could go with them until the end of the season.' I liked both John Philliben† and Miodrag Krivokapić; they had been Motherwell players in their time, were very capable coaches and were both delighted to accept the opportunity.

---

* Billy and I met only once in the following decades, much to my surprise at a concert in Glasgow – I think it was U2. Again, his demeanour was cold but polite; I am not sure he had forgiven me over a decade later. He met Annabel at a Fleetwood Mac concert, however, and she reported that he couldn't have been more friendly.

† John had been captain of the Scottish Under-18s European Youth Championship-winning side I had played in all the way back in 1982. We both scored in the final.

I wasn't surprised that they did a good job in the short term – winning 2–0 against Hearts at home and 3–2 against St Johnstone away; victories that eased the pressure considerably on the entire club after the awful run of results we'd had – but I was a little disappointed when both made it plain they didn't want to work together in the long term. They both wanted the job for themselves, and the chance to bring their own people with them. That particular dream team looked good from the outside but it was just that, a dream. That was fair enough, but it shifted them both down the pecking order in my mind.

Soon I had a pile of applications for the post, and whittled it down to a shortlist that included Tommy Burns, who had managed Celtic, Kilmarnock and later briefly Scotland – I knew Tommy, liked him a great deal, rated him highly and trusted him implicitly – and Ian McCall, who'd put up with a lot at Clydebank and was also high on my list; having met up with him in Glasgow I immediately understood he would be a pleasure to work with. Stevie Clarke was a consideration, but even though we were friends I wasn't convinced he would leave the job he had down south with Chelsea. There was, however, another candidate, who came from an unexpected direction. George Adams, our new youth-development man, popped his head round the door of my office and said, 'I wonder if Eric Black might be interested in the job?'

I had known Eric from youth and Under-21 days for Scotland, and then the Scottish national team, before dealing with him as Derek Adams' agent. I had also watched his start in coaching following his superb playing career, which included a goal in the European Cup-Winners' Cup final win for Aberdeen against Real Madrid, under Alex Ferguson in 1983. Anyone I talked to who had worked with Eric thought he was a fabulous coach. 'That's an idea, George. Could you arrange a meeting with Eric?'

'Not a problem. Tomorrow night after the Celtic game?'

'It is a bit quick, but yeah, that'll do.'

As the team was doing pretty well under Mio and John, with those wins against Hearts and St Johnstone, there wasn't an immediate need to rush into such a big decision. I had met up with a few of the candidates in person already, so I knew I had some good options. But each time I told myself that, my mind kept going back to Eric's magnificent presentation regarding his agency work a year before – the players he could source in France, as well as his coaching skills. Another significant part of my thinking was that not only did we get on well when we had met over the years, but I was convinced his personality would impress the owner. It was vital for JB to stay invested in the idea of doing the best for Motherwell, both financially and personally. I needed to present a manager he could relate to on a few levels – and maybe even like – not just any old 'hired hand' employee.

Eric is urbane, liberal-minded, friendly and intelligent as well as being easy company in just about any gathering. More than just a 'football man', Eric had many characteristics that JB would warm to. The relationship between the manager and the board is as important as anything at a football club, especially when the previous one had crashed and burned so spectacularly.

In the meantime, many sections of the press turned on me for sacking 'poor young' Billy. I remember reading that in a newspaper and blurting out at the top of my voice, 'Yeah, right! After the stick he got from you lot, I'm not having that.' I was, however, annoying the media by giving nothing away about who I was seriously considering for the next manager. It was their job to find out, and in the goldfish bowl of Scottish football, secrets don't usually last long. But there were no leads because I told very few people who I was talking to – I didn't even tell the owner, JB. Tommy Burns hadn't said anything about our meeting and neither had Ian McCall. I respected that and it had done their chances no harm at all.

We had the game against Celtic live on Sky TV, with the broadcaster itching to get the inside track, just like everyone else in the media. I had briefly considered Colin Lee, an old Chelsea teammate who had done well managing at Wolves, but soon realised we couldn't afford him. I invited him up for the game anyway as he was an old friend. The fact that the cameras and the press guys spotted him in the directors' box may well have led to two plus two equalling five. It worked for Colin, as he got the limelight and, OK, I admit was having a bit of fun too. I was getting a bit of press hassle, so decided that Colin sitting there might just tempt the cameras away from Eric Black, who was quietly sitting elsewhere in the ground having a close inspection of the team before I was to meet him later on.

The real reason for the cloak-and-dagger stuff was less frivolous. I seriously feared that if anyone found out that Eric was available and interested in getting back into the managerial side of the game, he would have been snatched away from me before I could get his signature on a contract. His time at Celtic as assistant to John Barnes* hadn't ended well, and he had said to quite a few people that he didn't fancy going into management now – but I had been given that inside information others didn't have, from George Adams. I spoke to John Barnes confidentially to put my mind at rest about Eric's Celtic period, and John said he thought Eric was superb and would be a great appointment.

And so I met up with Eric at his flat in the stylish part of the west end of Glasgow, with his wife and George in attendance. After an hour of talking I thought, 'If I don't get him as my new manager, I wouldn't mind hanging about with him as one of my best mates.' We got on famously, trusting each other immediately and implicitly. Then I was thinking, 'I could have Eric in place alongside George Adams and Chris McCart too, but who would be assistant manager? That might be a tricky one to sort out.' I was just about to ask Eric if he was considering anyone as his assistant and, if not, would he like me to make some suggestions, when there was a knock at the front door of Eric's flat. It opened and ducking slightly in the doorway, in walked the impressive frame of Terry Butcher, the former England captain, a huge name in Scottish football after his time with Rangers and, bizarrely, a distant cousin (through marriage) of mine. I would have seriously considered him as manager himself had he

---

* The final nail in the John Barnes Celtic era was the 1–0 defeat by Inverness Caledonian Thistle, leading to the famous headline, 'Super Caley Go Ballistic, Celtic are Atrocious.'

applied for the job. Eric then said he would like to bring Terry with him as his number two. Getting those two would be the absolute dream-team scenario. I couldn't believe my luck!

There were others I still had to consider, but I was almost sure in my mind then and there. They weren't officially offered the post that night, but I made it perfectly clear using an old Brian Clough line: 'I'm not saying you are the best team for this job, but you are definitely in the top one.'

That evening it was perfectly clear that they were interviewing me as much as I was interviewing them. The questions were intelligent and considered. Can we trust the owner? What will the budget be? Is there a long-term plan? Sensibly, neither wanted their reputations damaged by getting involved with something that wasn't right for them. I understood it perfectly; I would have felt precisely the same way myself.

Before I could offer the position to them officially, I first had to explain my decision to the other serious candidates. Those men deserved the respect of being told personally that they hadn't got the job. I wouldn't allow them to find out in the press when someone else was announced. Happily, when I officially offered Eric and Terry the roles a couple of days later, they accepted, and I was thrilled. I'd had dealings with caterers that were far more complex, time-consuming and pressured than the deal to get those two on board at Motherwell. It was a huge relief that they had agreed to come, and to a large degree I think they did so because, over and above everything else, we simply liked and trusted each other.

All that was needed now was to clarify things with the owner and his people. This was the new start, the clean slate we all wanted. In John Boyles' offices, with my new team in tow, I explained that I wasn't going to ask Eric and Terry to sign the contracts now sitting directly in front of them on the table if the weekly budget-changing madness continued. I had made Eric and Terry promises. We needed certainty, professionalism and trust going forwards. I still had the unpaid bill story niggling around in my consciousness, so trust was an issue.

As soon JB met the new team he was reinvigorated and gave his assurance that there would definitely be stability this time. JB liked Eric and Terry right away, as I absolutely knew he would. These were people he would enjoy working with; he wanted his colleagues to be his friends as well, and those two would be a perfect fit in that area. I could imagine JB, Eric and Terry sitting at a nice restaurant in the west end of Glasgow, along with their wives, having long conversations and forgetting to mention the football altogether. This could work; this, after so much hard graft, was the possibility of a bright new dawn.

22/
HAPPINESS

Within a week of Eric Black and Terry Butcher walking through that front door at Fir Park everything had changed for me. For the first time in my tenure, right back to the day over three years earlier when I first signed, I started to look forward to coming into work. I walked through those doors smiling, anticipating the day, enjoying working with the people there and planning the project ahead. That seems like an incredible admission, but it is painfully true.

The new management team supplied the classic breath of fresh air that was needed. After I introduced them at a press conference I took a seat at the back of the room and left Eric and Terry to get on with it. Both were intelligent, disarming and certainly didn't need any help from me in front of the press pack. So that was another job gone; more pressure alleviated. It was a fantastic first week, the place was alive with positivity.

It was also a huge relief that we could at last work with a sensible financial plan. JB and Hamilton Portfolio generally had been incredibly enthusiastic and were keen to underline that this was a new direction. I trusted them a little more each day to keep their promises; I hoped I wasn't being naïve. But even this wasn't the last weight lifted from my shoulders. The new backroom team felt it was their job to take as much responsibility off me as possible, instead of me working on their every little problem and chasing my tail doing 14-hour days, every day.

I could see that most of the players liked and respected the new leadership too. That didn't surprise me at all; they exuded professionalism and honesty. George Adams didn't come into my office to tell me that the Under-14 strips were missing and the parents were upset; he just went over and sorted it out himself. Terry Butcher was ultra-positive and great fun to be around, as well being a natural leader – as any Rangers, Ipswich and England fan will tell you. They wanted to work out everything themselves, and there was the most incredibly positive vibe about the whole club instantaneously. Eric himself was bursting with ideas for players he could tempt to the club, but not in a demanding way. He just underlined that he had huge knowledge and fantastic contacts that could provide very good players – and, critically, many of them were within our budget range.

I knew that it hadn't been barrels of fun before, but now I could see that I had been merely surviving in this job, instead of living it and trying to like it. There had been good moments, of course – and I'm generally cloaked in a positive disposition – but when I'd been asked in the odd media interview previously if I enjoyed it, I had never once answered yes. I would add the line that it was interesting, educational and sometimes exciting, especially when we won games or played well, but I would never say I liked the role. Now with the right atmosphere and surrounded by people with a similar life view as mine, then maybe, just maybe, it could be, dare I say it, enjoyable.

The budget for the coming three years wouldn't be exceeded and, once again, JB was in generous mode. The £1.5 million per annum players' budget wasn't huge – in fact, it was medium-to-low for the league we were in – but there were opportunities to use Eric's contacts and abilities. The team still had some very capable talents in place. Our goalscorer from Glentoran, Stuart Elliott, was still hitting the net regularly, as well as trying to organise Christian meetings for his church in the stadium. The atmosphere inside the club was unrecognisable from before.

Ned Kelly was popping them in at a decent rate as well, even though his mate Billy Davies was gone. And one or two of the exciting kids were getting close to the first team, midfielder Keith Lasley becoming among the first to cement his place. JB liked the new vision: he loved the new 'football department' and he bought into the way the whole atmosphere around the place had been lifted so quickly. He liked it so much that he promised Eric an extra £500,000 on top of the budget to help things along in his first season. It was accepted but, as we know, I wasn't a fan of this way of working. I preferred steady dependable security, no lurching up and down, even though declining that sort of generosity to the new manager would have looked churlish, ungrateful and maybe even divisive. I didn't like it when John giveth, because he was just as likely to taketh away. But this time, I shut up about it.

I still felt uneasy, however – not least because I feared going back to where we had been the previous season, having to have a fire sale, and I couldn't face doing that all over again. It worried me so much that it led me to contact the local prospective owner I had spoken to previously. My thinking was that if the club started being financed haphazardly again there had to be a safety net – it was only prudent. Tommy Coakley said he did still have some interest, so I told him I would let him know if and when things went downhill again. 'You can't be too careful,' I thought, especially with the TV deal dispute still rumbling on in the background. Until that was sorted out, we could never be totally sure of our financial position.

With the new management team in place Miodrag, who had been first-team coach, and John Philliben, who had been assistant manager to Billy, sadly had to be let go – but, once again, both accepted that this was just the way of things in the football world. Both were good men, whom I liked and, in better financial circumstances, I would have found jobs for at the club – but that wasn't possible now. If only they had been willing to work together as a duo, I might have been tempted to stick with them for the rest of the season, at least. But I understood and respected the fact that it wasn't what either man wanted.

We bounced around in the bottom three in the league for a while, but St Johnstone were being dropped from the pack, and with only one team going down, it meant relegation was unlikely. We had just about enough points to have some breathing space once again – so, as the panic to stay up receded, it was time to get the new plan up and running. Eric brought in some players for us to check out. Éric Deloumeaux was a class act as a defender, as were a few others, but apart from 'French Éric', the wages of the best ones were no longer in our price range. Some agents mistakenly still thought we had a mega-rich owner throwing his fortune around, which made my bargaining tougher. But ultimately it didn't matter anyway – as there was no way I was allowing the budget to be overspent. I had never gone over the given budget before, and wouldn't do it now, even if it was nearly half of what it had been in the early days.

Another great character and excellent player that Eric tempted in was striker Dirk Lehmann.* I had a good relationship with his agent, Tommy Langley, a former Chelsea legend, so it was an easy deal to do. There were other positive signs. Young Stephen Pearson was edging towards the first team and James McFadden's claims could no longer be ignored. Billy Davies had put 'Faddy' on the bench for his last game in charge but Billy hadn't enjoyed the benefit of his prodigy's talents. Eric felt young Faddy could be trusted with first-team football just about right away, and he wasn't wrong.

Faddy arrived in the first XI and immediately lit up the club and the fans. For a 17-year-old wide attacker – he had long since been moved from left-back – his seven goals in his first nine league games were astonishing at this level in Scotland, especially in a team struggling at the wrong end of the league. On top of that were his assists and some spectacularly skilful play. Faddy had – indeed, still has – that lovely mix of confidence and humility. He has a strong character, but with no overbearing attitudes, and has a cheekiness that is always affable. He fitted in perfectly because of his likeable demeanour as much as his phenomenal raw talent. Scottish fans in time would call his play *'gallus'*,

---

* Yes, he was a footballer even if he sounds like a porn star.

a Scottish word that means skilful, imaginative, utterly self-confident, and with a little cockiness thrown in for good measure – but still loveable. His on-field attitude was swathed in that cockiness, but he removed it with his number 26 shirt in the dressing room.

Faddy was also a hard-working team player and, when he scored, his goal celebration didn't involve a self-promoting, self-indulgent pointing at his own name on the back of his shirt, but a euphoric outlet of pure uninhibited shared joy with his teammates and the fans.

I had trained with him quite a few times and could see his match awareness wasn't up there yet, but restraining him would only have hampered him as a player. He needed to be free, to be allowed to play on instinct – and it was a joy to watch him tearing top defences to shreds.

Of course, he reminded me of my younger self, particularly back at the time when I had suddenly broken through in a very similar position, though at a very different level in Scotland! Although we were different types of players there were many moments that did make me smile internally with deep recognition; he even managed to look as bedraggled as a young me at times, when he turned up for training and even for games. In one early first-team match he had two players marking him closely, right up against the touchline. I thought, 'There is only one way out of that.' It was a very specific move, involving a twist and a drag-back, that I specialised in myself. Moments later he had made precisely that move and was off down the line, his markers mesmerised. I had learned it early in my career by studying Jimmy Johnstone. My dad and I had gone home after watching Celtic and worked on it for weeks to perfect it. Throughout my career I kept it polished by practising it, making sure it was in good working order. Michael Mols, the Dutch Rangers forward, was also highly proficient at this specific turn, which started with your back to the opponent. Even Lionel Messi did it for the third goal in the semi-final of the 2022 World Cup against Croatia! After the game I caught up with Faddy and said, 'The move you did on the touchline in the second half was technically brilliant. How long have you been working on it?'

He gave me a blank look. 'What move was that?'

I described the brilliant perfectly executed twist, roll, drag-back and dummy that he had performed.

'Did I?' he replied, with a confused smile.

Great! I was allegedly a 'naturally' very gifted player, but had to work on that particular skill for years, manipulating situations to allow me to use it. Yet Faddy apparently just threw it in 'off the cuff' and forgot about it. I was impressed, and maybe also a wee bit miffed by his effortless brilliance.

As the 2001–02 season progressed there was still pressure at Motherwell, but it was eased massively by the feeling that we looked like we were heading in the right direction again. It might also be an entertaining and even fun journey with the new management team and the exciting new young players.

It was also the case that the dilemmas landing on my desk weren't doing so with such a heavy thud – even if they didn't always have obvious or easy answers. One afternoon I was in my office interviewing about a dozen people to find a new part-time physio for the first team. As the afternoon wore on I had one candidate who was head and shoulders above the rest. Not only was his medical background perfect but he sounded like he could fit in well with the lads too. I was perfectly happy that I had my man – until the last candidate was shown in. Thirty minutes later I had a second candidate who was just as good as him and equally well qualified, but there was one obvious difference between the two: 'she' would make some waves in the dressing room.

It was not that she was a woman that was the concern, it was the fact that she could have been Claudia Schiffer's younger and even better-looking sister. For me it made no difference at all. If she could do the job as well as anyone else, she would be considered on nothing other than her ability and suitability. I switched to full-on earnest mode.

Just then the manager walked past my glass-fronted door, glanced in the window and spotted us chatting. He motioned to say, 'Could I have a word?' Now, Eric is as 'right on' as anyone you will meet in football and doesn't have a hint of sexism about him, but he looked me straight in the eye and said, 'You are joking, aren't you? Are you seriously suggesting that she comes and works in our treatment room every single day?'

I was smiling, as was he. 'What is the problem? She has just performed perfectly in the interview. She is well qualified, and has no deficiencies as far as I can see.'

'Too right, she has absolutely no deficiencies at all – and that's the problem!'

'I don't understand, please explain,' I replied again with faux naïvety. We could have danced round the subject a bit longer, but Eric decided to end it there.

'What chance have I got of getting any of those young lads out of the treatment room if she is in there. Half the team will be pretending to be injured every day!'

He had a point, but I made it perfectly clear: 'You are almost certainly right. We would struggle to stop the boys chatting her up – and she would need to be able to deal with that – but we would make sure she was given the right protection and environment, because if she is the right person for the job, I will give her it. Physical appearance shouldn't affect a person's employment opportunities.' Eric left, shaking his head but smiling too. In reality he felt the same as I did. I have to admit that back in those less enlightened days, although we had the same moral positions, he was being more of a pragmatic realist.

I went back into the room, apologised for the intrusion and asked the final question to the prospective perfect candidate. 'So, if we gave you this job, is there anything that would affect your working here? We have odd hours in football with games at unusual times.'

She answered honestly: 'I am a Jehovah's Witness, so the only day I can't work is Saturday.'

Being available on a Saturday afternoon at 3 o'clock was kind of crucial in football at the time. Our fabulous physio John Porteous wouldn't be getting his glamorous assistant, after all.

*

My own job was still hugely time consuming, with the minimum four-hour commute each day really beginning to wear me down after three and a half years of it. Father-in-law Bill had helped with the driving for a period, but not since I'd stopped playing. So even though the job was now more enjoyable, the club back on an even keel, the future finally being planned in a way I liked and felt comfortable with, and the trust in the ownership sticking to the promises was growing daily, Annabel and I again discussed the idea of me carrying on beyond the season's end. We both agreed that even though the circumstances had changed, and this was my most pleasant time at Motherwell so far, neither of us thought we should change the original decision. The end of the season would be the right time to go. But I wanted to allow the new group time to settle in and, in the meantime, I could give them a few pointers. It was a huge relief that both Annabel and I still felt the same way about it.

I had already chosen the successor I would champion for my role, though I hadn't told him yet. George Adams had been exceptional in organising everything that was thrown his way – he would be perfect. A few more months at this level then Eric, Terry, George and Chris wouldn't need me any more. In football, people habitually fear being replaced, so it was unsurprising that the chairman wouldn't have guessed my thoughts, that my exit had been planned and I wouldn't be changing my mind.

I did have the luxury of alternative income by then, which others in my position didn't have, and I knew how fortunate I was in comparison. My appearances on Channel 5 paid enough for us to get by, and I loved doing that work. BBC Radio 5 Live were also giving me work, so kicking about at a loose end at home wasn't going to be a problem. If I was lucky I thought, 'The Beeb might eventually even send me to some European games, World Cups and Euros on top of the Scottish and English league stuff. Wouldn't that be the most perfect job imaginable?' Even those exciting work possibilities were a distant second to the fact that I wasn't seeing enough of the family, and this was finally going to be fixed.

Lucy, by now only known to us by her pet name, 'the Cat', was growing up: at six she was no longer a toddler, her complex personality was totally engaging and developing daily. She also had a few traits she shared with her dad, including a deep desire to keep everyone around her together and have them all be mates with each other. Most delightfully we were like two friends and had a lovely relationship already. She also appeared to be quite sporty and rather good at her schoolwork.*

Simon was always going to have challenges, and it was grossly unfair of me to leave Annabel to deal with almost all the difficulties his autism threw up, none of which was his own fault or indeed anyone's. Now, however, being a family was at last within touching distance. Football had dragged me in too deep, deeper than I ever wanted it to. It was only December, but there would be no backtracking. I would enjoy the last few comfortable months, until my last day in May.

---

* It turned out Lucy was much smarter than me – or I should say, Dr Lucy was way smarter than I ever was.

23/
RIP IT UP

I was sitting again in my office with a comforting mug of tea at my right hand, doubtless sifting through the figures to make sure the accounts were balancing under the latest budgetary conditions. I might even have been musing about Eric and Terry's suggestion that I come to train with the team now and again, just for the fun of it on a Friday morning for the light training and games session. My phone rang bringing me back to reality. It was our football secretary, Betty Pride. After alerting me that it was the holding company for John Boyle's business, Hamilton Portfolio, she put their call through to me. These calls had a habit of delivering bad news. They usually arrived out of the blue, with the whole conversation conducted in a tense voice with just enough panic in the delivery to allow me to understand the seriousness of the situation.

Clearly Andrew Lapping, the chap on the other end of the phone this time, had decided not to let the team down and effortlessly returned to the company's favoured playing style: 'We need you to sell some players right away. We need some money immediately! As in, now! We've employed some outside agents to sell Andy Dow, Kevin Twaddle, Roberto Martínez and at least one other player – it doesn't matter who, we just need money. The budget going forward has to be looked at again.'

Once again our finances were lurching alongside those of JB's companies on the high seas of high finance, and our steady, sensible budgeting was being dragged along in the swell.

That was bad enough. But this time, there was the added doozy that even though sales and acquisitions at Motherwell were supposed to be my responsibility, they had arbitrarily handed that job to an outside company without talking to me first! I suspected a pushy agent had made promises to the club that he doubtless wouldn't be able to keep.

Above all else, though, the promises that Eric and I had been made were clearly not going to be kept. As I sat there that morning I knew we were in serious danger of falling back into the madness of the previous season. I didn't finish that mug of tea, as I legged it down to relay the bad news to the manager. I was devastated and angry at the thought of what might happen as I went into Eric's office. I felt I was letting him down personally – after all, it had been me who'd tempted him to the club in the first place, under what now felt like false pretences. At this point my open trust felt like childlike naïvety.

Eric took the news stoically and said he needed time to think it all through, but I could tell that his generally calm demeanour was already being tested by the Motherwell *modus operandi*. Andy Dow and Kevin Twaddle were openly furious, not having been consulted on their impending exits, and they were not slow to show it, or indeed to come to see me and tell me how they felt. Both were fine with me, as I was trying to be the honest broker, but it led to some more difficult and unnecessary friction in the dressing room, as they were righteously indignant about their situation.

Andy and Kevin were surplus to requirements for Eric and Terry anyway. I knew the feeling well enough – I had been there myself as a player; it always happens to someone in the squad when new decision-makers come in. There are always a few disgruntled players who aren't in the team, it is unavoidable. Rile them too much, however, and they dig their heels in, usually with the routine demand, 'Pay up every penny I am owed to the end of my contract, and I'll leave. Otherwise I'm staying put.'

There is often the unspoken suggestion that these players might also cause as much trouble as possible in the meantime, leading to a war with the management team. Such entrenched views from the players were understandable and legally sound. They were contracted, they were demanding their rights and, as a former union man, I was with them in spirit. I did, however, suggest, 'C'mon, lads. Try to be sensible. Get another club if you can. I'll push to get you as good a pay-off as possible in the circumstances. Careers are bloody short, I know that only too well myself. Football forgets you when you aren't playing in the first team. Get yourself into a club somewhere, anywhere, while you can.'

They weren't for budging, though, and their stubbornness wasn't going to cheer up an owner who, when the financial flames were back licking at the door, desperately wanted to get rid of what he thought was any costly dead wood on the premises.

On the field we got a superb 2–2 draw with the mighty Rangers live on Sky, a team whose budget would have been around 20 times the size of ours. But the moment couldn't be enjoyed now we were being thrown straight back into the financial maelstrom. After the match I went to Eric's office and sat down for a debrief, along with big Terry, but the game wasn't even discussed, we each knew it was secondary. Eric had given himself time to think for a day or two and was measured with his thoughts: 'How can you work in these conditions, with this constant ever-changing madness all around? How can I work with this uncertainty around the budgets, the way the club is run and changing the rules every few weeks? It's impossible.'

The one thing that was solemnly promised would not happen had happened already, and with bells on, only months after Eric had accepted the job. I was extremely upset for Eric and his team, who had come in good faith.

The last thing I needed at that point was a further internal problem – but that is exactly what I got. After a cup defeat at Dunfermline in early January I came down from the directors' box to be told that there had been a brawl in the dressing room. Eric was boiling with fury: 'I want you to sack Ned Kelly immediately. If you don't, I am resigning in the morning.'

'What happened?'

'He was shouting and bawling at me after the game, calling me a prick and much worse. As well as saying I was hopeless, undermining me in front of the entire team, he was also physically threatening. Then he was just as offensive to Terry. It escalated, and if the players and staff hadn't held Terry back, he would have ripped Kelly's head off.'

Considering Eric's mild-mannered nature, this was clearly serious. I had witnessed Ned's temper up close already, but I had to hear his side of the story. You can't just sack people on hearsay and on one point of view. I got in touch with Ned and told him to meet me in my office first thing in the morning. In the meantime, I got information from some of the players who were in the dressing room, and it was obvious Ned was clearly in the wrong.

To my surprise, the next morning Ned admitted he was totally at fault, saying he would apologise to Eric and Terry and, indeed, the entire team. That sounded reasonable to me – things can get fractious in dressing rooms, especially after a defeat. I have witnessed plenty of fist fights that have cleared the air at football clubs and been forgotten about quickly. However, he had massively undermined the new staff, and that was way beyond the pale. I hoped rather than expected that his expressions of deep regret would be accepted. I asked Eric if our joint top scorer's misdemeanour could be forgiven if he apologised. I wasn't surprised by the answer: 'I said it last night and, if anything, I feel even stronger about it this morning. Either he goes, or I do.' Terry piped up, 'He can come back into the dressing room if he likes, but he will not get back out in one piece if I'm in there.'

There was no option. Obviously, the press already had the story, and it was down to me to decide. I checked the legal position, and there was a good argument that Ned's behaviour could be considered gross misconduct. From my former life as PFA chairman in England I knew the club was on strong ground – but also that the player hadn't been given a first written warning, although I could have done that following his 'meeting' with me just after he'd arrived. I decided to be up front and straight with Ned, no politics: 'There is only one outcome here, Ned.

You will be leaving, and we can do it the hard way, legally, or try to come to some sort of sensible settlement.'

Ned's personality came to the fore. Apparently, I was weak, pathetic and immoral for not sticking by him. I tried to reason with him, but it was pointless. He is a strong character, and now I was the one at fault in his eyes. If his reaction didn't manage to make my decision pleasurable, it certainly made it simple. There was no way I was losing the entire management team when they had clearly done nothing wrong. Ned was ushered out of the club in short order, ending up at Mansfield and I thought, in the circumstances, with the fairest deal possible – but, obviously, he wouldn't agree with that.

It didn't cut out all of the bad feeling in the dressing room, though, as Dow and Twaddle were also in Eric and Terry's bad books for perceived lack of effort in training. I got on well with 'Twads', regularly picking him up as I passed his place near Edinburgh, taking him to and from training. He was dealing with his own addiction demons at the time; something he understandably never uttered a word about to me. Both sides dug their heels in and it led to the usual war of attrition. The 'lepers' weren't happy at now being told to train with the kids on adjacent pitches and even at different times from the first team. The Scottish players' association were unsurprisingly displeased at their treatment. The SPFA underlined the legal position that they had to be trained by a first-team coach, which then backfired spectacularly. Terry took Twaddle and Dow outside in the afternoons and, while they did laps of the pitch, Terry sat at the side in a comfy chair, having cups of tea brought to him while reading a newspaper.

I would have to sort this out. I couldn't accept this ridiculous situation but, before I could get it fixed, the ownership, having already delivered one bombshell regarding cost cutting, fired more ordnance in our direction.

John Boyle was so frustrated by his treatment in the press on the issues of Kelly, Dow and Twaddle that he sounded as if he wanted to dump the club there and then. This was when someone in JB's circle first openly used the word 'administration' in my presence – not as a business proposal, but just as a way to get rid of those players. The idea was being floated around back then in parts of the football community that clubs could go into administration, allowing some of the higher earners to be kicked out at no cost whatsoever and with no legal comeback. You could then try to rehire only the wanted players, and then get others in on cheaper contracts. On top of that, some of the debts to other companies could be all but written off. If you kept ownership post-administration, new staff could be hired at a lower cost, because average player wages were likely to decrease in the economic climate at the time. From my perspective, that argument made solid business sense, despite being morally dubious bordering on reprehensible.

Many companies were using 'pre-pack' administration to do precisely that; eight English professional clubs went into administration in 2002 alone. If you did it in a certain way, you could cut the costs, cut the debts and then just start again while retaining the ownership and the valuable assets – in the case of football clubs, those were the young players coming through. At Motherwell, from January 2002, the word 'administration' started to be bandied about with increasing frequency, and it was destabilising for us all. Anytime the conversations turned to the TV deal that had still not been agreed by the SPL, the spectre of going into administration grew larger. The speed of change from comfortable control to panic mode was stomach churning.

In early February another instruction from Hamilton Portfolio came through. This time, again, we were told that there had to be even more cutbacks to the budget: 'Get Twaddle and Dow off the wage bill and that might help a bit but get on with it and get rid of more players.' They had a real problem with those two that seemed frankly personal. For my part I looked around yet again for areas to reduce costs, but asking players to buy their own boots – the level that was being suggested – wasn't going to fix the larger financial problems. Two weeks later there was another meeting hastily arranged in the boardroom at Fir Park. The original promise of a decreased wage bill was to be parked; it would now be slashed even further than that. You could feel that the hysteria was bubbling over, the money men looked more fraught than ever and, despite already having been through this dance a few times, this time things felt much more sinister. It was becoming impossible to remain professional in the circumstances. On the other side of the boardroom table all I could see were the uninterested disdainful looks in the eyes of the people from Hamilton Portfolio, who appeared miffed at having to waste their time listening to me. Even though they had clearly made their decisions, I tried to explain the position from my side: 'Is there any chance of a plan here? Just consider the ability of the youngsters, McFadden and Pearson in particular; they will be very valuable in good time. This all feels like poorly planned short-termism yet again and, anyway, the budget has already been halved. I delivered millions from sales and wage cuts last season; it is cut to the bone already and it's impossible to do any more just now with the contracts in place.'

A fortnight on, Eric and I were summoned to a further meeting in the Hamilton Portfolio HQ in central Glasgow. Going into those offices decorated in corporate minimalist art and furniture now elicited a Pavlovian response, and it wasn't a good one. We knew it was going to be bad news; the only question as we sat waiting for the verdicts from the other end of their boardroom table was, how bad? By this point it was pretty clear, just by the way the chairs were set out, that Eric and I were the football department and those at the other end of the table were not on our side, in any sense.

This wasn't a discussion, just another set of edicts, purely business in a soulless corporate setting with no room for debate from the Glasgow 'city boys'. The original promise of the season's money was now officially gone.

Then it got worse: 'We want you to stop planning things like a pre-season tour, or even any pre-season games around Scotland after the summer. They are to be cancelled forthwith.'

This was savage stuff for a football club, but it wasn't over yet. They had some questions: 'Why can't we just sack the players we don't want any more, like Twaddle, Dow and a few others, and decrease the wage bill that way? They can't afford to sue us, and the Scottish Players' Union is too weak to do anything, aren't they?'

This was a step too far for me; they were crossing lines I wouldn't even have approached: 'Maybe that is the way some businesses work, but not football and certainly not me. Contracts are promises made on both sides, and I will not work for a company that sacks people on a whim. Some players aren't behaving perfectly well from your perspective, and they are clearly a drain on resources. But if we sacked them for that, it's a short steep path to madness and anarchy in the game. I will not be party to that and, what's more, it's immoral.'

On the way out of the meeting Eric said to me, 'They have consistently changed everything; they have broken every promise. These are unbearable conditions to work under. I can only say again, how and why do you put up with this?'

For once, I had nothing to say.

By now I knew how all this worked. There would be cash-flow issues in another part of JB's business empire, and Motherwell was undoubtedly an extra drain on those finances. But that drain was slowly but surely being sealed up from my side, by my actions and frugality. Eric and his team continued to try to be professional. Everyone at the club itself, despite Hamilton's best efforts, was pulling in the same direction.

Underlying everything was the uncertainty around the still not completed broadcasting deal. Everybody knew that if the TV money failed to arrive then the hole in the club's debt would soon look like the super-massive black one at the centre of the universe.

Many other SPL clubs felt the same; the Old Firm were squeezing us all until the pips squeaked. This could not only destroy some clubs, but it could also set Scottish football back years, or possibly decades, if they didn't get it sorted before the market crashed completely. With no decent TV deal, not only would servicing the current contracts be impossible, we potentially couldn't reinvest in the future of the national game. That final, rather important point seemed lost on the myopic actors involved. The SPL had initially gone to the wider sports TV market, where the accepted value of the deal within the industry was agreed to be around £60 million per year. Considering the previous deal was around £12 million per annum, this was a game-changer in every respect, news that had been originally received by everyone involved with great excitement.

So, it came as a bit of a shock, once Celtic and Rangers had finalised their dual position, to learn the Old Firm were demanding that 80 per cent of all the money be ring-fenced for themselves, with no one else having a chance of seeing any of that. Among other details that were viciously punishing for the smaller clubs, was that they also wanted a cut of the remaining 20 per cent depending on their final league positions. This last point, especially, left us smaller clubs incredulous, with the realisation that we could actually be worse off than we had been under the previous much smaller TV deal!

Roger Mitchell at the SPL couldn't go to tender until he got an agreement between the clubs on how the money would be shared – but the two sides wouldn't budge. Unsurprisingly, the big two Glasgow 'rivals' were always inseparable in the voting. They had habitually won on these issues against the smaller clubs in the past, and most observers thought they were powerful enough to bully their way through again. This time, though, I really thought that they were mistaken.

It was then 'leaked' yet again that the Old Firm might be on the verge of joining the Premier League in England – but I knew that still to be arrant nonsense. It wasn't the hefty bargaining chip they either thought or claimed it was. I knew that, and the other Scottish clubs also knew it by then, even if those in green and blue didn't or were simply deluding themselves.

We wanted to negotiate, but nothing was forthcoming from the other side and, as the days and weeks rolled by, disaster felt more and more like an inevitability, or more precisely a number of disasters.

The ITV Digital* deal that had been in place in England with the lower league clubs began to falter, and soon that agreement disintegrated.

---

* It is worth noting that the SPL might have signed with ITV Digital at one point, and that would have been catastrophic too.

This was the market that the SPL were trying to deal in. Suddenly, for the first time in history, previously agreed TV deals looked a lot less robust than before. On top of that, if the value of football rights had dropped considerably in England, it would be unthinkable to suggest that the Scottish Premier League would obtain anything like the £60 million they were anticipating. The collapsing ITV Digital deal sent shockwaves through the game – and first to be hit was the nearest market, ours. And yet, somehow, it still didn't manage to spark any worthwhile dialogue on our Old Firm versus the 'other ten' disagreement.

Other wider markets were having a tangential effect on business generally. The dot-com bubble had burst, with some stock markets down nearly 80 per cent from their high of a few years earlier. Tech companies, followed by advertising and then the media companies suffered in turn, which hugely affected every sector. I suspected JB's company Hamilton Portfolio were badly hit around then too: they were heavily into tech venture capitalism, but, crucially, the TV companies were also far from immune. The SPL's revenue expectations were now being openly and publicly questioned. The outlook was getting more dire by the day.

More palpably, the real-life disaster of the Twin Towers in September 2001, just months earlier, was having far-reaching consequences on the global economy. The horror that New York and America suffered in the cruellest way had rippled out in a series of negative waves for commerce – even if the tragedy of those who died was clearly more critical. In almost every sphere imaginable, economies shuddered. The tsunami eventually reached Scotland. The £60 million per year that Scottish football was hoping for – was expecting and, to some degree, depending on – began to evaporate before our eyes. Months had been wasted in petty squabbling, yet, unbelievably – even in this perilous situation – the arguments still raged on.

By early spring the reality was there was now no realistic competition for TV rights from anyone: the rest of the market had crashed as advertising revenues were slashed. And Sky didn't like the idea of paying top dollar when there was clearly no competition to speak of. SPL chief executive Roger Mitchell was asked by the clubs to go back, cap in hand, to the various TV companies to see what he could get. I recall saying to him at the time, 'I don't fancy your chances, mate. You're being sent into a gun fight with a water pistol.' He didn't answer, he just nodded his assent.

In the spring of 2002, there was still a serious chance that the concept of our own channel would be pushed forward to see how Sky, the only other player in town, reacted. But instead of agreeing to the ploy at the next crucial SPL meeting at Hampden, Celtic and Rangers asked for some time out to talk with one another. Moments later they walked back into the room and announced they would not support the SPLTV idea, finally killing it, and its possible use as a bargaining chip, stone dead on the spot. And with that Scottish football arguably scored the most spectacular own goal in its entire history.*

The ramifications would be huge in the game, but at Motherwell, without exaggeration, matters now tipped over officially into a full-blown crisis. We hadn't invested with the expectation of a £60 million deal (even given the Old Firm's anticipated £48 million lion's share of that) but JB, myself and all the other clubs had banked on there being at least *some* television revenue increase. Scottish football hadn't merely shot itself in the foot; it had blown its own legs off with a rocket-propelled grenade, and we had been caught in the blast.

---

* In the end, some months later, Sky, to their credit, kindly agreed to pay the same as they had in the previous deal, which was 20 per cent of what had been on the table before the bickering began over a year earlier.

24/
HUMILIATION

Motherwell football club's immediate crisis mode meant that every meeting with the owner's company financiers was now worse than the one that preceded it. Where once the relative merits of what were the best things to do for the team had featured on the agenda, such things were now no longer even considered worthy of debate. Sometimes there were board meetings at the club, other times ad hoc crisis talks were held in Glasgow – or, just as likely, a cold telephone call would announce, 'There's no money. What can you sell to get some cash in? Are there any more ways you can think of to stem the flow of losses?'

The annual budget was cut arbitrarily each week to an extent that there was no longer even the pretence of a coherent plan. If something brought in money, we could do it; if not, then we were told not to acquire anything. Bills were not being paid, and anything at all thought superfluous to the actual survival of the business was basically ignored. If something wasn't nailed down as essential, it was to be flogged. Everything was brutally questioned by the owner's company. After a while the phone calls became daily – then several times a day: 'Do you really need a physio or a doctor employed by the club?'

'Yes we do, it is in the league's rules.'

'OK. Can they go part-time to save money? Actually, that's a thought: can you think of anyone on the payroll who is currently full-time, who could go part-time if they really don't have to be on full-time contracts by the league's rules?'

I was even told to get rid of the computers at the club and dump the website to save costs. Also, could I give up my car? We had come a long way from relaxing on Lear jets, to returning loan cars. Administration was now being talked about openly by the money men as the next logical step. I tried to argue with the disembodied financiers from JB's company on the other end of the telephone line for some sort of longer-term strategy: 'I will get rid of the car and strip back as much as possible, no problem. I will get what I can for anything lying around to help out. I appreciate this is a crisis, but none of this looks like a company that has any thoughts about the future.'

The reply would be ominous bordering on threatening: 'How do you know there will be a future,? Plenty of other companies have gone under.'

I couldn't give up. The club had to survive, and come out the other end of this with at least some value. I tried again: 'At least let me sign the talented youngsters coming through on new contracts. That is the only thing that is going to give this club a chance in the future after this meltdown. If you don't sign them, they'll go for nothing, and then you won't even have a foundation in place to rebuild from the ashes.'

That much was grudgingly allowed – good business sense prevailed on this one single point – but with just about everything else, if it wasn't illegal to sell it, then it could go. There was more than a stench of asset stripping about the whole period, but when I mentioned such a phrase they argued it was merely 'cost cutting' – to the bone. What was clear was that there was a sense of panic growing around me, and all the normal rules, if you could call our previous business model normal, had been lobbed out the window. It was agreed we would organise an emergency board meeting at the club as soon as was practically possible.

This was clearly now a battle to save the club. When I say 'the club', I mean the staff, its history and its place in the community – and, of course, what the club meant to all its fans. None of them had done anything wrong. The players had worked hard, as had the staff at all levels. The fans had kept supporting the team through what had become a sickening rollercoaster of a period over the last four years. Yes, they had complaints now and again, but all fans do, it is their right, and I found no fault in that. Motherwell's fan base might not have been as numerous as some other clubs', but it didn't make their plight or their fears any less crucial.

For true fans their football club, and belonging to it, is hugely important – as important as family, sometimes more so. It is also how fans define themselves, often over and above anything such as religion, political persuasion or nationality. Those fans didn't deserve this madness and uncertainty. I wanted to fight for them as hard as I could for as long as I was working there.

Maybe, somewhat surprisingly, the relationship between JB and me was still outwardly fine – certainly civil, at the very least – because I understood his plight. I also understood that, to a large degree, he had handed over the financial decision-making to others. I suspected that he had been told by those close to him that his generosity had cost him too much already and, if he didn't stand back, it might cost him even more. The original warnings from Annabel's uncle were, however, ringing in my ears throughout: 'Businessmen will take care of themselves in the end.'

By late March I was told there would be no money moved to cover the players' wages that month, which is when the whole episode stopped being perilous and then became obvious. This ship was sinking – or maybe being scuttled – and fast. It was now time to try any desperate ideas that I had previously toyed with. I had kept in touch with Tommy Coakley, the Lanarkshire businessman whose son was a young player at the club, knowing that this state of affairs had always been a possibility, and hastily arranged an emergency meeting with him. After quickly driving the 15 minutes to his very plush, I've-clearly-made-it-in-life home near Hamilton, I didn't waste time on pleasantries: 'I think John Boyle is bailing out of Motherwell, and soon. Do you think you might fancy working up a takeover plan?'

At this point Roger Mitchell, the now slightly disgruntled chief executive at the SPL, was also showing some interest in joining the venture. Both of us wanted to work together, and we liked and admired Eric, Terry and his team, and Roger knew Tommy Coakley as well. Tommy's reaction was positive, if not an entirely easy listen. It was hard-headed, business-minded and involved a 'buy out' that Eric, Terry and I would be involved in. He gave me a brief no-nonsense outline: 'If I bought into this, the club would be run at cost with no chance of extra loans from me. If you make a mess of it financially, I might just sell the ground and build houses on the land to recoup my outlay! But, yes, I'll make an offer to John if it comes to it, so he can walk away and we can take over.'

It was just what I wanted to hear: 'I'll arrange a meeting as soon as I can.'

The last thing I wanted was any part in ownership of a football club, as I was planning to leave, but if there was a choice between letting Motherwell die or at least trying to save it, I couldn't let that disappear without making an effort to do something.

As the crisis picked up momentum, there were a multitude of other things going on every single day, not least of which involved trying to get a team to win games of football against the likes of Celtic and Rangers! We did get three points from both Hibs and St Johnstone but, incredibly, those were no more than secondary considerations, even while they were happening. It is the only time I can remember, at any point during my career in the game, where my team winning left a completely empty, bereft feeling. I was happy for the players – I was particularly pleased for Eric and his staff because they were having to operate under near impossible conditions and still stay utterly professional – but, as I sat in the stands among the roaring crowd, I just thought, 'What's the point?'

Sections of the press had got wind of the deepening problems. As soon as it got out that wages were not being paid on time, it was a huge clue that there was a major crisis. I wasn't even trying to hide the problems by then – why should I? I certainly wasn't going to lie; there was nothing to be gained from trying to spin a positive line at this point.

When football players are not being paid they will complain to anyone and everyone, and I didn't blame them for a second. Those who came to speak to me directly quickly realised that not only was I in the same circumstances as them but I was clearly on their side. Openness was the only sensible policy at this point. I was impressed by the coaching staff, however: they were still managing to get performances amid all this uncertainty and fear, while trying to care for those working under them and never, at any time, mentioning their own financial concerns. It wasn't just the players knocking on my door, of course: many staff members were coming to me fearful of not only losing their jobs but also of losing their homes, as they would have no way of paying their mortgages. Worried contractors and local businesses that Motherwell owed money to also started calling the club incessantly. Alasdair Barron was flak-catcher in chief; all I could say to them was that I would keep them informed with everything I knew, which I did – but by this point I clearly was no longer one of the real decision-makers. I dealt with everyone who came to me honestly, but could give little reassurance. What was noticeable was that every single staff member was courteous and dignified, which was amazing considering their fears.

I had another personal problem myself at this point, just to add an extra layer of discomfort. I was suffering a lot of pain in my upper left leg. It felt like a very bad groin strain, but with all the work and stress I hadn't been running much and couldn't recall damaging it. Amid all the incredible goings-on I just hadn't found the time to see the doctor for months on end. Eventually, when just walking without a pronounced limp was becoming difficult, I did manage ten selfish minutes in the club doctor's surgery, but only at the end of a meeting to explain why the club wasn't paying his medical bills: 'Doc, is there any way you can decrease the time you spend seeing the players on match days, just to save a few quid in the short term at least?'

'I don't think that would be sensible, Pat. And I think you know that. It's not safe. I understand you have to ask, in the current circumstances, but you know the answer.'

'Just so you know, wages aren't being paid and administration is possible, so I am not sure your bills will be paid for the foreseeable future. I hope we can still come to you for emergencies in the short term? Also, your payment for attendance at games isn't certain. If it helps, neither is mine nor anyone's!'

He was as helpful as he could be: 'You know I care for the club and the players, just keep that in mind.'

That was some relief, but I was also looking for personal relief and asked one of those questions you only ever ask a doctor: 'Now there was just one other thing. Could you have a look at my groin?'

After a quick examination he said, 'I'm quite worried about that. You need an MRI scan immediately, and you must see a specialist right after that. I am seriously concerned about your lymph nodes.'

I am not a medic, but football folk have many meetings with medical people, and we can sense when they are truly troubled. They become quite formal and use phrases like 'seriously concerned'! I said to him, 'You sound more anxious about my health than you do about not getting paid. Now I know it could be serious.'

I might have affected a light-hearted attitude but I knew fine well what he was saying. I had to be checked out for cancer in that area, and he was clearly uneasy. The problem was, with the club on the edge of a precipice, there was no chance of me getting the time off just then. The club couldn't afford an MRI scan anyway, so I would also have to organise it in my own time, of which I didn't have any, and sort it privately. I can hardly believe my attitude, looking back, but at the time my priorities were self-evidently clear. The lymph nodes would have to wait – I didn't even tell Annabel about it.

Three days later, on 8 April 2002, after more meetings and one final hopeless effort by Roger Mitchell to resurrect the SPLTV idea, the final decision was made by Celtic and Rangers to now 'officially' vote it out of the question permanently. With no other bidders and the deal with Sky in tatters, financial Armageddon was now all but certain.

A few days later there was a major meeting at Hampden, and the other clubs from the SPL, excluding Celtic and Rangers, finally decided on the nuclear option. We announced our intention to resign en masse from the SPL by giving our statutory two-year notice period. Everything around me in the league and at the club felt as if it was in meltdown or, at the very least, utter turmoil.

I knew by then that JB and his team were moving swiftly towards administration. I hoped Tommy Coakley might be a trump card at this moment but, realistically, it would more likely be a last throw of the dice: I hadn't even had a chance to check out his financial credibility. It was a long shot and nothing more.

Why was I trying so hard and even forgoing my own health when I wanted to leave the club myself? I didn't *want* to stay, but something about my make-up, or the promises I felt I'd made to people, made me absolutely driven to do whatever I could to save Motherwell and be fair to everyone who was working there in such good faith. I wanted to honour the debts not only regarding players' contracts, but also repay the money owed to local companies that would struggle if they didn't get what they were rightfully due. I also wanted to safeguard those jobs for the rest of the management staff currently at the club. Someone had to do all this, and I couldn't see anyone else taking this on other than me. The good news was that Eric and Terry were interested in keeping the club going too, so I approached JB when I got him on his own during one of his now fleeting, blustering visits to Fir Park. I guessed he had been warned by his advisers about being pressured at the club, or just having his 'good nature buttons' pressed, so it wasn't that easy to get him on his own. I managed to stop him very briefly in a corridor: 'John, I know this is a terrible time for you and for everyone, but maybe there is another way out of this. If you can't or won't keep the club going, how much would you sell it for?'

Considering there was debt, though the amount was very much disputed, and the lion's share was from the club to JB himself, in some respects it wasn't a valuable looking asset, especially with the threat of administration hanging heavily in the air. He off-handedly, without any consideration, said, 'Between one and two million would do it.' I don't think he had the first idea that I was about to present him with a buyout concept, one I hoped would resolve everything.

'I might have someone willing to take it off your hands. Would you meet him?'

He didn't seem excited by the idea, but he agreed that he would consider every avenue.

I relayed the vague figure to Tommy, but the meeting between us and Boyle wasn't to happen for a few days. More stress. In the meantime, I finally managed to go for my MRI scan – but the results also wouldn't be ready for a few more days. 'I'll park that concern for the moment,' I thought. Every hour, something possibly life-changing seemed to come flying towards me.

John's wife Fiona, who was a director of Motherwell but until that point rarely involved day-to-day, met up with me alongside the money men at Hamilton Portfolio. Their minds were clearly made up in the direction of travel: the most frequently used word throughout was 'administration'. To be fair, I fully understood why Fiona wanted the financial and emotional drain taken away from her husband and her family – I didn't blame her for a second. I also guessed they were keeping John out of the way because he was finding it difficult to watch the suffering the decisions were causing.

After the meeting, on the way out of the building, from nowhere Fiona asked me, 'Would you consider resigning?'

I was taken aback; the meeting had been about searching for more increasingly fruitless ideas for raising funds and saving money. My answer was simple, 'I have always had an agreement with John. If he wants me to leave at any time, I will walk out the door that instant. I will not ask for a single penny in compensation, so resigning isn't necessary. Just say the word and I will leave.'

I knew I was leaving at the end of the season in a few months anyway and the only thing that would stop that was being part of a consortium taking over the club. Fiona just said, 'Oh, I didn't know that.'

Should I have been shocked and annoyed at her suggestion? Maybe, but I wasn't, she was a sleeping club director who was within her rights to ask about any possible savings. Getting rid of my salary would decrease the wage bill a bit, so maybe that was her, admittedly blunt, thinking. There had been many weirder cost-cutting suggestions than that one over the past few weeks anyway, so I let it go. It wasn't a time to be concerned with personal slights. There were other bigger problems.

That same day, I got another blunt message, this time from the medical consultant: 'Mr Nevin, can you come and see me as quickly as possible?'

I simply didn't have any time in the middle of everything that was going on at the club. I was speeding between meetings but driving when he called. 'Actually, I can't see you for a few days. Could you just tell me the results over the phone? That'll be fine with me.'

He sounded surprised but kept up the serious monotone impressively: 'I can't do that, Mr Nevin. It would be unethical, particularly when you are driving. If you can't come to the hospital, could you come to my house at any time after work?'

This didn't sound great. Consultants are among the busiest people in society – well, they tell you that anyway. The idea of him asking a patient to visit him in his downtime, at home and as soon as possible, was not a great sign, but my health, even if it was cancer, had to wait until other people's problems were dealt with: 'There is an important job I have to do for a few days, maybe longer. I'll come to see you after that.'

He sounded surprised that I had something more important than my health, but said, 'Just don't leave it too long!'

Again, definitely not what I wanted to hear.

There were constant media questions to deal with, contracts to sort out for the younger players, reports to write, a board meeting to prepare for – all while keeping everybody, including the manager, informed about what I knew, which certainly wasn't the whole story. There was also a bunch of football teams still to organise. I remember driving home late one night when Irma Thomas popped up on the radio singing 'Time is on My Side' and me shouting, 'Well, it bloody well isn't on mine!'

I made my last desperate attempt at a final emergency board meeting to underline that I thought the administration route was not only unfair, but unnecessary and immoral. One by one, each member from the Hamilton Portfolio side stood up and spoke, making the case for administration, aided by a raft of spreadsheets and a slew of graphs. By the time I rose slowly to speak it already felt like a lost cause, even if a few other board members who were still hanging on from the old days hadn't made their positions clear yet. Maybe I could sway at least some of them.

I took a moment, looked at my notes, then tossed them on the table and ignored them. Instead, I delivered what turned out to be more of a soliloquy than a report: 'The wage bill has been reduced radically over the past eight months. I originally thought the spending was too high, so I have been very much on board with getting it down to manageable levels that will not cost the ownership any further huge sums of money. I have managed to get in over £1.6 million in transfer fees already with the sales of McCulloch, McMillan, Goram and Brannan. All the big earners, including John Spencer, are now gone; the wage billed is slashed and there is great value in the young lads coming through such as McFadden and Pearson, along with Steven Hammell and the young David Clarkson, even if it will take a year or two to realise that value.'

I had a brief look round and, although I had an audience that was clearly listening, nobody seemed to be looking in my direction. Most were staring down at their own papers and wouldn't catch my eye.

I carried on.

'There is also huge value in the management team of Eric Black, Terry Butcher, Chris McCart and George Adams – they are a very special group. There is a youth set-up with great people who are now developing a production line of real talent. If you decide on administration, are you sure they will all stay on? If you insist on going down this road, I wouldn't blame them if they left and took their talents somewhere more stable. For these reasons, I urge you to reconsider this decision.'

The uncomfortable shuffling around the room had little effect on me. By now I was getting closer to home truths and further away from financial forward planning.

'There is another way out – or we should at least try every other avenue before making this momentous and damaging decision for this proud club and its history. Surely we can't let local companies down, companies from this community who are depending on getting paid what they are owed by the club. Most importantly, we should do the right thing for our fans and for our staff who have been promised contracts too. They are all relying on us.'

It was an honest attempt that, in my heart, I knew was extremely unlikely to succeed. I droned on for some time longer trying to stay on the right side of being earnest without slipping into pomposity, but I could tell this was about the least receptive audience I had ever spoken to. The moral argument about honouring contractual promises the club had made got little response other than from the secretary Alasdair Barron who accepted that it was a very reasonable position. Without going native, he had gained some respect for at least some of us football folk.

When I sat down again the next board member stood up and made his suggestion to the room with more effortless pomposity than I could ever muster: 'In that we all agree how we are going to proceed . . . except for Pat. Why don't we just blame everything on him? If we all stick together, we can make him the fall guy with the press and say that he was the one who spent all the money, without our prior knowledge?'

To be fair, everyone else was as shocked as I was by his little speech – and his downright stupidity, arrogance and bad taste to actually say it in my presence! I 'politely' explained, 'That's fine by me. But with the information I have to hand, it probably won't hold up. Apart from being incorrect, it is also very easy for me to prove it is a barefaced lie that you are proposing, which I will be delighted to share with anyone who asks.' Happily, JB and the rest of the board seemed as outraged as I should have been at the brazen suggestion and immediately made their feelings clear to the oaf. That individual should have had a political career – it would have suited him well.

The question was then formally asked, 'Do you agree that Motherwell football club should be placed in the hands of an administrator?' There was nothing else I could do. I had played my last available card at that point. The vote was then taken by a show of hands. Had I pricked anyone's conscience? I hoped rather than expected that I had.

One by one, every single other hand went up, some of them slowly and sadly, others with more enthusiasm. I was on my own, hands flat on the table, head down, the only naysayer right to the end. The club was duly voted into administration, the deed was done. Then and there it felt like almost four years of hard work by everyone involved at the club had been tossed to the winds. In fact, it felt like it had all been a huge waste of time.

25/
AN ENDING

As we trooped out of the final board meeting in a sombre mood, I made for John on the way downstairs. I still wasn't furiously angry with him and the rest of the board, only disappointed in the situation and devastated for those working at the club who stood to lose so much. We had disagreed but we were still cordial. He was also candid. As I approached him he caught my eye and said, 'This was the only business decision I could make, Pat. I couldn't carry on the way it was: the financial burden was too much, there was simply no other option for me if I am going to save the club.' The most important thing I gleaned from that short discussion was that he clearly didn't sound to me like he was walking away completely. That was made even clearer when he offered Eric Black and I very healthy rewards if we would stay in post and rebuild the club back up after administration, with a version of the plan Eric and I had already suggested, of a reduced budget but more reliance on kids and Eric's continental contacts.

Being asked if I wanted to resign by his wife, then days later being offered a generous deal going forwards by John himself, just underlined how mixed up the general thinking was. It was either a kindness for the situation we had been put in, or an understanding that it was a very special group of people that I had brought together over the past few months.

Eric and I made it perfectly clear that this wasn't how we worked. We couldn't watch people being summarily sacked and then callously pick up healthy salaries and bonuses ourselves. Both of us said we would resign and leave our jobs directly. It took only a few seconds to deliver, and it was no more than a single sentence, but it put an end to my almost four-year stint working for John Boyle at Motherwell. It may have been said, with no ceremony, in the manager's office, but it was a day of such mayhem that I can't honestly remember where it took place. Terry, on the other hand, was keen to stay on as manager and fight on, which both Eric and I encouraged him to do with our best wishes.

After officially resigning from my post, I didn't walk out the door and leave Fir Park immediately – and it was telling how the two opposing parties then acted in the following critical hours. I knew exactly where my priorities lay: someone had to tell the staff and explain the situation to them; to my mind, the club having a press conference to give the spin to the media was of secondary importance. The workforce shouldn't find out about the situation through whispers, gossip or, God forbid, the press. It's at times like these when you must do the right thing; you should consider others positions first and give them due respect. However hard it would be for them to hear the message, and for me to give it to them, I was dreading it – but I wasn't for sidestepping it.

I rounded up everyone: the management, the players, the office staff, the catering staff, the cleaners, the kit man, and anyone else who worked at the club. It was important to me that they should all hear this at the same time – the highest-paid football player was no more important than the lowest-paid member of the ground staff. That was the original message when we arrived, and it was mine still.

We gathered in the dining room, a low-ceilinged space that always felt gloomy, however many lights we put on. I had made many speeches and stood up at many meetings before then, but this felt like the most important of my life, because it would affect every one of their lives.

It was a hushed room, with just the odd whisper audible as I waited for the last of the stragglers to come in before I explained that there was no easy way to say this but, 'The club is going into administration, and I will try to explain what I understand is likely to happen now, with the limited information I have. The future is, however, incredibly uncertain for all of you.'

After imparting all I could I finished by saying, 'After today I personally will not be staying to pick up wages when some players and maybe some of you will lose your jobs. You can still come to me with any questions, though, and I will use all my knowledge and influence to help you in any way I can.'

My legal knowledge from my PFA work could help in some instances. I would use my inside knowledge of the workings of the industry and any contacts I had to try to get anyone in that room re-hired elsewhere if the administration affected them. I carried on, though I could feel the despair and shock in the room growing: 'I must make it clear to you all that I disagree with the action of going into administration, and will do my best to find another solution over the coming days and weeks. I can't make any promises and I do not want to raise any false hopes. None of you deserve this, and none of you have done anything wrong to cause this state of affairs.'

At that moment I must have looked and sounded much more like a union shop steward talking to his members than an executive talking to his staff. In truth, that role had always sat far more comfortably with me. The poacher had never been a gamekeeper at heart. There were no negative comments from those in the room when I stopped speaking, but lots of questions, a great deal of fear and quite a few tears. All these people saw the possibility of their livelihoods disappearing in front of them, as well as the fear they had for their club. The most common question and the most pertinent, particularly from the players, was: 'How can John Boyle break his promises to us and refuse to honour the contracts we agreed and signed? We are ruined financially, but he is still a multi-millionaire many times over!'

I could only say, 'You'll have to ask him that question.'

I stayed as long as there were questions being asked, and for a few hours I spoke to many of them on a one-to-one basis. I was desperate to help as many as possible but was devastated that I couldn't give them more comforting answers or indeed anything concrete at all. It was incredibly moving when some of the staff waited afterwards to thank me for being a decent person to work with, and for my honesty with them. Some players also stuck around to speak to me and even though it was a traumatic time for them, they were considerate enough to be interested in how I was and what I was going to do now. I explained that it was of no importance! Anyway, I knew their jobs at Motherwell meant far more to them at that moment than mine did to me.

I will never forget the integrity and the kind heartedness of Derek Adams, Roberto Martínez and Stuart Elliott, among quite a few others, around that time. Our keeper Stevie Woods was, as ever, perfect for the moment, making me laugh while not undermining the seriousness of the situation. He was, and is, a truly selfless and caring person. Woodsy was a man after my own heart throughout my time at the 'Well, always intelligent enough to know when it was important to have fun or be a little silly to ease the tension. I thought of these guys as friends and teammates, more than employees.

After the meeting, emotionally exhausted, I went outside for some air, and sat on the steps, not knowing a photographer was lingering, catching the moment perfectly. When you see the picture, which was used in a few of the newspapers the next day, it is a perfect illustration of my feelings at that moment. I am totally worn out and worn down. All the dejection, exhaustion, stress and the desolation is there, more so than in any photo taken of me as a player after losing an important game. What you cannot see is that I am not despondent for myself or my own situation, but only for the others still inside Fir Park to whom I had just broken the bleakest of news.

The buyout idea had been a last small ray of hope to save the jobs and the money owed to contractors. I was, however, totally shocked by what happened when we – JB, Tommy and I – reached the stairs outside the building where the meeting was to take place. It was a dull office block, done out in the brutalist Soviet style that municipal councils in Scotland seemed to favour in the late 1960s. These were the last buildings I usually enjoyed entering but, to my dismay and shock, I wasn't going to be entering this one anyway. I wasn't to be involved in the discussions – both JB and Tommy said they wanted to conduct the business on their own without me! This felt very wrong and had me seriously questioning whether I should be involved with either of them. I obviously wanted to know what was being said and if I wasn't trusted to hear that discussion, then I wasn't comfortable with the situation at all.

I had to make do with waiting in my car outside in the drab car park, not knowing how long the meeting would last. It didn't last long before Tommy came striding out. 'He's moved the goalposts. I am not interested in dealing with him any more.' He jumped in his car and sped off. And that was that: the very last chance of saving Motherwell evaporated there and then in just a few minutes.

I have never found out what happened or what was said from either man's point of view. I ran it over in my mind: how would these two – businessmen at heart – consider any deal in the cold light of day? Maybe Tommy saw the value in the real estate at Fir Park. If it didn't work as a business, the ground itself was worth enough to cover his costs if he knocked it down and sold it for housing. There was also the value of the players, especially the young ones. They would cover his initial outlay, if it was going to be just 'north of £1 million'.

John, for his part, wouldn't have been dim enough not to see the intrinsic value in the kids – I had told him often enough. Maybe JB wanted £1 million and also the debts owed to him taken on by Tommy. That could have quadrupled the cost at the very least. I have absolutely no idea because I wasn't invited in! Judging by the demeanour of both men, I would have had absolutely no effect on the outcome had I been inside anyway. Many years later JB did indeed waive the debts owed to himself.

It didn't matter now and, in hindsight, if I am brutally honest, had the buyout gone ahead it may have been a case of 'out of the frying pan and into the fire'. Would Tommy have been any better than JB in the long run?

I had no way of knowing. I didn't want to stay in the role, I didn't want to work with those types of people, I just felt I had a duty to try to save the jobs and honour everyone's contracts. That had been my last long-range shot and, as I had suspected all along, it didn't land in the net – in fact, it was so high and wide it probably went over the roof of the stand.

I was in my office clearing out my desk when the press conference was announced and the news was to be broken that the administrators who John had chosen would be coming into the club the next day. The board asked if I was ready to face the press conference on the top table alongside them, to show a united front. 'That's fine,' I said. 'The press and the fans should know what's happened here. I have never ducked an interview before, and I'm not about to start hiding now.'

The PR company that had been chosen to spin the news for Motherwell then explained the party line to me, and wanted to make sure I was happy, while sitting at the top table, to give their version of the story. I was annoyed at the thought they were paying a PR company when they weren't willing to pay people to whom they owed money. At this point I had to rein in my anger: 'I am absolutely happy to be on the top table alongside the rest of the board, but I will be giving my "line" and nobody else's. I will answer every question brutally honestly and if the press wants to ask me about the figures that are being mentioned, particularly regarding debt, I will be giving them far more detail than you are currently suggesting. Why should anyone be afraid of the whole story as opposed to a part of it?'

John's exasperated answer, as he overheard me, amounted to possibly the only angry words exchanged between the two of us over the near four-year period at Motherwell: 'Oh, why don't you drop the Saint fucking Patrick act, just for once.'

I understood his frustration, I understood the pressure he was feeling, but I also realised that he could never have fully understood my commitment to always at least trying to do 'the right and honourable thing', whatever effect it might have on me. In retrospect, one harsh sentence in three and a half years of almost constant pressure isn't that bad, and it was a quite a good line, I thought.

Unsurprisingly, my invitation to sit beside the rest of the board at the press conference was immediately revoked! I had nothing to run and hide from, so I waited afterwards to see if any of the journalists wanted to chat to me outside. They would be in touch anyway, so I might as well do it now rather than later. The press guys and the news people did want to ask me some questions, but they weren't of anywhere near the complexity I expected. The story that day concerned the administration; maybe the deeper questions would come later.

To my amazement that examination never arrived. I am still surprised, because when you consider the forensic work done week after week and even year after year following Rangers' demise some years later all the way to liquidation, the Motherwell administration details were never pondered in depth. It was doubtless a smaller story in comparison and a different one in some respects, but the indifference confused me. There seemed to be a distinct lack of interest in the backstory. Considering how much press scrutiny there had been in us over the previous years, this was a surprise. Maybe it was just yesterday's news already, and there was now only one story of importance – what happens next?

26/
DON'T LOOK BACK IN ANGER

As I settled into the last long drive home from Motherwell that day, I couldn't help turning the events of the last couple of years over and over in my mind in an attempt to understand it all. Was there anything I could have done differently that would have changed the outcome? When Billy Davies asked my advice about buying Tony Thomas, who I'd played with at Tranmere, my answer was, 'If fit and his knees hold up, he'll be the best full-back in the league. But if they don't, he could be a complete waste of money.' He played less than 20 games before his knees gave up. Would that have made any difference to Motherwell's downfall? Absolutely not.

Should I have relieved Billy Davies of his duties earlier, as the rest of the board had wanted, and even demanded, many months before? There is a reasonable argument there, but I still felt he deserved the chance to show if he could cope after the monumental decrease in his budget. He went on to manage in the Premier League in England, so he was a good coach. Would it have made a difference with administration had I removed him earlier? Not a chance.

Should I have tried even harder to stop John Boyle spending big early on? Maybe, but it was his choice, his money, and he was warned. If I had been a more hard-headed boss, who didn't care about the players' and workers' rights, would that have changed the final outcome? Hardly.

When I left, was I worried that this proud club with its long history might go into liquidation and disappear from history the way Third Lanark had?* Absolutely not. I knew John Boyle wouldn't allow that – it wasn't his style, but, more pertinently, it wouldn't make business sense. There were people willing to take the club on, albeit at a knock-down price. In the worst case scenario Boyle might eventually have to write off the debt owed to himself, but letting it die completely was nonsensical due to the value of the land, the players and its history, as well as its position in football.†

How did I feel leaving behind the youth system for which I had such high hopes? I had worked hard to get the best people on board, and in the end it was a huge long-term success. Scotland's best away result in generations was a 1–0 win in Paris against France in 2007. Our team that night included three graduates from Motherwell's youth system in Stephen Pearson, Lee McCulloch and the scorer of that screamer from 25 yards, James McFadden. Stephen McMillan could have been there too, had his progress not been hindered by injury.

There were many more questions and, of course, no one gets everything right, but as I drove home I instinctively knew that I did feel comfortable on most of the decisions I'd made over the last four years. And those internal inquisitions didn't last too long – if I am honest, they faded away in an indecently short time.

---

* Third Lanark were a top-level Glasgow club formed in 1852 who went out of existence in 1967, following liquidation only seven short years after losing in the Scottish League Cup final and finishing third in the top division. They never returned to the professional game.

† As I anticipated, JB did stay with the club and they managed to survive. He left in 2011, after 13 years as chairman, leaving it in the hands of the supporters' trust. The best possible outcome in my eyes.

There was the odd thought about how it might have been had John Boyle been able to continue funding us for more than just those first 18 months. We were very quickly battling for third place in Scotland, and there were more good things in the pipeline before the plug was pulled.

Somewhat surprisingly, even more than that successful period under Billy Davies, I do wish Eric Black, his team and I could have been given a decent chance at building Motherwell back up again. I suspect it would have been good and also quite enjoyable. These wistful thoughts were pointless and fleeting, though – the hard facts were what mattered. In the end John felt he had overstretched financially, spent more than he wanted to, and it was now history.

The non-arrival of the increased TV monies that we had been banking on was more than just the straw that broke the camel's back – that was a dumper truck full of ten-ton hay bales dropped on the dromedary from a great height. Had a reasonable deal been struck a few months before between Sky, the Old Firm and 'the other ten', then it would all have still made perfect business sense to John Boyle. In the end, yes, this was the real problem over and above every single other issue added together. My feeling was that Celtic and Rangers hadn't actually physically thrown us into the river, but they seemed perfectly happy to stand by and watch us all drown while they sailed blithely on.

The demise of Motherwell was painful for everyone involved, including John Boyle, but as one player said to me, 'That's all very well, but I bet he isn't going back to a one-bedroom flat or having to sell his family home that he can no longer afford. He will still be tucked up in his big mansion house – or one of them.' There was no argument – that was simply true.

The pain for me of leaving Motherwell right at that moment was that there were a lot of problems left behind for others to deal with, and I could no longer help with them.

There was no further communication with John Boyle, not for around 15 years. Even then it was a quick call from him after he had had some tough personal times. There was certainly no anger from either of us, but this has been the only direct contact: 'Pat, we used to be good friends and got on well. I don't want that not to be the case.'

He needn't have worried. I am not one to bear grudges, and didn't feel angry with him; I simply disagreed with his business methods and moved on. And, anyway, I understood what he had done at the end and, to a great degree, why he had done it.* I guessed that his other businesses hadn't done well for a while, though my only evidence for that, apart from the cash-flow panics at Motherwell over those last two years, was the money I lost when I was asked to invest in his company Northern Edge and related outfit Axeon.

I had no desire for power or to play the games needed to propel myself up those greasy poles. I didn't have anything close to the right personality and, deep down inside, I'd known that all along.

Now that I was driving away from Fir Park for the very last time I knew there was little point in worrying. As Reinhold Niebuhr famously said, '. . . grant me the serenity to accept the things I cannot change, courage to change the things I can, and wisdom to know the difference.' There was no longer anything I could do that would make any difference.

As I drove out beyond Motherwell and up past Cleland towards the M8 motorway, with administration disappearing in the rearview mirror,

---

* There was a further, indirect contact years later. In *The Accidental Footballer* I wrote about how, long before Motherwell, JB was interested in buying Celtic, with me helping him run it. In a newspaper article he said that was nonsense. The headline basically called me a liar, claiming it had never happened. Given the right to reply I said only, 'I stand by every word in the book, it's all true.' Some months later my wife was flicking through some old magazines and out fell a letter. Dated from that time, it was helpfully signed by John: 'Thanks for the tip-off on our friend Mr McGinn [the Celtic director], negotiations are proceeding with some of the shareholders at a slow pace, these have been exacerbated by the recent bad results which are increasing pressure on everyone. It is difficult not to show your hand too early, I will keep you posted.' I am not the bitter type, so asked the newspaper just to leave it. I have, however, kept the letter just in case I am challenged about my honesty again!

I already knew that it was time to think about myself, or more particularly, the Nevin family, at last.

Suddenly after a twinge in my groin, I remembered the MRI scan! I called the consultant, and he said I should come to see him right away. I swung the car round and headed back along the road I had been on. A short while later I was shown into his office and asked to sit down, with him at the other end of what I thought was an unnecessarily large and imposing desk. I was oddly relaxed, preparing for what was clearly going to be bad news. Whatever it was, I would deal with it and be calm. He looked sombre and certainly wasn't smiling to suggest there was any good news to soften the blow. His small talk was limited to, 'What do you do for a living Mr Nevin?' I answered honestly, 'As of today, I'm unemployed, for the first time in my adult life.' He said that this was a shame and clearly had no idea what my profession had been. Obviously not a football man, then. 'Mr Nevin, the results have come back and there is no doubt in my mind that you will need surgery soon.' Not a great start, but I waited for more. He paused, looked down at his notes, then over to some scans and then peered over his glasses to me again. 'I am afraid you will be needing a hip replaced.'

I raised an eyebrow, 'And? What else?'

'Well, nothing, that's it. Isn't that bad enough news for a man of your age?' He checked his notes again. 'Thirty-eight is a bit young for a new hip. I thought you'd be upset.'

He could see I was utterly unperturbed. With a grin I said, 'Is that all it is? Well, thank you very much, Doc.'

I figured it out in my mind immediately. My own doctor had suggested a concern with cancer, but obviously he hadn't passed that thought on to the consultant. The consultant was just checking an MRI scan, and from his perspective he was giving me bad news. I'd had many operations during my career and took this new information on board with the same level of concern that I would for being told that my car needed a service. It was doubtless a relief, because he spotted that I was almost laughing at the situation. I was, however, intrigued and asked him, 'Why do I need a new hip so early at the age of 38? Is it genetic, osteoporosis, or am I just unlucky?'

He said, 'The damage looks unusual to my eyes. Tell me, in your life, have you ever done a job that stressed the joint by twisting and turning?'

He seemed even more confused by my broadening smile as I thought of every full-back I had ever beaten, thinking to themselves, 'Serves the little bugger right, he is finally getting his comeuppance!'

I walked – limped – out of his office, delighted with the situation. I'm sure I was one of very few who'd reacted that way to this kind of news. The last thing I recall was a very confused, quizzical look from him. On that now leisurely drive back home, I was quite a bit happier than I had any right to be on that bleak day. In fact, I felt I'd been given a second chance.

It was the perfect moment to look ahead positively and be excited about what I could do now, albeit with a dodgy hip slowing me down for a while. It was time to consider family, friends, gigs, films, reading for pleasure, travel – and maybe even a little chance to sit back and simply enjoy life for the first time in a long while, without that constant pressure to win and perform at the top level. I'd been employed in sport for the past 21 consecutive years. Maybe a little break was just what I needed.

Almost every retired professional sports person knows that there is one question you are asked more often than any other, whether it is two years or 22 years after you've finished: 'Do you miss it?'

My honest answer has always been the same: 'Not really. I miss being super-fit, but I have never missed the job. Even if I loved playing football while I did, I have never yearned to have it back, even for a moment. I had my time, it was fun, now it's someone else's turn.' The truth of that answer reminds me, more than anything else, that me and my sanity, in the end, did manage to survive football.

Epilogue

I felt sure that Motherwell would pull through one way or the other, and I confidently said as much to any journo that I met in the following months. I'd learned a great deal in the previous few years, much that would inform any further journalism that I would go on to do myself. It occurred to me that few others had seen football from the inside, or from as many angles as me. I had been a successful professional player north and south of the border at numerous levels, an international footballer, PFA chairman, a chief executive; I'd served on most of the major boards in the game on both sides of the border, as well as being a columnist and a TV and radio pundit. The football CV didn't look too bad – or it wouldn't have done, had I ever bothered to type one up.

I was, however, content that at last I would be getting to live more of a life with my family.

Annabel had been beyond saintly coping with all the stresses at home for far too many years. It is all very well me getting the cheers and the roars of approval from the stands; she was as much a part of my career and she got no recognition for doing a much harder job than me, bringing up the children so well under often very challenging circumstances. Simon was and is a fine lad, but the challenges of autism cannot be underestimated. It was long overdue time for me to help and be more hands-on with him and his development.

Lucy was by now an inspiration and great fun to spend time with. She had certainly inherited my earnest desire to do the right thing and to help everyone she possibly could.

I had never meant to be a footballer, but at 38 I now had to finally consider a real job and another career. I wasn't the first ex-player to find himself in this position, so it didn't come as a shock – in fact, I saw it only as an opportunity. In many ways I had put off considering those life decisions for 21 years since I took a two-year sabbatical from my degree course. Now it was time to be positive.

I just loved the fact that I finally had the chance to have a more normal life – something that was summed up one Saturday afternoon a while later at Easter Road, the home of Hibernian. Simon, by then 12, had shown an interest in going to football games after not being able to cope when he was younger – but he didn't have a team and by that point I wasn't sure I had either. I didn't want us to follow a team I had played for in Scotland, and the only other obvious choice was the club I had supported all my life, Celtic. The complications of the religious and sometimes sectarian undertones that existed at the big Glasgow clubs ensured that this was not something I could conceive of introducing Simon to – and as I got older my tolerance levels for that sort of stuff had plummeted. The first team we tried was Hibernian, who had always been my 'other' Scottish club anyway.*

Simon and I went along and sat in the lower east stand one warm late-season Saturday afternoon, turning up at Simon's behest an hour and a half before the game started in an almost totally empty stadium. It was a smart piece of thinking, because it allowed him to slowly acclimatise himself to the noise and the excitement as it built up.

Before the game had begun I could see that Simon felt at home, while everyone who slowly arrived around us was keen to converse and have a laugh. With Simon relaxed as well as being excited, I fell into conversation with a few people around me and, within minutes, the chat wasn't about

---

* There is no truth in the suggestion I was just too mean to buy a new scarf, in that both teams play in green and white.

football . . . but the relative merits of David Bowie, Iggy Pop and Lou Reid and their effect on other modern artists. There followed a discussion about the comparative importance of the Fire Engines (from Edinburgh) and Orange Juice (from Glasgow). Clearly I was at home too. We quickly made friends with Ray, Craig, Steve, Bill Garrioch and old Davie Gillies. I sat and watched the game and didn't really comment greatly to the others around me, boring them with my professional outlook. Instead, I liked listening to what everyone else had to say and how passionate they felt. I loved the fact that, although they enjoyed winning, playing attractive football seemed at least as important to them, which chimed perfectly with my attitude to the game. The 3–2 victory against Dundee United with a 90th minute winner that day sealed the deal for both Simon and me.

I was able to rediscover the simple pleasure of going along and watching my team play, hopefully with some good football thrown in now and again. That was something I had missed hugely without realising it.

Mostly I loved watching the joy that Simon got from that game, the company, the friendship, the belonging, the camaraderie and the acceptance from everyone. He had found a spiritual home, even more so than me.

That first day at Easter Road, and every visit since, I have felt at home; I have felt normal and I am eternally grateful for the welcome and the happiness that the club and the fans have given to both Simon and me. Years later, in a huge moment for us – after immense and dogged efforts – Simon passed his driving test. It was one of the happiest and proudest days of my life, never mind his. Seeing him step out of the car in the Co-op car park and turn to me with that beaming smile, was more glorious than any goal I scored in my career at any major stadium.

Yes, it turned out that driving was one of Simon's superpowers, along with that astonishing memory. Even more, this meant that he was able to attend the Hibs games independently without me – especially useful when I could no longer get to their games due to my media work. Simon kept his season ticket and would drive 'old' Davie Gillies up from Berwick to Edinburgh for the home matches; something he did for the rest of Davie's life until that lovely man died, just short of his 80th birthday in 2022. They had become a fabulous help to each other, and they were true friends to the end. Losing Davie hasn't stopped Simon's passion, however. Simon is still a dedicated Hibee, always hoping for 'Sunshine on Leith' as he rarely misses a match, home or away.

Eventually, Simon got a job, becoming a driver for school kids, many of whom have special educational needs themselves. That trip to Gleneagles at John Boyle's expense years before while I was at Motherwell was a turning point in his life, and I'm forever grateful for that kindness.

I have never felt any antipathy towards any of the clubs I played for, but there was a residual feeling of some anxiety for a while when I was driving past the Motherwell turn-off on the M8. It wasn't the club, rather the stresses of the time there. That job was clearly never particularly suited to me or my personality, but I never let it turn me into a football cynic. In fact, it just gave me the fuller understanding that if I had spent more time in that area of the business, it could have destroyed my love and enthusiasm for the sport completely.

As it was, I got out just in time and retained my passion for the game, particularly when it is being played well. This was quite fortunate when you consider the next, again unexpected but hoped-for, part of my working life. This job covering football in the media meant I could once again experience the joy after the painful end to my two decades inside the sport at every level.

I had survived the career by grimly holding onto the belief in the beauty of the game, though, admittedly by the end, I'd only held onto that by my fingertips. I had learned a lot over those years about people, how they think and behave, particularly in stressful situations. I also learned a lot about myself. But the lesson I turned to now was one of football's great tenets: don't look back in anger, or indeed sadness or longing! Enjoy the moment you are in, always look ahead, and resist living too much in the past. When I quickly got my head round that, I knew it was time for the next big adventure.

But the one thing I never resisted looking back on, was what football had given to the relationship between me and my dad. We had gone through so many adventures together – from me dribbling around sticks and half-bricks with him as a very small boy on a red ash pitch at the back of our tenement home in Easterhouse, all the way to the Scottish national team. He followed me through the years of boys' club football all over Scotland, almost always by train or bus as we never had a car. If there was no public transport available he would use, as he put it, 'Shanks's pony'. That is, he walked to the games, even if it was a couple of hours there and a couple back.

He travelled to Clyde, Chelsea, Everton, Tranmere, Kilmarnock and Motherwell, seeing the vast majority of games I played throughout my entire professional career. We talked at length about the games but, more importantly, I loved how much joy watching me play gave him. I got as much pleasure from that as I did from playing the game myself – and I loved playing football. I wasn't going to miss football as part of my life, but I was going to miss it as part of our shared lives.

He was, however, happy when I left Motherwell – and with that, a career inside football. He could see that it wasn't something I wanted to keep on doing. He didn't give me any advice at this crucial time; he just did what he always did. He gave me his undying, ever-dependable support, just as he had done when I was training with him as a kid all those years before. And he was never pushy. If there is anything I could pass on to parents who have youngsters getting involved in football, or indeed any sport, it would be to follow his lead.

By taking this approach he showed me the right path to stay in love with the game and with life in general. And though he is no longer with us, I would like to say a phrase just one more time, one I said to him by dribbling in every game I played: 'Thanks, Dad.'

Chapter Titles Playlist

1. 'Upside Down' — The Jesus and Mary Chain
2. 'Clouds' — The Go Betweens
3. 'Apocalypse' — Cigarettes After Sex
4. 'High & Dry' — Radiohead
5. 'Don't Let Go' — Pink Industry
6. 'Race for the Prize' — The Flaming Lips
7. 'I Didn't See it Coming (Richard X Mix)' — Belle & Sebastian
8. 'Setting Sun' — Howling Bells
9. 'Different Stars' — Trespassers William
10. 'Do You Realize??' — The Flaming Lips
11. 'Soon' — My Bloody Valentine
12. 'Crushed' — Cocteau Twins
13. 'No Danger' — The Delgados
14. 'You Never Can Tell' — Chuck Berry
15. 'Movin' on Up' — Primal Scream
16. 'Don't Let Problems Get You Down' — Horace Andy
17. 'Higher than the Stars' — The Pains of Being Pure at Heart
18. 'Time to Pretend' — MGMT
19. 'I Don't Recognise You' — New Dad
20. 'Blindness' — The Fall
21. 'The Promised Land' — Johnnie Allan
22. 'Happiness' — The Blue Nile
23. 'Rip it Up' — Orange Juice
24. 'Humiliation' — The National
25. 'An Ending' — Brian Eno
26. 'Don't Look Back in Anger' — Oasis

Index

Acknowledgements

Thanks to those who helped me edit this book and deliver it in the form you see here. Principally Jake Lingwood once again but also Ian Preece, Leanne Bryan, Giulia Hetherington, Matthew Grindon, Megan Brown, and everyone else who played their part at Monoray. Thanks also to the legal reader Jan Clements, for hopefully ensuring I don't get sued.

Thanks to Vivienne Clore for being a friend all these years, for her wise counsel and help throughout the writing, principally by taking all other concerns away. The perfect literary agent yet again.

All the players and coaches at Tranmere Rovers, Kilmarnock, Motherwell and the Scotland national squad for putting up with me and slowly but surely making me take myself less seriously every day. You have my heartfelt thanks for all those years and all your patience.

The PFA were always a helpful and conscientious bunch to a man and a woman and they have my gratitude for the help they gave me that isn't noted in these pages.

The biggest help in finishing this book were the many people who went to the trouble of reading my previous work *The Accidental Footballer*. Without the fabulously kind reactions, this second part would have been a far more difficult task.

Many currently working in the media were also good enough to contact me with kind words; each was appreciated. Some of the readers who got in touch were football fans, but others were not. It didn't matter; each positive message lifted my spirits and, even though there were many of them, every single one helped. You cannot know how important you were and are.

My adventures in medialand during and after my football career haven't made it into this book, but all of you who made that part of my life exciting and enjoyable are not forgotten; you may well get your own stories told by me soon enough.

Richard Bignell helped me enormously over the last decade while we worked together at Chelsea TV. His encouragement was unfailing, his kindness unequalled and there was no one I wanted to share this book with more than him. I never will share it; we lost him in January 2022 and I miss him every day. Tricky, you were far too good a human being for that brutal business.

In these pages are stories about our children, Simon and Lucy. In very different ways they have had some phenomenal teachers, specialists and helpers in various areas of their lives. My boundless admiration and thanks go to all of those who have helped them.

My family are, of course, a constant inspiration and I hope they all know this by now.

This **monoray** book was crafted and published by Jake Lingwood, Leanne Bryan, Ian Preece, Mel Four, David Eldridge at Two Associates, Katherine Hockley, Jouve, Giulia Hetherington, Matthew Grindon and Megan Brown.